Economic Models for Managing Cloud Services

Sajib Mistry • Athman Bouguettaya • Hai Dong

Economic Models for Managing Cloud Services

 Springer

Sajib Mistry
School of Information Technologies
University of Sydney
Sydney, NSW, Australia

Athman Bouguettaya
School of Information Technologies
University of Sydney
Sydney, NSW, Australia

Hai Dong
School of Science
RMIT University
Melbourne, VIC, Australia

ISBN 978-3-319-73875-8   ISBN 978-3-319-73876-5   (eBook)
https://doi.org/10.1007/978-3-319-73876-5

Library of Congress Control Number: 2017964374

Printed on acid-free paper

This Springer imprint is published by the registered company Springer International Publishing AG part of Springer Nature
The registered company address is: Gewerbestrasse 11, 6330 Cham, Switzerland

To my parents, Sunil and Mili, and my wife, Pragga, and my daughter, Aapti.

Sajib Mistry

To my wife and best companion and friend, Malika.

Athman Bouguettaya

To my parents, Jianwen Dong and Aiying Yang.

Hai Dong

Foreword

Cloud computing is inexorably making large inroads to becoming the technology of choice among small and large businesses via provisioning IT infrastructure resources and hosting applications. A significant advantage of cloud computing is its economic benefits to both service consumers and providers. From a consumer's perspective, cloud computing is a model for providing computing resources as a location-independent and highly scalable service that is acquired on demand with little or no fixed capital investment. Cloud is ideal for those organizations with fluctuating computational resource demands. It is able to fulfill those demands with dynamically provisioned resources. From a provider's perspective, cloud computing provides economies of scale through a distribution of costs among a large pool of consumers, centralization of infrastructures in locations with lower costs, and improved resource utilization.

Cloud service management is a critical aspect of cloud computing. In cloud computing, a complex business process can be realized by outsourcing its involved tasks to the cloud and then composing the resulting component cloud services against each of these outsourced tasks. The cloud service management from the consumers' perspective aims to select the optimal provider for each component cloud service to minimize consumers' total cost while meeting consumers' Quality of Service (QoS) requirements. Similarly, cloud providers require an effective cloud service management process to achieve their business goals, e.g., specific revenue or profit expectations. In this regard, the cloud service management process can be realized by selecting and composing more profitable services to fulfill consumers' demands while ensuring delivery of the promised QoS. From here, we can see that cloud computing management is mainly driven by economic factors. Employing economic models to design the cloud service management framework is a right way, as it perfectly fits the way in which business is conducted.

There are a variety of books on the market that cover many interesting issues related to cloud computing. However, none but this book provide a comprehensive analysis of economic models in the long-term cloud service management from the providers' perspective. This book is a first attempt to design quantitative and qualitative economic models for an Infrastructure as a Service (IaaS) provider. It provides an efficient, market-driven, and competitive environment for cloud providers and consumers to maximize their profit and minimize their costs, respectively, while meeting their long-term QoS requests. This is crucial if we want to unlock the full potential of cloud computing which has largely remained closed and proprietary. This book also covers fundamental technical details concerning optimization, prediction, and machine learning models in the cloud service management. The state-of-the-art technologies described and the references included in this book will also help the interested readers gain knowledge on these topics.

This book can be utilized as a useful reference to anyone who is interested in theory, practice, and application of economic models in cloud computing. This book will be an invaluable guide for small and medium entrepreneurs who have invested or plan to invest in cloud infrastructures and services. Overall, this book is suitable for a wide audience that includes students, researchers, and practitioners studying or working in service-oriented computing and cloud computing.

School of Computer Science and Engineering   Professor Boualem Benatallah
The University of New South Wales
Sydney, NSW, Australia
September 18, 2017

Preface

Cloud computing is increasingly becoming the technology of choice as the next-generation platform for conducting businesses. Cloud solutions are represented as services, i.e., a higher level abstraction of computing resources. An effective cloud service management framework has the potential of creating a sustainable cloud service market. It enables the wider adoption of the cloud at a greater scale and faster pace by considering economic perspectives of service consumers and providers. The long-term cloud service composition is an essential element to designing an effective management framework. The composition from the consumer's perspective aims to minimize total costs while meeting Quality of Service (QoS) requirements by selecting the best set of cloud providers. The composition from the provider's perspective aims to maximize profit for a long-term period by selecting an optimal set of service requests. Developing an efficient and long-term cloud service composition framework from the provider's perspective is very important to sustaining and growing demand from a large number of service consumers in the market.

In this book, we develop an economic model-driven long-term cloud service composition framework from the Infrastructure as a Service (IaaS) provider's perspective. The provider-consumer relationships in a cloud market are usually long term and economically driven. In this regard, using economic models to optimize the composition of service requests fits perfectly well with the way in which business is usually conducted. First, a new quantitative economic model is developed that maximizes the provider's long-term revenue and profit by selecting an optimal set of IaaS requests in a dynamic economic environment. We propose a new multivariate Hidden Markov and Autoregressive Integrated Moving Average (HMM-ARIMA) model to predict various patterns of runtime resource utilization. A heuristic-based Integer Linear Programming (ILP) optimization approach is proposed to maximize the runtime resource utilization. We deploy a Dynamic Bayesian Network (DBN) to model the dynamic pricing and long-term operation cost. A new Hybrid Adaptive Genetic Algorithm (HAGA) is developed that optimizes a nonlinear profit function periodically to address the stochastic arrival of requests. Next, we develop a qualitative economic model which is a preference-driven approach to enact on high-level business strategies, such as service menu creation and pricing. We propose the Temporal Conditional Preference Network (TempCP-Net) to represent the high-level IaaS business strategies. The temporal qualitative preferences are indexed in a multidimensional k-d tree to efficiently compute the preference ranking in runtime. A three-dimensional Q-learning approach is proposed to find an optimal qualitative composition using statistical analysis on historical request patterns. Finally, we propose a new multivariate approach to predict future Quality of Service (QoS) performances of peer service providers to efficiently configure a TempCP-Net.

We have evaluated the efficiency of the proposed framework using Google Cluster data, real-world QoS data, and synthetic data. Experimental results show that the proposed composition framework efficiently maximizes the provider's long-term economic goals in runtime. The proposed models in this book are expected to play a significant role in creating an economically viable and stable cloud market.

Sydney, NSW, Australia   Sajib Mistry
Sydney, NSW, Australia   Athman Bouguettaya
Melbourne, VIC, Australia   Hai Dong

Acknowledgments

I owe a huge debt of gratitude to my wife, without whose love and support, I would not have finished this book. I would also like to thank my parents, parents-in-law, brother, and sister-in-law for their encouragement. I would also like to thank all my friends who directly or indirectly supported me.

Sydney, NSW, Australia   Sajib Mistry

I would like to thank my family for their unwavering support during my work on this book.

Sydney, NSW, Australia   Athman Bouguettaya

I would like to acknowledge with gratitude the love and support of my family members and friends along the way.

Melbourne, VIC, Australia   Hai Dong

The authors of this book would like to extend their sincere gratitude and appreciation to their collaborators for the contribution to this book. In particular, we would like to acknowledge Dr. Kai Qin, Dr. Abdelkarim Erradi, and other collaborators in the Sensor Cloud Services Laboratory (SCSLab) at the University of Sydney.

Contents

List of Figures

List of Tables

Chapter 1
Introduction

Cloud computing is inexorably becoming the technology of choice among big and small businesses to deploy and manage their IT infrastructures and applications [8]. The primary drivers for this *paradigm shift* include the fast increase in the costs of maintaining in-house IT infrastructures, non-adaptability of traditional paradigms to changing business requirements, achieving better scalability and ease of management. On the part of IT resource providers, the higher and cheaper network bandwidth and commoditization of data storage and computational resources provide significant economies of scale. Large companies such as Amazon, Google, Microsoft, and IBM are providing cloud solutions to consumers [21].

Service computing is the preferred mode of delivery of cloud computing solutions [8, 101]. It is a fairly recent paradigm where services are treated as first-class objects which constitute computing proxies for a wide range of artifacts, such as applications and data. A key benefit for using services is the ability to *compose* them based on *functional* and *non-functional* requirements [139]. Functional requirements are usually defined via resource requirements such as CPU, memory, and network bandwidth. Non-functional requirements are commonly defined via Quality of Services (QoS) such as availability, response time and throughput.

An effective *cloud service management framework* may create a sustainable and efficient cloud service market [96]. As both service providers and consumers are growing quickly in the cloud market, the cloud market requires management frameworks to meet the expected large demand [139]. Existing research mainly focuses on the management framework from a consumer's perspective [140, 142]. The service management framework from a *consumer's perspective* selects services according to that consumer's functional and non-functional requirements. It plays a significant role in the continuous growth of consumers in the market.

Service providers are the backbone of the cloud market. An economically viable cloud market should maximize the long-term economic expectations of the providers while ensuring the delivery of the promised *prices* and *required QoS* to the consumers. To achieve such efficiency in the cloud market, we require a service

© Springer International Publishing AG 2018
S. Mistry et al., *Economic Models for Managing Cloud Services*,
https://doi.org/10.1007/978-3-319-73876-5_1

management framework from a *provider's perspective*. It composes service requests according to the provider's long-term economic expectations, such as revenue and profit. Current management frameworks from a consumer's perspective [140, 142] are not well suited to compose requests from the provider's perspective. *In this book, we aim to build economic models for a new cloud service management framework from the provider's perspective, i.e. to find an optimal composition of the service requests that closely meets the provider's economic expectation (e.g. maximizing long-term profit) by considering certain constraints, such as resource limitations and Service Level Agreement (SLA) violation penalties* The proposed economic models are significant for three reasons:

(a) The proposed models will provide the necessary impetus for the wider adoption of the cloud on a greater scale and at a faster pace.
(b) The proposed framework will enable an economically viable cloud market. As the IaaS composition maximizes the long-term economic expectations, investors in IaaS resources should feel more confident about their return on investments.
(c) The proposed models provide the foundations for the *market-driven* selection and provisioning of cloud services based on the consumers' and providers' long-term requirements.

1.1 Cloud Service Management

Cloud services are mainly categorized in *three layers* in a cloud market: *Software as a Service (SaaS)*, *Platform as a Service (PaaS)* and *Infrastructure as a Service (IaaS)* [21].

- *Software as a Service (SaaS)*: A SaaS provider delivers software or applications to the end users through web browsers [8]. SaaS users do not need to buy software licenses or install software on individual machines. The life cycle of a SaaS application (e.g. upgrading, bug fixing, and accounting) is fully maintained by the SaaS provider. Examples of SaaS applications include Salesforce.com CRM and Google Email [81].
- *Platform as a Service (PaaS)*: A PaaS provider offers different platforms, i.e. application programming interfaces (API) and operating systems (OS) as services to develop applications in the cloud. The typical consumers of PaaS services are SaaS providers. A PaaS platform provides different tools for easier deployment of SaaS applications [8]. For example, Google App Engine provides different automatic scaling and load balancing tools to the application developers [61]. PaaS consumers control the hosting environment configurations, rather than the underlying infrastructure including network, compute or storage resources. Examples of PaaS providers include Google's App Engine, Salesforce's Force.com [61].

- *Infrastructure as a Service (IaaS)*: An IaaS provider delivers physical resources (CPU, Storage, and Network) as services using virtualization techniques [101]. A virtualization technology abstracts and isolates the underlying hardware as virtual machines (VMs). PaaS and SaaS providers are the typical consumers of an IaaS provider [42]. The general specifications in a VM are the number of processor cores, the volume of RAM, storage, I/O write throughput, etc. The IaaS provider is responsible for maintaining and allocating the resources to the VMs. Examples of IaaS providers include Amazon EC2, Windows Azure, and Rackspace [55].

We define the following concepts to describe the environment of a long-term IaaS service management framework.

- *Service providers*: *"The providers" refer to IaaS providers. In this book, we target service composition for a single provider.* The services refer to infrastructure services, such as computing, memory and network services. Amazon EC2, Windows Azure, and Google Compute Engine are examples of such providers. However, we assume that the provider does not advertise predefined virtual machine (VM) sizes and their prices, as does Amazon EC2 [3]. Instead, it allows creating custom VMs with the shape (i.e. vCPU and memory) that are right for the consumers' workloads. Such a model is already running in Google Compute Engine [52].
- *Resources*: *"The resources" refer to the capacity of physical machines running in a cloud data centre.* A physical machine incorporates CPU, storage units, and network interfaces. The VMs are provided as a service using hypervisor technology on top of the physical machines [52]. *An important assumption on the resources is that they are limited and fixed in the time interval of composition, i.e. 1 or 2 years.* For example, the IaaS provider Rackspace can host about 80,000 machines, and a machine specification is similar to a Dell PowerEdge 2970 [51].
- *Consumer Requests*: *"Requests" refer to the requirements of custom VMs sent from consumers to IaaS providers. The consumers targeted in this book mainly refer to various SaaS providers.* For example, computing intensive IaaS services are typically requested by scientific SaaS providers, such as Human Variome Project and 3D virtual cityscape project [92]. Network-intensive IaaS services are preferred by online community SaaS providers, such as Microsoft 360, Facebook, and email services [3]. Such a request has both functional and non-functional properties. Functional properties refer to the specification of resources in a VM, i.e. CPU, memory, and network units, while non-functional properties refer to the desired Quality of Services (QoS), i.e. availability, throughput and response time. *In this book, we only consider requests in the form of long-term (no less than 1 year) reservation.* Due to the nature of the cloud consumers, e.g. multi-tenancy and dynamic business and cost requirements, their functional and non-functional service requirements change from time to time [140]. For example, a university CRM may request to reserve VMs containing 100 units of vCPU, 1 TB storage and 2MBps network with 100% availability, 0.9 Throughput, and 2 ms response time in the first half of a year (January to June). In the second

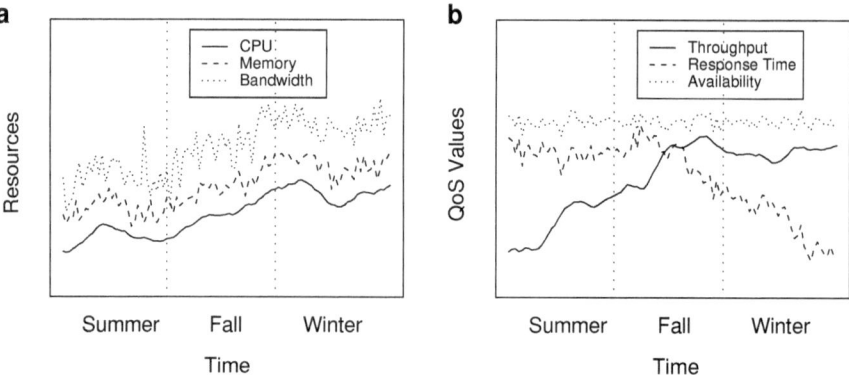

Fig. 1.1 Long-term consumer requirements for (**a**) three resource attributes, and (**b**) three QoS attributes

half of the year (July to December) it may request to reserve VMs containing 90 units of vCPU, 0.5 TB storage, and 1MBps network with 98% availability, 0.9 Throughput, and 3 ms response time.

The *multivariate time-series* is an intuitive technology to represent the long-term consumer requests [140]. Figure 1.1 depicts a possible time-series representation of requirements in a school management SaaS application. As schools typically remain closed over summer, the application should receive lower workload demands in that period. Hence, the functional requirements, i.e. CPU, Memory, and Network Bandwidth should be less in the summer than the rest of the year (Fig. 1.1a). Similarly, the QoS requirements, i.e. throughput, availability, tend to stay low in summer for the school management SaaS (Fig. 1.1b). Another important aspect of the long-term request is that once it is committed by the provider, the service should be provided for the whole term. Partial provision of services is treated as an SLA violation.

- *Arrival models of consumer requests*: The service requests are generated from different consumers. Hence, the provider may receive service requests at various times. The provider has to consider different arrival models of service requests in the composition. In the *one-time* arrival model, all the long-term requests are available at the time of composition (Fig. 1.2a). The type of future requests and their arrival times are known to the IaaS provider at the start of the composition interval in a *deterministic* manner (Fig. 1.2b). In the *stochastic* model, both the request types and their arrival times are stochastic in nature (Fig. 1.2c). In these situations, the key challenge is to determine whether to offer a service for sale or reserve it to wait for a more profitable set of consumers.
- *Service Price*: *The price of a service is determined by the provider*. As the services are customisable, the price is advertised on a per-unit basis. For example, the custom type of Google Compute Engine charges $0.03492/vCPU per hour

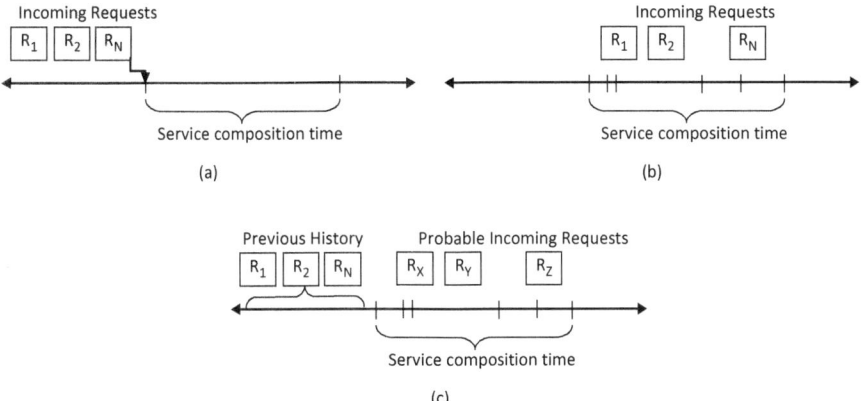

Fig. 1.2 Arrival models of incoming requests. (**a**) One-time arrival of requests. (**b**) Deterministic arrival of requests. (**c**) Stochastic arrival of requests

[52]. *We do not consider consumers' bid prices in this book.* If two or more consumers send similar requests, the provider will charge them at the same price.

- *SLA violation*: *An SLA violation occurs when a provider fails to deliver a committed service to a consumer.* Also, if any committed service property value is not reached in the offered service, it is treated as an SLA violation. For simplicity, *the intensity of a violated SLA is ignored in computing service credit.* For example, Amazon EC2 returns 30% service credit if the monthly server uptime is less than 99% [3]. In this book, if 100% availability is promised, the SLA violation costs on 98% or 90% availability are the same.

1.1.1   Cloud Management Using Service Composition

The cloud provider-consumer relationship is usually *long-term* and *economy driven* [140]. A cloud service is economically efficient for organizations, especially small and medium enterprises (SMEs) that have *fluctuating* demands on computational resources [139]. The *on-demand provisioning* and *elasticity* of cloud services enable service consumers to automatically adjust resource usages according to fluctuating demands [51]. For example, during different periods of a year, universities need different amounts of computational resources to offer services to students and staff. By outsourcing these needs to the cloud, universities could avoid the costly over-provision of computing and storage resources when the demand for these services is lower, e.g. during university holidays. Under-provision could also be prevented when the requests for these services surge at the beginning of each academic semester. Outsourcing tasks to the cloud usually include the use of simple multi-

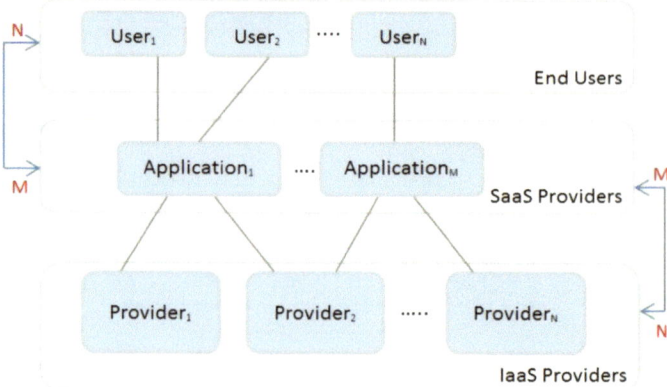

Fig. 1.3 A cloud service composition architecture

tenant applications (e.g. Gmail), complex workflows (e.g. US academic promotion evaluation cases) and facilities for computing and data storage.

Figure 1.3 depicts a typical cloud service composition architecture. In this architecture, cloud consumers are organizations who would like to outsource their IT applications or infrastructure needs to the cloud. Their functional and non-functional (QoS) requirements would be addressed via the composition of cloud services. *For simplicity, we omit the PaaS layer, assuming that it is included in the IaaS layer.* Usually, service providers compete in the market according to how well their services meet both the consumer's functional and, more importantly, non-functional requirements. Consequently, a QoS-based cloud service composition is required for selecting SaaS and IaaS providers to form an optimal composite service which best meets the consumer's economic expectation. More formally, a *cloud service composition* from the *consumer's perspective* is to compose various cloud services from one or many cloud providers [140]. Its objective is to find the *"best"* provider for each component cloud service and to *minimize* the consumer's total cost subject to consumer's QoS requirements on the composite service over *time*.

The composition from the *provider's perspective* has a different meaning to that from the consumer's perspective, but both views share the same long-term aspect of the composition. From the provider's perspective, the composition treats service requests as the object of composition for the purpose of meeting its economic expectations, i.e. profit and revenue. *We focus only on the composition from the IaaS perspective.* More formally, the cloud service composition from the *IaaS perspective* is to select an *optimal* set of long-term IaaS service requests that maximizes the IaaS provider's economic expectations. The IaaS composition may *reject* providing a service to a consumer if the consumer's economic model (reducing cost) does not align with the provider's *economic model* (increasing revenue and profit).

In the IaaS composition scenario, the provider receives long-term requests from different consumers. We assume that the provider has limited resources to provide services to those requests. The key question is, "Should it commit SLAs on all the incoming requests or consider a subset of requests from future incoming requests?" In a greedy approach, all incoming requests are composed that may cause excessive virtualization of the constrained resources and increase the number of SLA violations resulted from degraded QoSs of the offered services [135]. There are two ways to solve this problem.

(a) Adding additional resources from a cloud federation to maintain the SLA [51].
(b) Selecting and composing an optimal set of service requests.

Cloud federation has internal issues such as service heterogeneity, i.e. machine and platform mismatch [27]. *In this book, we assume the provider is not a member of a cloud federation and cannot borrow resources from other cloud providers. In this context, the key challenge for the provider is an optimal composition of the service requests that closely meets the provider's economic expectation (e.g. maximizing long-term profit) by considering certain constraints, such as resource limitation and SLA violations.*

1.2 Economic Models for Better Cloud Service Management

An *economic model* is a mathematical or conceptual framework to determine economic decisions [70, 96, 99]. For example, the supply-demand economic model regulates the price of commodities based on the flow of consumers and the competition of suppliers in the market [70]. The behavior of a market is the key determinant to form an economic model [51]. A *short-term* economic model controls the decisions of the actors in a market to achieve a short-term revenue and profits. On the other hand, a *long-term* economic model determines effective strategies to achieve long-term economic goals. In the cloud market, a long-term economic model may be constructed from both perspectives of provider and consumer. To the best of our knowledge, existing research has focused on developing long-term economic models mainly from a consumer's perspective [139, 140]. Such economic models use decision trees or influence diagrams to represent the long-term strategy of the consumers to maximize their financial expectations. *In this book, we focus on developing long-term economic models from a provider's perspective.*

Cloud providers usually create economic expectations for a long-term period [34]. They take various decisions to achieve their goals. We divide economic decisions into two categories: (a) *quantitative*, and (b) *qualitative*. The long-term profit and revenue maximization is an example of quantitative economic expectations. Providing discounts on service prices for long-term consumers is a case of qualitative financial decisions. We consider developing two types of economic models based on the characteristics of economic decisions.

• *Quantitative economic model*: The profit, SLA violations, and resource utilization can be considered as key components in the long-term quantitative economic model. Different business factors such as time, operation costs, and reputation influence the economic expectations of a provider [51]. For example, a provider may find that SLA violations in the summer period influence the reputation more than in the other periods.

• *Qualitative economic model*: This model should capture the long-term business strategies of the provider. For example, the provider may treat the short-term and long-term consumers differently. The long-term consumers may get a discounted rate on service prices that is not given to short-term consumers. It may also have a promotional strategy in the first year and a profit maximization strategy in the following years. The acceptance or rejection of an incoming request should follow such strategies as accepted requests are committed for the whole period.

We identify the key research challenges in long-term IaaS composition from both the quantitative and qualitative economic model perspectives. The research challenges are stated in the following subsections.

1.2.1 Challenges in Developing a Quantitative Economic Model

The provider should analyze the long-term economic benefit, i.e. profit, resource utilization and SLA violations of a composition, before accepting the incoming requests into the system. To the best of our knowledge, existing approaches only consider the composition of short-term service requests [42, 134, 138]. These methods optimize the allocation of available resources at the time of compositions and maximize economic gain locally. These approaches are not *applicable* to the long-term composition as short-term compositions select consumers based only on *current* requirements. The consumers who maximize economic expectations at present may not adapt to the dynamic nature of composition environment and thus *minimize the global economic gain* in their future requirements. We identify the following *long-term factors* that are missing in the existing approaches.

• *Dynamic behavior of consumer requests*: SaaS providers' run-time service requests may be different from the initial requests. Such dynamism may occur in *resource utilization, QoS fluctuation tolerance level* and *early contract termination*. SaaS providers estimate the required long-term IaaS resources and add headroom over these estimates. This estimate may lead to gross under-utilization of IaaS resources in the runtime [120]. The under-utilized resources may be allocated to other suitable consumer requests to maximize the profit. If other requests are unavailable, the operation cost may be reduced by turning off the under-utilized resources to save power. Consumers may early terminate contracts for various reasons [65]. In this situation, the free resources may be allocated to new consumers to maximize profit. Similarly, *QoS fluctuation tolerance* is another important runtime behavior of consumer requests. When the IaaS provider advertises QoS, some consumers may tolerate QoS changes in delivered services to some extent [65]. The IaaS provider, therefore, prefers consumers who are more likely to tolerate QoS fluctuations to reduce possible SLA violation penalties. To the best of our knowledge, prediction models for IaaS consumer behavior have yet to be studied.

- *Long-term economic behavior of the IaaS provider*: The IaaS provider performs several operations in its runtime. Such operations are: (a) run VMs using local resources; (b) turn on off nodes; (c) turn off idle nodes, and (d) cancel execution of VMs [7]. Such operations may directly affect long-term profit management. The economic model calculates the economic valuation of such operations [70]. In contrast to the short-term economic model, the long-term economic model relates the present valuation of an operation to future behaviors, which include dynamic pricing and future operation cost. According to [51], electricity prices are the most influential variable in IaaS provider's operation cost. Electricity price, employee wages, etc. fluctuate in the long-term according to the demand and supply in the market. The future operation cost of a service may not be measured using current environment variables such as the current electricity price. Hence, an economic model is required for estimating the long-term profit in the service composition. To the best of our knowledge, such an economic model has yet to be developed in the context of long-term IaaS composition.

- *Design of an efficient optimization and resource allocation process*: When an IaaS provider has specified resource constraints, it is important to allocate resources optimally to maximize the profit [135]. For example, composing only CPU-intensive services may rapidly exhaust the CPU quota and under-utilize the networking resources. Further, composing services using over-provisioned resources may cause SLA violations [133]. The future service demand also needs to be considered at the time of composition. In the *deterministic* situation, all the long-term requests are available at the time of composition. The types of requests and their arrival times may be accurately predicted by the composer using deterministic models. In the *stochastic* situation, both the request types and their arrival times are stochastic in nature. Therefore, a service composition task is to determine whether to offer a service to an immediate consumer or to reserve it for more profitable requests in future.

  An optimization algorithm is a procedure which is executed iteratively by comparing various composition solutions until an optimum or a satisfactory composition is found [141, 147]. In our context, the optimization formulation becomes complex and multidimensional due to different attributes in the long-term service requirements. Besides, the economic model may not be linear in nature [51]. To the best of our knowledge, multidimensional optimization for non-linear objective-based IaaS economic models has yet to be studied. As we are performing long-term optimization, we may need to perform the optimization process several times. We define two types of optimization methods in this context.

– *Memory-less optimization*: In this regard, the results of the previous optimizations are not used in the next optimization process. In other words, each
   optimization process considers only the current and future conditions. The
   one-time optimization directly performs the optimization process once for
   the whole composition time. The provider sticks to the output plan despite
   changes in the environment. The *fixed interval optimization* performs the
   optimization process at regular intervals and updates the composition by
   following the changes in consumer behavior.
– *Memory-full optimization*: In this context, the results of the previous optimizations are forwarded to the next optimization process. The last result influences
   the heuristics in the next optimization process. Here, the functionality of
   fixed interval optimization is similar to the memory-less optimization except
   that the previous result is used in next optimization process to speed up
   the convergence process. In addition, the interval time of *adaptive interval
   optimization* is not fixed. When an optimization process is performed, it sets
   the checkpoints for the next optimization based on previous results.

• *Effective multidimensional service composition*: The service requests are multi-
  faceted over different attributes such as response times, availability and throughput. To the best of our knowledge, how the service requests are composed and
  transformed into an IaaS economic model is yet to be studied. The transformed
  economic valuation needs to be matched with the IaaS multidimensional economic expectations. Here, *time-series matching* across all the dimensions are
  not computationally useful. Hence, we require an effective *dimension reduction*
  technique considering the *inter-dependence* of QoS and resource attributes.

We summarize the key *research questions* on developing the *quantitative economic model* for the long-term IaaS composition.

(a) *How can the dynamic runtime behavior of the service requests be effectively
    predicted?*
(b) *How can the long-term QoS and resource requirement be transformed into IaaS
    economic attributes such as SLA violations, revenue and operation costs?*
(c) *How can we design an effective optimization technique for the optimal compo-
    sition in a relatively large solution space with a non-linear objective function?*

1.2.2 Challenges in Developing a Qualitative Economic Model

We may consider the long-term IaaS composition as a decision-support system.
Such a system provides logical, cognitive and automated models to achieve a certain
goal [37]. It supports organizational decision-making activities such as choosing
from different alternatives based on user preferences. Such preferences are either
quantitative or *qualitative* [111]. In an IaaS composition, the provider's qualitative
preferences will be complementary to its quantitative preferences. Usually, the

provider's quantitative preference is to maximize its long-term profit. We may consider the provider's service provision strategies as its qualitative preferences. An IaaS provider may have long-term business plans, i.e. qualitative preferences to maximize its revenue and profit. For example, the provider may have a reputation-building strategy in its first year and may prefer to provide higher QoS at relatively lower prices. In the second year, the provider may have a profit-building strategy and may prefer to provide greater QoS at relatively higher prices.

To the best of our knowledge, existing qualitative economic models represent the consumers' qualitative preferences [111, 126, 139]. They do not consider the following issues related to the long-term composition from the provider's perspective.

- *Dynamic temporal semantic preferences*: In a typical short-term composition, the qualitative preferences remain *static* during the composition time [111, 126, 139]. The relative ordering of the provider's preferences may *vary* over the longer term. For example, a provider may prefer providing CPU-based services over Network-based services in the first year but prefer the opposite in the second year. It creates a set of temporal segments of preferences in the economic model. The semantics of preferences may not be static during the whole period of composition. It is about the competition in the market [51, 87]. For example, 10 ms response time is treated as a high QoS in this year, but it may become a moderate QoS in the next year because of an upgrade to the hardware in the market.
- *Temporal mismatch between the service request and the provider's preferences*: The long-term service requests may not have an exact *temporal match* with the temporal segments of the economic model. For example, the provider has a choice of provisioning CPU intensive services in January and Network intensive services in February. If a service request spans from the middle of January to the middle of February, an economic model could not be applied directly to evaluate the merit of the requests.
- *An effective sequential optimization process*: We may consider both the global and local optimization approaches to select the optimal composition. A typical Dynamic Programming (DP)-based global approach considers all requests at the time of optimization [74]. The global optimization may pose a *scalability issue* in the runtime due to comparisons among a large number of candidate solutions. However, an efficient sequential local optimization approach accepts or rejects requests in each segment so that *local decisions* are collectively converged to an acceptable approximate global optimal composition [125]. To the best of our knowledge, finding the best sequence of local IaaS composition has yet to be studied. Historical request patterns may be used to generate knowledge about the sequence of local optimizations [128]. There can be different distributions of historical request patterns such as normal, left-skewed and right-skewed distributions [108]. Hence, we require statistical analysis to identify the knowledge of the sequence of local optimizations for a particular distribution in a set of incoming requests.

We summarize the key *research questions* on developing the *qualitative economic model* for the long-term IaaS composition.

(a) *How can the long-term qualitative preferences of the provider be effectively modeled?*
(b) *How can we design an effective sequential optimization process for the qualitative economic model?*
(c) *How can we effectively find a heuristic to reduce the long-term influence of local optimizations for new consumer requests without behavioral history?*

1.2.3   Economic Model Based Cloud Service Composition

We propose quantitative and qualitative economic models based on long-term IaaS composition approaches. Both the deterministic and stochastic consumer requests are composed in the quantitative IaaS composition. Only deterministic requests are composed in the qualitative IaaS composition. The key aspects of a better service management framework are described as follows:

- *Predicting Dynamic Request Behavior for Long-term IaaS Composition:* We propose a novel composition framework for an IaaS provider that selects the optimal set of long-term service requests to maximize its profit. Existing solutions consider an IaaS provider's economic benefits at the time of service composition and ignore the dynamic nature of consumer requests over a longer term [24, 98, 138]. The proposed framework deploys a new multivariate Hidden Markov Model (HMM) and an Autoregressive Integrated Moving Average (ARIMA) model to predict different patterns of resource utilization and QoS fluctuation tolerance levels of existing service consumers. The dynamic nature of new consumer requests without history is modeled using a new community-based heuristic approach. The predicted long-term service requests are optimized using Integer Linear Programming (ILP) to find a proper configuration that maximizes the profit of an IaaS provider. For simplicity, we model an IaaS composition using a short-term economic model [51] and assume that it remains constant over the longer term.
- *Metaheuristic Optimization for Dynamic Quantitative IaaS Composition:* We propose a novel dynamic metaheuristic optimization approach to compose an optimal set of IaaS service requests to align with an IaaS provider's long-term economic expectation. This method is suitable for situations where IaaS provisioning is subject to resource and QoS constraints and is qualitative in nature. Also, the IaaS service requests are characterized by their dynamic resource, QoS requirements and stochastic arrival times. A new quantitative economic model is proposed that matches the provider's long-term economic expectations with compositions of service requests. The evaluation incorporates assessing dynamic pricing and operation costs of service requests. The proposed economic model is constructed in the form of a Dynamic Bayesian Network (DBN) [121]. The DBN

not only depicts the correlations among resource utilization, QoS provisions, and service pricing but also describes the changes in correlations over time.

An innovative hybrid genetic algorithm is proposed as an optimization process that incorporates the economic *inter-dependency* among the requests as a heuristic operator and performs repair operations in local solutions to meet the resource and QoS constraints. The proposed approach generates dynamic global solutions by updating the heuristic operator at regular intervals with the runtime behavior data of an existing service composition. The proposed metaheuristic algorithm is a hybrid of Genetic Algorithm (GA) [141] and Ant Colony Optimization (ACO) [147]. GA [141], as one of the most popular metaheuristic algorithms, is especially useful to find globally optimal solutions to a combinatorial optimization problem. However, GA is *memory-less* in nature and requires optimization from scratch in a dynamic environment [12]. The *memory-full* character of the proposed metaheuristic optimization provides runtime efficiency for adapting to the dynamic IaaS composition.

- *Reinforcement Learning for Qualitative IaaS Composition:* We propose an approach to compose an optimal set of infrastructure service requests based on a provider's qualitative preferences over a long-term period. The qualitative preferences are modeled in a Temporal Condition Preference Network (TempCP-Net) which incorporates decision variables to deploy different business strategies for both short-term and long-term service requests. Condition Preference Network (CP-Net) [18] is a compact and intuitive formalism for representing and reasoning with conditional preferences under the *ceteris paribus* ("all else being equal") semantics. The dynamic semantics of the preferences are indicated using a Conditional Preference Table (CPT) [18] of the temporal CP-Net. The temporal mismatch between the service requests and the provider's preferences is solved through the semantic temporal segmentation of the requests, which preserves the inherent dependencies among the attributes in the original long-term requests. The multidimensional qualitative preferences are indexed in a k-d tree to compute the preference ranking of a set of incoming requests. The k-d tree is widely used for a multidimensional point query in different applications [5].

  We propose a three-dimensional *Q-learning* approach to find the optimal composition using historical request patterns. The model-free reinforcement learning approach, called *Q-learning* [129] is widely used to model the decision process in a dynamic environment. The proposed three-dimensional Q-learning approach considers the execution order of the local selections in the time segments to find the best sequence of selecting the incoming requests. Statistical distribution-matching algorithms [44] are applied to map the request patterns with corresponding *Q-matrices*. We propose a heuristic based approach using the *aggregated* learned Q-values to compose the new or non-matched request patterns.

- *Service Providers' Long-term QoS Prediction Model:* It is important to monitor the performances of cloud providers for the growth of the cloud market. It gives confidence to consumers to perform long-term compositions [139]. We find that such a prediction and monitoring tool also plays an important role in the

IaaS composition. It will help providers to analyze their peers' performances and to design their economic models based on market performance. In this context, we propose a multivariate prediction model for QoS values. The long-term QoS provision of a service provider may change for various reasons, e.g. a change in resource allocation policy, resource sharing, multi-tenancy or economic models [68]. Existing QoS prediction models do not usually consider existing correlations among the QoS attributes in *time-series* of providers' performances [84, 98, 144, 148, 151, 152]. These correlations, however, are prevalent in cloud service composition where a QoS attribute is correlated with one or many other QoS attributes. We analyze the effectiveness of the proposed multivariate prediction model in the IaaS composition.

1.3   Outline of the Book Chapters

The remainder of this book is organized as follows.

- In Chap. 2, we present the background and related works that are closely related to cloud service management and composition. Related work helps differentiate the proposed approach with existing composition approaches.
- In Chap. 3, we study several consumers' long-term requests pattern from Google Cluster Data [109] and real world cloud QoS performance data [67]. We propose a new multivariate HMM and ARIMA model to predict the future behavior of IaaS consumers. We compare the proposed prediction model with the univariate HMM, ANN and univariate ARIMA models. We also propose a heuristic based Integer Linear Programming (ILP) approach to compose the predicted consumer requests. We also compare the profitability of the proposed heuristic-based service composition with a greedy approach and an ILP without heuristics.
- In Chap. 4, we consider the long-term quantitative IaaS composition for the stochastic arrival of the requests. We propose a DBN to model the dynamic service prices and operation costs. We analyze the runtime performances of traditional optimization approaches, i.e. Genetic Algorithm (GA) and Ant Colony optimization (ACO) in the dynamic environment. We propose a hybrid adaptive genetic composition approach for the stochastic arrival of the requests. The efficiency of the proposed approach is compared to a greedy approach, the traditional GA, ACO approaches and a brute-force approach.
- In Chap. 5, we consider the long-term qualitative IaaS composition for the deterministic arrival of the requests. The long-term business strategies of an IaaS provider are modeled in a temporal CP-Net. We analyze the effectiveness of the sequential composition process over the global composition. We propose a three-dimensional Q-learning approach to find the best sequence of local compositions. We also analyze the effect of request distribution patterns in the reinforcement learning. The efficiency of the proposed approach is compared to

the two-dimensional Q-learning approach and a global Dynamic Programming (DP) approach.

- In Chap. 6, we analyze IaaS providers' long-term service performances and service level agreements. We propose a multivariate QoS forecasting model for the cloud service composition. We compare the efficiency of the proposed approach with ARIMA, Holt-Winters and Vector based multivariate time-series prediction (VAR) approaches.
- In Chap. 7, we provide the concluding remarks and discuss possible future work.

Chapter 2
Background

An introduction to the research fields related to the management of services in cloud environments is given in this chapter to help readers gain a better understanding of the work described in this book. In particular, an overview of cloud service composition and economic models are presented in this chapter. Furthermore, we discuss existing prediction models and optimization techniques for developing economic models for an efficient management framework. Finally, we discuss the research gaps in existing approaches and possible directions to develop the economic models for a better cloud service management.

2.1 Cloud Service Management from an End User's Perspective

The composition from an end user's perspective is defined as finding the best component service based on the user's preference [139]. End users such as enterprise organizations and government agencies usually require service composition when a single service cannot meet their requirements. The requirements from the end user have different types of properties: *functional* and *non-functional* [139]. Those requirements may also span from a *short-term* period to a *long-term* period. We discuss different approaches to the service composition from the end user's perspective in the following subsections.

2.1.1 Service Composition with Functional Requirements

The cloud service composition approaches based on functional properties usually focus on finding the component services that are functionally matched to the

© Springer International Publishing AG 2018   17
S. Mistry et al., *Economic Models for Managing Cloud Services*,
https://doi.org/10.1007/978-3-319-73876-5_2

requirements of end users. To the best of our knowledge, most existing approaches focus on enabling a cloud platform as a *Service Oriented Architecture (SOA)* [123]. Such methodologies use *cross-enterprise workflow* and *AI planning* for the service composition [107]. Cross-enterprise workflow enables Infrastructure usage to be managed and tracked from different platforms [121]. Usually, two steps are performed in workflow-based approaches. The composer first generates an abstract composition plan. The concrete services are then matched with those abstract plans. Two approaches are typically followed to generate the composition plan: (a) *manual*, and (b) *automatic*. In the manual approach, end users or composers need to design the control flow and data flow of the composite services. Automatic methods learn the pattern of workflow composition and find appropriate concrete services from the cloud market. EFlow is a composition platform developed by HP that runs on top of the traditional Web service model (service provider, requester, and registry) [26]. The workflow (graphs) of different composite services are created manually. However, eFlow provides the automation for binding the nodes with concrete services [25, 79].

Classic AI planning methods use a state-action sequence where each execution of action alters the state of the composition. The user only specifies the desired output of the composition and the AI planners automatically generate a composition plan [56]. Various semantic matching algorithms and business process integration methods are proposed to automate cloud service discovery and composition, based on the functional properties [142]. Besides, AI-inspired planning techniques are suitable for the composition in the deterministic real world environment [131]. For example, the STRIPS-style planning algorithm usually assumes the deterministic behavior and a sequential state-action models orchestrate the composition plan [97]. In the stochastic environment, important heuristics update the composition plan by predicting the unexpected behavior of web services (e.g. failures) [117]. For example, OWL-S process models automate the composition of Web services to deal with non-determinism, partial observables and multiple goals [76]. A Model Driven Planning (MD-Plan) approach encodes conditional operators and iterations in the composition of services as a synthesis of plans [118]. The MD-Plan approach also translates OWL-S service descriptions to the SHOP2 domain [118]. A Hierarchical Task Network (HTN) system plans the set of OWL-S descriptions using SHOP2 and then executes the resulting plans over the web [31].

2.1.2   Service Composition with Non-functional Requirements

In a cloud market, different providers may provide different non-functional properties (QoS). The QoS-aware cloud service composition finds the optimal component services that are best matched to end users' QoS requirements. The short-term composition considers QoS values only at the time of composition. It is usually modeled as a Multiple Criteria Decision Making problem [143]. The QoS-aware composition approaches typically use Integer Linear Programming (ILP) and

Genetic Algorithm (GA) [140]. An ILP consists of a set of variables, a set of linear constraints and a linear objective function. After translating a composition problem into an ILP problem, a particular solver software such as LPSolve generates a composition plan [14]. One fundamental limitation of this approach is that the QoS attributes need to be linearized to fit the LP solver. A Mixed Integer Linear Programming (MILP)-based QoS-aware composition is proposed to overcome this issue [57]. It allows the QoS aggregation rules to be non-linear.

Although constraint-based programming, e.g. MILP, allows a certain degree of flexibility in the aggregation rules of a composition, evolutionary algorithms are found to be more applicable in the generic QoS-aware compositions [22]. Genetic Algorithm (GA) is the preferred technology for short-term service compositions [141]. Although the GA approach [141] is slower than integer programming, but it is a more scalable choice and better suited to handle generic QoS attributes. A modified GA method [80] computes the QoS uncertainty for pruning redundant services while extracting reliable services. The GA based approach composes at different levels, such as applications and computing [22, 80]. The GA-based approach could be improved further by incorporating a skyline optimization approach [2]. This selects services for composition by efficiently reducing the number of candidate services to be considered in the GA solutions.

2.1.3 Service Composition with Long-Term Requirements

The long-term composition considers the end users' long-term QoS requirements. Existing long-term based research usually focuses on two kinds of composition approaches: (a) *economic model based compositions*, and (b) *cost optimization based compositions*. A time series-based composition framework represents the long-term requirements of the end users is proposed in multivariate time-series [140]. It formulates the long-term composition problem as a time-series similarity measure problem. Dimension reduction techniques, e.g. Principle Component Analysis (PCA), are used in the runtime similarity measure [140]. Another efficient way to represent economic model is the Bayesian Network (BN) [139]. BN models consider the temporal dependency among the QoS attributes. The BN-based economic model uses Influence Diagram (ID) to deploy the concrete services in the composition [139].

Long-term cost maximization is another important aspect from the end user's perspective. End users expect to receive the right-provision of cloud services according to their work-loads and pay only what they use. Although cloud services are elastic, on-demand provision is often costlier than reservations. For this reason, the cost optimization is defined to reserve the right amount of resources. However, such advanced reservation is difficult to perform due to the uncertainty of end user's future demands. An optimal cloud resource provisioning (OCRP) algorithm is proposed [28] which formulated a stochastic programming model to handle dynamic workloads. The OCRP divides the long-term plan into several segments and decisions are made in multiple provisioning stages. A two-phase algorithm minimizes the service provision cost [63]. In the first phase, the composition is mathematically formulated to derive upper and lower bounds for VM configurations. In the second step, the Kalman filter and Linear Programming (LP) predicts resource demands and VMs are dynamically configured according to the prediction. A machine-learning technique predicts the future workload and automatically adjusts the resource cap [66]. The resource auto-scaling scheme decides the trade-off between cost and latency [66].

Although our target is cloud service composition from the provider's perspective, we still need to consider the composition from an end user's perspective. It provides insight into the long-term expectations of the end users. This knowledge will eventually help service providers to select the best service requests.

2.2 Cloud Service Management from a Provider's Perspective

To the best of our knowledge, existing approaches mainly focus on the short-term resources utilization and satisfy the end users' QoS requirements. Key techniques used are resource allocation, job scheduling, and admission control. We discuss these in the following subsections.

2.2.1 Resource Allocation Approaches

A greedy resource allocation algorithm minimizes infrastructure costs and SLA violations for SaaS providers [134]. The algorithms are designed to ensure that SaaS providers can manage the dynamic demands of customers. These algorithms map customers' requests to the infrastructure level parameters and resolve the heterogeneity issue of virtual machines. A distributed architecture, Multiple Criteria Decision Analysis (MCDA) is proposed to manage the resources and to prevent their under-utilization and over-utilization [138]. The MCDA correlates resource allocation with energy efficiency and SLA violations. Low utilization of servers in a datacenter is one of the biggest factors in low power efficiency of the data center. For example, Google datacenter was reported to be 30% energy-efficient [53]. Resource optimization should not violate the SLA as it incurs penalties. One essential technique for resource optimization is consolidation which involves power-performance tradeoffs. If servers consolidate the workloads, fewer servers are needed to service VMs, and the active servers will be highly utilized. However, it may affect performance due to the reduction of available physical resources (CPU, memory, I/O bandwidth) [11]. The key idea is to migrate VMs from the hosts without compromising the user-specified QoS requirements. Such migration ensures the optimal resource utilization and minimizes energy consumption, i.e.

operation costs [11]. An efficient heuristic algorithm based on convex optimization and dynamic programming minimizes the total energy cost of cloud computing system while meeting the specified client-level SLAs in a probabilistic sense [53].

Auction mechanism is also a traditional method for resource allocation. Spot VM instances are offered in an auction-based mechanism in the cloud market [3]. Providers expect to increase consumer demand by lowering service prices which are under-utilized in a spot market. However, as the request of each type of VM can fluctuate, the allocated resources to each VM type should be correctly provisioned to maximize the total revenue. An adaptive resource controller [146] uses prediction models for the dynamic capacity in each VM. The Model Predictive Control (MPC) takes into account capacity constraints in the adaptive resource controller. Next, the optimal resource allocation is modeled in the Optimal Control Theory (OCT) predicting runtime demands in the spot market. A cloud service provider collects all the users' bids and determines the price in a sealed-bid auction based cloud resource allocation approach [88]. This system simplifies the cloud service provider's decision rules by transforming a resource problem into an ordering problem.

To the best of our knowledge, existing resource allocation approaches in a cloud service composition maximize the short-term profit of the provider and optimize the efficient resource utilization. It requires the full knowledge of available resources and the associated static demands from consumers. However, we focus on the long-term resource utilization in a cloud provider. Usually, consumers' runtime resource utilization behavior get changed in the long-term period. Hence, short-term approaches may not be applicable in the long-term period. Besides, existing resource allocation approaches do not consider the long-term economic models of consumers. Hence, these approaches may cause more SLA violations in the long-term IaaS composition.

2.2.2   Task Scheduling Approaches

An efficient scheduling of all tasks of an IaaS provider is an important research issue to optimize resource utilization and operation costs. The IaaS's consumers can be divided into two classes: (a) computing-intensive, and (b) data-intensive [100]. In data-intensive applications, it is desirable to decrease the data movement, which means decreasing the transferring time. In the computing-intensive tasks, it is advisable to schedule the data to the high-performance computers. Besides, tasks are often heterogeneous in nature, e.g. some jobs may require fewer computing resources at a lower, while some tasks may take more bandwidth and computing resources. The target of an efficient task scheduling algorithm is to minimize the total executing cost and transferring time in IaaS physical servers. A modified Particle Swarm Optimization (PSO) algorithm solves task scheduling in cloud computing and minimizes the overall time of execution and transmission [100]. A task scheduling algorithm is proposed [42] that uses the analytic hierarchy process to allocate optimal resources. Upon receiving a pool of tasks, an evolutionary algorithm compares them pairwise, according to network bandwidth, completion time, task costs, and reliability of the task [42]. The weights of tasks are then calculated and computing resources are allocated accordingly. Different criteria, such as execution time, policy and utility function are also considered to design a scheduling algorithm [102].

To the best of our knowledge, existing task scheduling approaches in a cloud service composition consider only deterministic arrival of the incoming requests. The future jobs are not considered while a set of submitted jobs are scheduled to meet the deadline. However, the stochastic arrival of requests is a realistic phenomenon in the long-term IaaS composition. We may have to update the compositions in the periodic intervals considering the dynamic and new requests which are not considered in existing task scheduling approaches.

2.2.3   Admission Control Approaches

Admission control in the cloud can be viewed as the upper layer of the resource management. Admission control mechanisms filter the requests that are not wanted by the underlying resource manager where the resource management only works with the admitted service requests. A SLA-based admission policy is proposed [135] whereby heuristic algorithms determine if a new request can be admitted without affecting accepted requests and available resources. The admission policy algorithm operates on a First Come First Served (FCFS) basis. It only admits a request if there are enough resources to complete the request within the deadline. A policy-based admission control mechanism is proposed for elastic cloud services [77]. The model allows for partial acceptance of the services and possible federation with other cloud providers. An autonomous scheme for admission control ensures right-provision, minimum response times [82]. It uses an adaptive feedback control scheme to compensate for changes in system capacity with the admitted workload.

To the best of our knowledge, existing admission control approaches do not consider higher level long-term business strategies of a provider. Such business strategies include reputation building, profit maximization, and risk management. These strategies are usually constructed based on different environment variables such as available resources and number of consumers. Besides, the provider may invest in increasing new resources or sell a part of existing resources to other providers in the long-term period. Hence, the existing short-term admission control approaches are not applicable in the long-term IaaS composition.

2.3   Economic Models

Economic modeling is at the heart of economic theory. An economist explains chains of cause and effect among numerous interacting elements in a market using economic models [69]. For example, a beverage company increases the price of its product using its economic model. In this context, the economic model explains and predicts what will happen to the sale of beverages if the price of the product increases. Economic models find both short-term and long-term correlations among economic variables. A long-term economic model predicts long-run influences of the variables [39]. For example, if a bank decides to increase the rate of a home loan, the economic model can be used to predict how this would affect some homes purchased in future.

We treat IaaS cloud resources as services. They provide a higher level of abstraction and a human concept to computing. In the real world, IaaS services are delivered using several economic operations such as service menu creation, dynamic pricing, advertising and committing to service level agreements. IaaS providers often perform business operations over a long term. As IaaS providers invest heavily in developing the infrastructure, sometimes it takes years to get the return on investment (ROI) [130]. Hence, economic models naturally fit IaaS service provisions. The IaaS provider can decide if the incoming consumers are expected according to its economic model.

We first discuss economic modeling in the research field of operations research. Such models should provide useful insight into developing economic models for the cloud providers. Later, we discuss the existing economic models in the cloud market.

2.3.1 Economic Modeling in Operations Research

Operational research (OR) usually involves a wide range of decision-making techniques to improve the profit and performance of real-world objectives [132]. The major sub-disciplines in modern OR are transportation, simulation, yield management, and financial engineering. The business structure of cloud providers is reasonably similar to these sub-disciplines [145]. We can consider cloud resources as having limited capacity and as a perishable asset, which is similar to airplane seats or hotel rooms. In this context, we review some economic models in OR. Our focus is the economy model of yield management, whose objective is to maximize the revenue or yield of an organization. A good yield management system will help it to decide the amount of inventory (e.g. seats on the airplane, rooms in a hotel or cars in a rental car fleet) being allocated to different types of demand [72]. Three distinct problems are identified for yield management in the airline industry: *overbooking*, *discount allocation* and *traffic management* [119]. Over-booking is the practice of intentionally accepting more reservations than the available seats in an airplane. Discount allocation is the process of determining the number of discount fares to be offered on a flight. Traffic management is the process of reserving seats in different markets [10]. Existing approaches not only focus on revenue maximization but also consider perceived fairness [54]. Yield management for perceived fairness is discussed in [73]. A perceived fairness or reference transaction is how customers think an operation should be conducted and how much a given service should cost.

To the best of our knowledge, existing approaches in Operation Research are resource allocation driven and do not consider services as the first-class objects in the decision making. Services present a higher level of abstraction providing a human concept to computing. In that respect, the key aspect of the service approach is its ability to elegantly provide real-world problems with a naturally congruous solution. Long-term quantitative and qualitative economic models are challenging to design using the approaches in Operation research. In this book, we first create the abstraction of cloud resources (i.e., CPU, Memory, and Network bandwidth) using the service paradigm and then complementing it with the use of QoS (i.e., Availability, Response time and Throughput). We focus on developing the long-term QoS-aware quantitative and qualitative economic models for IaaS services.

2.3.2   Quantitative Economic Modeling in the Cloud Market

Economic models in cloud computing are characterized in two groups: microeconomic models and macroeconomic models [36]. Microeconomic models are for individual service producers and consumers. It helps them to maximize their economic goals. Macroeconomic models are for the whole market analysis.

The existing service delivery models are microeconomic in nature. Cloud service delivery models have the following three typical properties.

- *On-demand Provision*: In this model, computing resources are made available to the user as needed. Service consumers can allocate a service at any time in the absence of a long-term contract with the provider [6].
- *Elasticity*: Elasticity in the cloud is the ability of an application to automatically adjust the infrastructure resources usage to accommodate varied workloads and priorities. The elasticity is used to overcome the challenge common to enterprises: being able to meet fluctuating demands efficiently while maintaining availability and performance in a context-aware environment. Because an enterprise's demand on computing resources can vary drastically from time to time, maintaining sufficient resources to meet peak requirements can be costly. Conversely, if the enterprise cuts cost by only maintaining minimal computing resources, there will not be sufficient resources to meet peak requirements [21].
- *Flexible Pricing Model*: The prices of the services are determined by different models. The Pay-as-You-Go (PAYG) model is designed for on-demand services. In this model, customers subscribe to a service on an hourly or monthly basis and only pay based on their usage. In the reservation model, consumers can reserve services for a long-term period at relatively cheaper rates than PAYG. In spot markets, the consumer bids a maximum price for a service. If the service's market value is less than the bid price (market value is determined by supply and demand), the service is provided to the consumer. The service is stopped by the provider when the market value of the service becomes greater than the bid price [96].

The long-term QoS economic model of a service consumer identifies how QoS requirements of end users change over time [139]. The service providers' economic models are further categorised into two types: *cost modelling* and *price modelling*. An economic model for self-tuned caching is proposed to model the cost of cached queries in cloud databases by practicing the theory of altruistic economy [34]. The economic model is altruistic in the sense that its intention is not to increase the cloud's profit but to provide good quality query services at low cost. Another cost modeling of cloud database query is proposed where the main objective is to optimize query management in a cloud database based on various economic policies [78]. An economic model for profit maximization of cloud service providers is proposed that analyzes the total cost of ownership (TCO) of cloud providers [121]. An economic model of a federated cloud [51] evaluates the cost of using resources from a cloud federation and develops a resource management core for profit maximization. Apart from cost modeling, pricing is another type of economic model used in the cloud. A dynamic pricing scheme describes the relationship between price and demands of a cache service in a time-efficient manner [71]. A market-driven dynamic pricing mechanism is proposed that considers stochastic demand and perishable resources to set prices of the services for revenue maximization [136]. Dynamic pricing of a service is determined through a non-cooperative stochastic game among cloud providers in [122].

Existing economic models do not consider long-term relationships among composite QoS, resource utilization, and operation costs. The price of the service, QoS provisions, and user satisfactions are also not modeled for any long-term period. We focus on developing a long-term and QoS-aware economic model for the service providers in Chap. 4.

2.3.3   Qualitative Economic Modeling in the Cloud Market

The qualitative economic model is critical to a service composition [1]. It determines how the composition is performed. This model is a form of user-preference where relative ordering among preference attributes are determined by economic variables such as cost and profit [4, 16]. For example, in the case of airline booking, a qualitative economic model may specify several domain-specific non-functional properties such as the choice of a particular carrier, the time of flight, a price range and a minimum trust level.

To the best of our knowledge, existing qualitative economic models are constructed for the service composition from a consumer's perspective. A Conditional Preference Network (CP-Net) [18] is a dependency graph that represents consumers' preferences qualitatively. The total preference ordering over attributes are described in a Condition Preference Table (CPT). A CP-Net based economic model is proposed for the service composition from the consumers' perspective [111].

The quality of the composition depends on the density and semantic consistency of the CP-Net. When preference specifications in a CP-net are sparse, a composition generates too many candidate solutions which may not be useful in the real world. The Weighted CP-Net (WCP-Net) and the concept of Violation Degree (VD) [127] are used to fine-grain consumer preferences in a qualitative service composition. Considering the weights of all attributes, the VD quantifies the dissimilarity of a service pattern from the provided WCP-Net. The composition approach from incomplete consumer preferences [126] performs preference amendment, i.e. the similar consumer detection and historical preference voting.

As objectives of IaaS providers are different from service consumers, the qualitative preferences of the consumers are not analogous to the preferences of providers. The long-term IaaS business strategies may have several temporal objectives, such as the first 2 years are to build reputation while the later years are for profit maximization. We focus on developing a long-term qualitative economic model using the IaaS business strategies in Chap. 5.

2.4 Prediction Modeling in Service Composition

The long-term service composition requires predicting service performance from their history. Predicting future resource utilization also requires prediction models or machine-learning techniques. First, we discuss different types of prediction models in various applications. Then we discuss the integration of prediction models with service compositions.

2.4.1 Time-Series and Probabilistic Prediction Models

Time-series prediction models are used in different sectors such as stock forecasting and population growth prediction. There are different time-series prediction models that work on various time-series patterns. ARIMA [19] is the most commonly used model in the autoregressive (AR) analysis. It integrates both the AR and moving average (MA) parts. In the AR model, the current value of a time-series is determined by the previous values in the time-series. In MA, the present value of a time-series is determined by the past prediction errors in the time-series [20]. In a recursive analysis, Holt-Winters exponential smoothing is mostly used in practice [47]. Holt-Winters' model is an extension to exponential smoothing that can detect level, seasonality, and trend [29]. A vector-based multivariate time-series prediction approach (VAR) is proposed with AR and non-adaptive coefficients [35, 75]. With vector AR models, it is possible to approximate the actual process by arbitrarily choosing lagged variables.

Probabilistic models have different applications in various sectors. A Bayesian Network (BN) is proposed to model long-term QoS requirements [139]. Different uses of Dynamic Bayesian Network (DBN) and the algorithms for learning and inference are discussed in [93]. Both BN and DBN ignore incorporating time intervals in their states. A Continuous Hidden Markov Chain (CHMC) incorporates the time dimension in the states [106]. Another popular probabilistic model is Hidden Markov Model (HMM) and used in different domains such as speech recognition and financial predictions [40]. An HMM is a statistical Markov model where it is assumed that the observations have Markov properties and they follow unobserved (hidden) states.

2.4.2 Web Service QoS Prediction Frameworks

Most existing approaches for Web service QoS predictions are based on univariate analysis. Table 2.1 summarises some of these prediction models in the web service composition. An Artificial Neural Network (ANN)-based learning agent and AR technique are used to predict QoS [17, 68]. The agent-based approach [68] assumes linear correlations between the observed QoS and time. A personalised web service prediction framework is proposed using the MA method, which usually models simplistic non-linear models [148]. The ARIMA model predicts higher levels of non-linear trends in univariate QoS performances efficiently [85]. Although ARIMA is extremely efficient, the Holt-winters method is usually preferable to model seasonality in the observed sequence of QoS predictions [23]. The predictions model is very useful to forecast trends or seasonality. However, sudden increases or decreases in demand or workload are not efficiently handled by ARIMA or Halt-Winters. A random walk approach augments the ARIMA and handles such spikes in the workload [62]. A web server workload forecasting framework is proposed

Table 2.1 Different prediction models in the service composition

Name	Used in	Type	Purpose
AR	[68]	Univariate	Predicting linear trend
MA	[148]	Univariate	Predicting non-linear trend
ARIMA	[85]	Univariate	Predicting non-linear trend and seasonality
Holt-winters	[23]	Univariate	Predicting high-frequent seasonality
Random walk	[62]	Univariate	Predicting linear trend
VAR	[124]	Multivariate	Predicting non-linear trend and seasonality
BN	[86]	Univariate	Predicting non-linear trend
DBN	[84]	Multivariate	Predicting higher-level non-linear trend
HMM	[98]	Univariate	Predicting high-frequent seasonality
ANN	[17]	Univariate	Predicting high-frequent seasonality
CHMC	[149]	Univariate	Predicting high-frequent seasonality

using VAR models, which apply multivariate analysis and are useful to predict non-linear trends and seasonality [124]. The HMM and queuing models are also useful technology in resource planning to predict QoS performances [98]. A fuzzy logic algorithm is fused with the CHMC for a financial time-series prediction [149]. An iterative algorithm for maximum likelihood is proposed in [9]. Both the HMM and CHMC predict high-frequent seasonality in univariate time-series. The BN, designed for multiple observation spaces, works with univariate observations and predicts non-linear trends [86]. However, a Dynamic Bayesian Network (DBN) incorporates a multivariate analysis to predict higher-level non-linear trends [84].

The long-term attributes in IaaS composition should be highly correlated. For example, an increase in QoS often follows an increase in service prices. To the best of our knowledge, the correlations among different dimensions are not considered in predicting service performance. Further, non-adaptive coefficients and lack of MA features make VAR and DBN models less efficient in the time-series with high random seasonality. Hence, there is a possibility of developing faster and better multivariate prediction models. We propose new multivariate prediction models in Chaps. 3 and 6.

2.5   Optimization Approaches in Service Composition

Optimization techniques are a set of tools that are important to efficiently manage an enterprise's resources. These techniques are used to find the action that optimizes (i.e. maximizes or minimizes) the value of an objective function. For example, in a price-output decision-making process, a company may be interested in determining the output level that maximizes profits. We define the IaaS composition to maximize the long-term profit using the quantitative economic model and to follow the decisions from the qualitative economic model. The IaaS composition could be transformed into an optimization problem to maximize the quantitative or qualitative objective functions. We can divide the existing optimization approaches into two categories: (a) global optimization, and (b) sequential local optimization.

2.5.1   Global Optimization Approaches

A global optimization approach creates a global objective function and considers all in-put options at the time of optimization. Table 2.2 summarises some existing global optimization approaches in web service compositions from the consumer's perspective. Differential calculus methods are used in unconstrained optimization where no constraints are imposed on the decision variables [60]. Often, the constraints in an economic decision-making process are in the form of inequality relationships. For example, limitations on the resources, such as personnel and capital of an organisation, place an upper bound or budget ceiling on the quantity of

Table 2.2 Different global optimization approaches in the service composition

Name	Used in	Objective function	Category
Differential calculus	[60]	Linear	Constraint-based
ILP	[113]	Linear	Constraint-based
QP	[105]	Linear	Constraint-based
GA	[141]	Non-linear	Evolutionary
ACO	[147]	Non-linear	Evolutionary
PSO	[150]	Non-linear	Metaheuristic
DP	[46]	Linear	Combinatorial
GD	[89]	Linear	Stochastic
BRST	[15]	Linear	Stochastic
OCBA	[30]	Linear	Stochastic

such resources. In this situation, Linear Programming (LP), Integer Programming (IP) and Quadratic Programming (QP) are mostly used as optimization techniques [110]. A constraint based Integer Linear Programming (ILP) is proposed to compose services from the consumer's perspective [113]. The selection of candidate web services are transformed in a QP method in [105].

Sharing resources and multi-tenancy is the usual way of provisioning services by IaaS providers [63]. Such approaches often create non-linear objective functions when operation costs are calculated [51]. Due to the non-linear objective function in long-term service compositions, evolutionary algorithms, i.e. Genetic algorithm and Ant-Colony optimizations are used in service composition from the consumers' perspectives [141, 147]. An improved discrete immune optimization algorithm based on particle swarm optimization (DIPSO) combines the features of a proportional clone to find the global best fit in the web service composition [150].

Dynamic Programming (DP) is an algorithmic paradigm that solves a given complex problem by breaking it into sub-problems (overlapping sub-problems) and stores the results of sub-problems to avoid repeated computation (optimal substructure) [74]. A DP-based solution finds the longest path in a Weighted Multi-stage Graph for the composite service in [46].

The dynamic environment is inherent in the service composition, i.e. changes in service prices and the stochastic arrival of the requests. A collaborative service composition is proposed considering the local connectivity between web services users and geographical information [89]. The Gradient Descent (GD) technique searches the local minimum of a matrix factorization in the composition [89]. The Boender-Rinnooy-Stougie-Timmer algorithm (BRST) is an optimization algorithm that involves sampling, clustering and local search in a stochastic composition environment [15]. An optimal computing budget allocation (OCBA) is proposed to maximize resource allocation through using an asymptotic framework and analyzing the structure of the optimal allocation in [30].

To the best of our knowledge, existing optimization approaches do not consider non-linear objective functions from the IaaS perspective. It is also important to analyze the effect of dynamic consumer behavior in the optimization process. We discuss the transformation of the linear IaaS composition into a heuristic based ILP process in Chap. 3. We also consider the optimization process in the stochastic arrival of requests in Chap. 4. We focus on evolutionary algorithms in the stochastic IaaS composition as existing dynamic optimization approaches do not consider non-linear objective functions. Besides, existing non-linear evolutionary approaches do not consider storing the information of the previous optimization and using it to facilitate the forthcoming optimization in a dynamic environment. We develop an efficient dynamic optimization technique for service composition from the providers' perspective in Chap. 4.

2.5.2 Sequential Local Optimization and Machine-Learning Approaches

A local optimization approach creates a local objective function and considers a fragment of input options at the time of optimization. The main idea is that local optimizations are executed in a sequence, and it approximates to the global optimization. The key benefit of this approach is scalability and runtime efficiency [59]. Sequential local optimization is a common practice in operations research where it is often required to determine the consequences of any given action regarding high-level criteria [59]. A Sequential Minimal Optimization (SMO) algorithm is proposed to train Support Vector Machines (SVM) and to model the state-action sequences [103]. Another state-action model is the Markov Decision Process (MDP). A MDP-based approach optimizes software on mobile phones to enhance the performance [32]. The MDP framework incorporates user preferences into decision-making at or about runtime and optimizes the given utility or reward functions [32].

Machine-learning is a widely used technology that determines the parameters in state-action sequences in sequential optimization [137]. As we are considering the dynamic composition, a model-free learning platform should be more efficient than the model-based learning algorithms [48]. Reinforcement learning is a useful model-free technology for the adaptive service composition from consumers' perspectives [128]. A service composition is modeled as a Markov Decision Process (MDP) incorporating multiple alternative services and workflows [128]. A modified Q-learning algorithm is designed for optimal adaptive controllers through a sequential decision process [83]. Q-learning is an off-policy method that approximates an MDP by updating the information after each experience of actions [43]. It constructs the optimal policy by using the rewards of actions to approximate the optimal function.

To the best of our knowledge, sequential optimizations in IaaS composition are yet to be studied. We analyze various model-free reinforcement learning for the qualitative IaaS composition in Chap. 5. We propose a three-dimensional

Q-learning approach to finding the best sequence of local optimizations for a deterministic request pattern in Chap. 5.

2.6 Conclusion

In this chapter, we have discussed the fundamental differences between the long-term IaaS composition and the existing short-term composition approaches. To the best of our knowledge, existing approaches do not consider the long-term service composition from the provider's perspective. The purpose of these approaches is to maximize the provider's short-term profit through efficient resource utilizations, task scheduling, and admission control. The long-term IaaS composition requires quantitative and qualitative economic models. Multivariate prediction models and multidimensional reinforcement learning are also essential components of an effective IaaS composition. To the best of our knowledge, these components have not been studied regarding the composition from a provider's perspective. In the following chapters, we consider several long-term features in the service composition: (a) dynamic consumer behavior, (b) stochastic arrival of the requests and (c) qualitative service provisions. In Chap. 3, we develop a long-term service composition framework considering the dynamic consumer behavior. In Chap. 4, we deal with uncertainties in service provision environment and maximize the provider's financial expectations. In Chap. 5, we incorporate the higher level business strategies in service provisions and transform the composition into a decision-support system. In Chap. 6, we predict the performance of an IaaS provider to minimize the SLA violations in the future service provisions.

Chapter 3
Long-Term IaaS Composition for Deterministic Requests

3.1 Introduction

The provider-consumer relationship between IaaS and SaaS providers is long-term and economically driven [140]. In the cloud, a large proportion of services are provisioned for a long-term period and are billed monthly or yearly instead of hourly. IaaS providers encourage long-term service requests by advertising lower prices on reserved resources. For example, a consumer can save up to 53% on a 3-year reservation plan compared to the on-demand scheme in Amazon EC2 [51]. Naturally, an IaaS provider receives long-term service requests from different types of consumers. The provider should analyze the long-term profitability for any relationship by composing service provisioning based on these requests before accepting them.

Our target is to achieve the optimal service composition that maximizes the provider's objective function, i.e. revenue and profit. *In this chapter, we focus on the profit maximization in the deterministic arrival of service requests.* We assume that the decision-support system for the IaaS composition does not have to consider future uncertainties. Although *stochastic* arrival of requests is more practical in the market, our findings of the IaaS composition for deterministic requests may provide a foundation for the dynamic IaaS composition.

To the best of our knowledge, existing approaches consider only the composition of short-term service requests to achieve a trade-off between profit maximization and consumer satisfaction [42, 134, 138]. Different methods, such as resource allocation, scheduling and admission control, are proposed to compose the short-term requests [88, 102, 135]. These approaches optimize the distribution of available resources at the time of composition and maximize the profit at that time. These approaches are not applicable to long-term compositions as the functional and non-functional requirements in the long-term service requests may change [140]. As short-term compositions select consumer requests based only on current requirements, the selected requests may not be profitable in future.

© Springer International Publishing AG 2018
S. Mistry et al., *Economic Models for Managing Cloud Services*,
https://doi.org/10.1007/978-3-319-73876-5_3

In this chapter, a new long-term IaaS service composition framework is proposed by considering the deterministic arrival of service requests. We consider two practical constraints in the composition process: *resource limitation* and *service level agreement (SLA) violation. We assume that the IaaS provider delivers services only from its data center which has a fixed amount of resources (CPU, Memory, Network Bandwidth, etc.).* This constrains the elasticity of physical resources. Although these restrictions can be removed through cloud federation [50], it imposes additional complexities such as platform heterogeneity and future pricing of services [116]. *Our next assumption is that the service provider maintains the SLA.* The consumer expects a long-term SLA from the provider which defines the boundaries of permissible values for QoS attributes, such as execution time, availability or cost over a period. An SLA violation incurs penalties and may cause profit or loss to the provider [64]. The selection process in the request composition requires a revenue and cost analysis model for the allocated resources and QoS provisions. The combined allocated resources to the consumers should not exceed the maximum allowable resources and should also produce minimum SLA violations. *Hence, the IaaS composition is regarded as a constraints-based optimization problem for the deterministic arrival of requests.*

Apart from the constraints, cloud consumers' long-term behaviors also influence the composition process. Such behaviors include QoS fluctuation tolerance levels and resource utilization pattern. Existing composition approaches consider the requirements as exact and allocate resources according to it [42, 134, 138]. The service selection usually follows the best match criteria in the real world [135]. For example, a consumer requires x units CPU and y units response time in z units price. In the market, it finds the best-matched service that provides x_1 units CPU and y units response time in z units price. If $x_1 > x$, the probability that $(x_1 - x)$ CPU units are under-utilized is very high. A consumer who under-utilizes its allocated resources may increase the provider's profit as the under-utilized resources can be allocated to other suitable consumers. Not only resource utilization, but the QoS fluctuation tolerance level is another important run-time consumer behavior. As the QoS fluctuation is advertised by the IaaS provider, it is expected that consumers may allow some QoS changes and still be satisfied over the long-term. Different consumers may have different QoS tolerance levels based on their application types and the times of operation. It is practical to assume that a consumer who is less tolerant to QoS fluctuations is more prone to report SLA violations. *Hence, an efficient prediction model is required for IaaS composition using consumers' runtime behavior as a heuristic.*

We formulate the IaaS composition problem for deterministic requests as follows. Let us assume an IaaS providers advertises its long-term functional and QoS properties of its services. The functional properties are the provision of CPU (C), Memory (M) and Network bandwidth (NB) as units. The QoS attributes of the services are Availability (AV), Response time (RT), Throughput (TH) and Price (P). The advertisement specifies a fluctuation range, i.e. maximum and minimum values of the QoS attributes. In a certain situation, N different Software as a Service (SaaS) providers may find the service advertisement to be the best in the market and send their specific requests to the IaaS provider. We denote the N consumers as $(U_1, U_1, \ldots, U_N)$. All the consumers require total T_{total} time units of services. A consumer may require different short-term service requests in this time interval. We define the jth short-term service request of the ith consumers as a tuple: $S_{ij} = \{c, m, nb, av, rt, th, t_s, t_e\}$, where c, m, nb are the required functional units of CPU, Memory and Network respectively. The QoS requirements av, rt, th specify the required units of Availability, Response time and Throughput respectively. t_s and t_e specify the respective starting and ending times of the service. The long-term service request of a consumer is formed by the combination of the different short-term service requests. The long-term service requests of the ith consumer can be formed using k short-term requests represented as $U_i = (S_{i1}, S_{i2}, \ldots, S_{ik})$, where $\sum_{j=1}^{k} (t_e - t_s) = T_{total} \mid t_s \in S_{ij}$ and $t_e \in S_{ij}$. The IaaS provider has finite capacity on CPU, Memory, Network denoted as C_{max}, M_{max} and NB_{max} respectively. The maximum composite QoS values it can provide are AV_{max} for availability, RT_{max} for response time and TH_{max} for throughput. **The target** is to analyze consumers' future run time behavior and to select the optimal set of requests $(U_i, U_j, \ldots U_l)$ from the N users that maximizes the long-term profit and minimizes the number of SLA violations.

We propose a new service composition framework that analyzes the behaviors of the consumers and imposes the heuristics in the selection process. According to [120], the long-term consumer behavior regarding resource utilization can be represented as *high-frequent*, *seasonal-trending* or *regime changing* time-series. Resource utilization time-series of stock market SaaS applications generally follow high-frequent patterns [86] (see Fig. 3.1a). SaaS providers such as Video Stream Services are likely to follow seasonal-trending (see Fig. 3.1b) or regime changing patterns [120]. It is difficult to use a specific model to realize different patterns. Additionally, service requirement attributes (VMs and QoS) are often correlated and *multivariate* in nature [140]. Hence, we propose a new multivariate Hidden Markov Model (HMM) and Auto Regressive Integrated Moving Average (ARIMA) model,

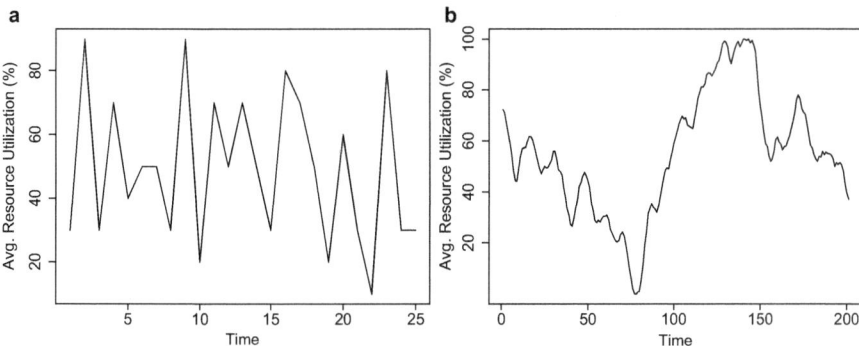

Fig. 3.1 The long-term resource utilization patterns: (**a**) High-frequent, and (**b**) Seasonal-trending

to predict the high-frequent or seasonal-trending long-term behavior of service requests based on historical evidence. In the case of new consumer requests without historical data, a novel community-based bootstrapping method is devised to predict future service usage.

Selecting the optimal set of long-term requests require combinatorial optimization techniques, e.g. Integer Linear Programming (ILP) and dynamic programming [110]. However, the combinatorial solution space is relatively large in our problem, as we consider the long-term aspects in a large number of variables and a high number of service requests. Once the incoming requests are transformed by projecting the dynamic behavior, we model the profit maximization problem using Integer Linear Programming (ILP) [110] by considering resource constraints (CPU, memory and network bandwidth) and penalty arising from SLA violations.

The novelty of the proposed framework is summarized as follows.

(a) The use of multivariate analysis on an HMM and ARIMA model for predicting the future QoS fluctuation tolerance levels, resource utilization and early exit patterns of the existing consumers, and community-based bootstrapping method to predict the dynamic behavior of new consumer requests.

(b) An ILP based solution for profit maximization taking transformed requests as inputs and considering resource constraints as well as SLA violation penalties.

The chapter is structured as follows. The heuristics on consumers' behavior, the service composition framework and prediction model are discussed in Sects. 3.2, 3.3 and 3.4 respectively. The optimization process, experiments and conclusion are presented in Sects. 3.5, 3.6 and 3.7 respectively.

3.2 The Heuristics on Consumer Behavior

We assume consumers' service requests are influenced by their behavior. We consider the following two heuristics on consumer's long-term requests.

- *QoS fluctuation tolerance level*: This is the fluctuation range in the QoS values that the consumer can tolerate and will not report a QoS violation. If a consumer's response time tolerance level is 5% at summer, a requirement of 100 task/hour throughput can be fulfilled by 95 task/hour throughput or above without the QoS violation report. The QoS fluctuation tolerance level of a consumer may change over time.
- *Resource utilization level*: This is the difference between the requested resources and their actual usage. If a consumer requests 100 units of CPU and uses 80 units of CPU, its resource utilization level is 20%. This level may also change over time.

One trivial question is, "Why a fluctuation from the requested values is still acceptable to the consumer?" We identify two stages in SaaS providers' request procedure that likely cause the heuristics.

- *Stage 1—IaaS service requirement determination*: SaaS providers require the IaaS services based on their workload. Typically SaaS architecture is multi-tenant. A workload mostly depends on the number of tenants on board at a particular time which is stochastic in nature [94]. Hence, SaaS providers typically use probabilistic models to assess their future IaaS service requirements [49]. Consumers choose a maximum confidence interval in the probable IaaS service units if it is feasible in their economic models [49]. The selected value is often greater than the actual usage. For example, a consumer may predict that 80 CPU units are sufficient for its workload at summer with a confidence interval of 90%, and that 85 units are also sufficient with a confidence interval of 95%. If the consumers have enough money to invest, it is more likely that the IaaS provider should receive an 85 unit request from the consumer. It imposes a 5% resource under-utilization level.
- *Stage 2—Best IaaS provider determination*: It is unlikely that consumers may find an IaaS service advertisement having an exact match with its requirements [140]. This influences the consumer to transform its request from exact requirements. For example, if the provider advertises 90 CPU units for 110$ and the consumer requires 85 CPU units for 100$, it is more likely that the IaaS provider should receive a 90 unit request from the consumer based on the policy of minimum QoS violation. Hence, around 5% resource is likely to be under-utilized.

3.3   The Long-Term Composition Framework for Deterministic Requests

The proposed service composition framework consists of three modules: the request transformation module, the economic model of the provider and the optimization module (see Fig. 3.2). The request transformation module applies heuristics to the SaaS requests to predict their future QoS tolerance levels and resource utilization. Here, we consider heuristics on *Resource utilization level*, *QoS fluctuation tolerance level* and *early exit from contract* in the consumers' long-term requests. The optimization module calculates the profit of the transformed requests using the long-term economic model of resources and services of the IaaS provider. The following example describes how the heuristics-based approach can maximize profit in service composition from the provider's perspective.

Let us assume an IaaS provider operates with two constraints: both the numbers of maximum resource and QoS units are 100. We only consider the "availability" as QoS for simplicity. The rule of determining the composite QoS of QoS_1 and QoS_2 is the maximum value of the two attributes. The provider has a fixed rate ($5/hour) for the service usage. The profitability of the provider is proportional to resource usage, i.e. the marginal operation cost per node reduces when the resource utilization increases at the node [51]. We assume that three SaaS Customer relationship

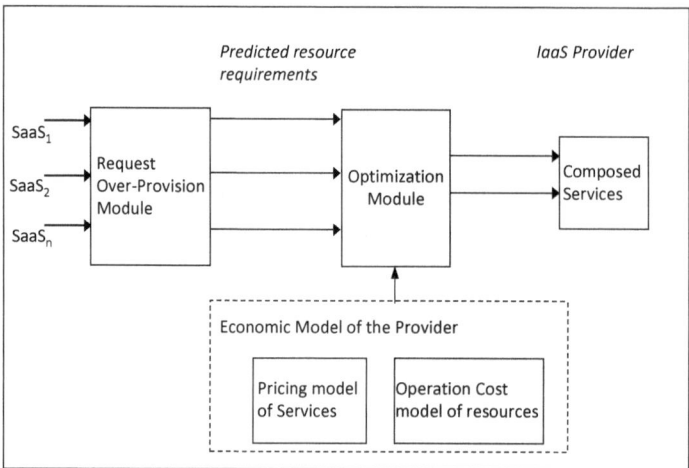

Fig. 3.2   The proposed service composition framework

management (CRM) consumers require services from the IaaS provider. The three consumers' QoS and Resource requirements change over times (solid lines in Fig. 3.3a, b). As there are three requests, an optimal composition can be selected from six combinations. At first, we consider optimization without heuristics, i.e. exact resource provisioning according to the requests. Here, only the following four combinations ($\{CRM1\}, \{CRM2\}, \{CRM3\}$ and $\{CRM1, CRM3\}$) satisfy the maximum resource and QoS unit constraints. $\{CRM2\}$ is a combination that maximizes the profit by \$110 in these specific provisions. We create the transformed requests based on previous history of the consumers (dotted lines in Fig. 3.3a, b). Considering the predicted resource utilization, we have five combinations with the transformed requests ($\{CRM1\}, \{CRM2\}, \{CRM3\}, \{CRM1, CRM3\}$ and $\{CRM2, CRM3\}$) that satisfy all the constraints. We find that the combination $\{CRM2, CRM3\}$ maximizes the profit by \$180. Hence, the heuristics-based service combination may generate more profit than the specific provisions.

3.4   Predicting the Dynamic Behavior of Consumer Requests

The long-term service requests are typically modelled in *time-series* [140]. We predict three types of dynamic behavior of the service requests: *Resource utilization level, QoS fluctuation tolerance level* and *early exit from contract*. We use historical data to build the prediction model for existing consumers. According to [120], different consumers generate different types of patterns in their service usage history. Two of the most frequent patterns in Google Cluster data usage are high-frequent and seasonal-trend [109]. HMM, and ARIMA models have proved to be

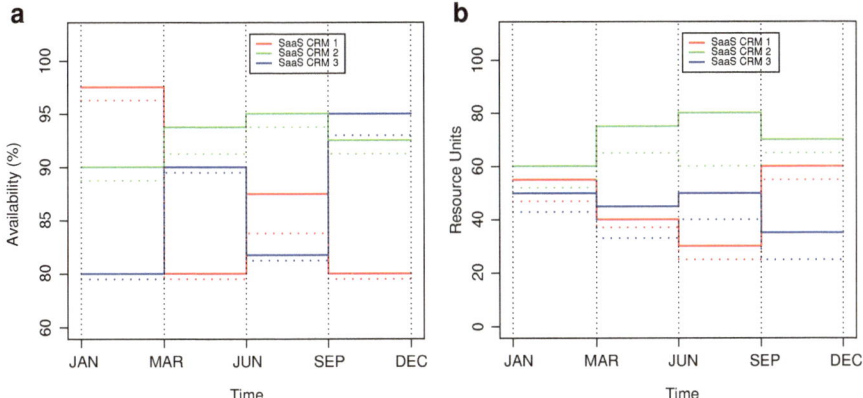

Fig. 3.3 (**a**) Original and transformed QoS requirements, and (**b**) Resource requirements

efficient for high-frequent and seasonal-trend univariate patterns respectively [98]. As the behavior of service requests is multivariate in nature, a univariate model would ignore the correlation effect among the attributes (e.g., relationships among computing, network, and storage attributes). We propose a multivariate HMM for predicting high-frequent multivariate patterns. This is used to predict errors in the seasonal-trend ARIMA model. Prediction models of the consumers' requests are aggregated in their corresponding community. This community prediction model is used to predict the behavior of new requests without history.

We formulate the prediction problem as follows. Let us assume that the IaaS provider receives long-term requests from N different consumers represented as $\{U_1, U_1, \ldots, U_N\}$. The consumers belong to a community from a set of predefined communities, COM. All the consumers require total T_{total} time units of services. The long-term requests are formed concatenating different short-term service requests in this period. In this section, the objective is to transform the long-term service requests of the ith consumer, U_i into $\acute{U}_i$ by applying QoS tolerance level and resource utilization heuristics. As both new and existing consumers can submit service requests, we generate the transformation heuristics for both the new and existing consumers.

3.4.1   Predicting Runtime Behavior of Existing Consumers' Requests

We generate the heuristics for an existing consumer using its history. Let us assume that there are n observations of requests $(U_i^1, U_i^2, \ldots, U_i^n)$ and service usage records $(\acute{U}_i^1, \acute{U}_i^2, \ldots, \acute{U}_i^n)$. The target is to predict future $(n+1)$th service usage record $\acute{U}_i^{n+1}$, given the $(n+1)$th service request U_i^{n+1}. Naturally, service utilization is correlated with service requests. Hence, for each resource or QoS attribute, q, we generate the normalized QoS tolerance or resource utilization sequences $\hat{q}$ in each observation using Eq. 3.1.

$$\hat{q}_t = \frac{q_t - \acute{q}_t}{q_t} \mid q_t \in U_i^n \text{ and } \acute{q}_t \in \acute{U}_i^n \tag{3.1}$$

As T_{total} is the length of request sequences, the past resource utilization and QoS tolerance of attribute q can be transformed into a $n \times T_{total}$ observation matrix $M(q)$. We consider two types of patterns in the observation matrix: (a) high-frequent, and (b) seasonal-trend. The multivariate HMM and ARIMA modeling of the observation matrix is described in the following sections.

$$\text{Observation matrix, } M(q) = \begin{bmatrix} \hat{q}_1^1 \cdot \hat{q}_t^1 \cdot \hat{q}_{T_{total}}^1 \\ \hat{q}_1^2 \cdot \hat{q}_t^2 \cdot \hat{q}_{T_{total}}^2 \\ \cdot \quad \cdot \quad \cdot \quad \cdot \quad \cdot \\ \hat{q}_1^n \cdot \hat{q}_t^n \cdot \hat{q}_{T_{total}}^n \end{bmatrix} \tag{3.2}$$

3.4.1.1 Multivariate HMM Modeling of High-Frequent Usage Patterns

One way to predict future QoS tolerance level and resource utilization in high-frequent patterns is to model the generated univariate observation matrix in an HMM. Each attribute has its own HMM. As external factors influence such patterns, regression analysis should perform more poorly than machine-learning techniques. Modeling HMM from the univariate sequences would ignore the correlation effect among the attributes.

We model a new multivariate HMM for QoS tolerance level and resource utilization level using the following modified Markov assumption.

- *Limited horizon on correlated sequences*: The probability of current state of an attribute depends on the previous state of the attribute and all the correlated attributes. We can denote it as $P(X_{t+1} = av_{t+1}|X_t, Y_{t-l}, Z_{t-l})$. l is the lagged value of correlated states. X, Y and Z represent the states of the three QoS or resource attributes respectively (Fig. 3.4).

Based on the modified limited horizon assumption, we define the multivariate HMM for QoS tolerance level and resource utilization as *Multi_HMM* = $(S_k, O_k, A_k, B_k, \pi)$ for all k attributes ($k \in AV, TH, RT, C, M, NB$). S_k defines the set of hidden states for the k_{th} attribute and m denotes the number of elements in S_k. Defining the number of hidden states in the HMM is often chosen based on the data nature [90]. We set $S_k = \{$very low, low, medium, high, very high$\}$ considering the relative changes in patterns over a period of time. O_k defines the set of observation states as a data sequence. n denotes the number of elements in O_k. As the data are normalized using Eq. 3.1, the values are in the range [0,1]. The state transition

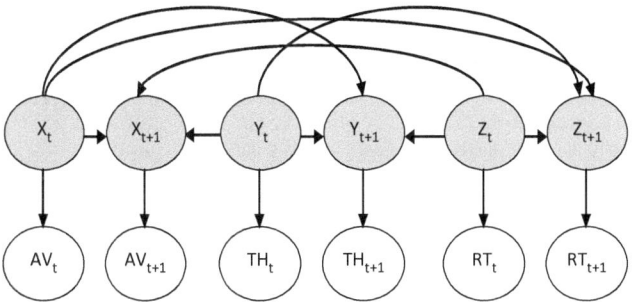

Fig. 3.4 Correlation among QoS attributes in the multivariate HMM

probability distribution matrix, A_k, is an $[m \times m]$ matrix denoting probabilities of transitioning from one state to another for the k_{th} attribute. The observation symbol (output) probability distribution matrix B_k is an $[m \times n]$ matrix representing the probability of producing n outputs for each of the m hidden states for the k_{th} attribute. π is the initial probability distribution of the states.

The generated multivariate sequences in the observation matrix could not be used directly for the lack of explicit dependence and appropriate lagged values in the sequences. We find the explicit dependence using the following definition of correlation operator:

- *Correlation Operator* $(CP_{x,y})$: Given $\bar{q}_x$ and $\bar{q}_y$ as the means of observation sequences of x and y attributes, and S_{q_x} and S_{q_y} as their standard deviations; the correlation operator between the attributes x and y is defined as a Pearson Correlation:

$$CP_{x,y} = \frac{1}{m-1} \sum_{i=1}^{m} \left(\frac{q_{x_i} - \bar{q}_x}{S_{q_x}}\right)\left(\frac{q_{y_i} - \bar{q}_y}{S_{q_y}}\right) \qquad (3.3)$$

The appropriate lagged value is found using the iterative method in Algorithm 1. We generate the multiple observation sequences for training the multivariate HMM with proper lagged values for the correlated attributes. For example, to train the HMM for the "availability" QoS attribute, we generate the sequence like $\{(av_i, av_{i+1}, \ldots, av_n),\quad (th_{i-l}, th_{i-l+1}, \ldots, th_{i-l+n}),\quad (rt_{i-j}, rt_{i-j+1}, \ldots, rt_{i-j+n})\}$. Here, l and j are the lagged values of throughput and response times respectively.

We use the procedure described in [86] to train the HMM. It uses joint probability distributions of the observation sequences as a weight factor to train the HMM. As there is no direction about how to determine the weights, we use the correlation operator from Eq. 3.3 to state the uniform dependence. We derive the combinatorial multiple observation probability of the attribute X with the generated lagged sequence of other $(k - 1)$ attributes from [86] as stated in Eq. 3.4. O denotes the multiple observations and $O^{(k)}$ denotes the observations from k_{th} attribute. λ is used for the short form of the multivariate HMM in Eq. 3.4.

Algorithm 1 Finding the lagged value l of the Y_{th} attribute in a multivariate HMM

Require: The normalized observation sequence generated by Eq. 3.1, $X = (x_1, x_2, \ldots, x_n)$ and $Y = (y_1, y_2, \ldots, y_n)$

Ensure: the lagged value l of the Y_{th} attribute for the X_{th} attribute

1: minimum standard deviation, $MS := MAX\_VALUE$.
2: lagged value, $l := 0$
3: **for** $i := 2$ **to** $n - 1$ **do**
4:     Generate $\hat{X} = (x_i, x_{i+1}, \ldots, x_n)$
5:     Generate $\frac{\hat{X}}{Y} = (\frac{x_i}{y_1}, \frac{x_{i+1}}{y_2}, \ldots, \frac{x_n}{y_{n-i}})$
6:     Find the standard deviation MS_1 of $\frac{\hat{X}}{Y}$.
7:     **if** $MS_1 < MS$ **then**
8:         $MS := MS_1$
9:         $l := i$
10:    **end if**
11: **end for**
12: Return l

$$P(O|\lambda) = \frac{1}{K} \sum_{k=1}^{K} (CP_{X,k}) \, P(O^{(k)}|\lambda) \tag{3.4}$$

The generalised training equations from [86] are also modified with the correlation operator in Eqs. 3.5–3.7. As the Baum-Welch algorithm [86] requires forward and backward operators, we denote the joint probability $\xi_t^{(k)}(m, n)$ as the probability of transition from states m to n at time t and $t+1$ for the k_{th} attribute. $\gamma_t^{(k)}(m)$ denotes the probability of the system being in state m at time t for the k_{th} attribute.

1. The state transition probability from state m to state n:

$$a_{mn} = \frac{1}{K} \frac{\sum_{k=1}^{K} (CP_{X,k}) \, P(O^{(k)}|\lambda) \sum_{t=1}^{T_k-1} \xi_t^{(k)}(m, n)}{\sum_{k=1}^{K} (CP_{X,k}) \, P(O^{(k)}|\lambda) \sum_{t=1}^{T_k-1} \gamma_t^{(k)}(m)} \tag{3.5}$$

2. The emission probability of the observation symbol x from state m:

$$b_{mx} = \frac{1}{K} \frac{\sum_{k=1}^{K} (CP_{X,k}) \, P(O^{(k)}|\lambda) \sum_{t=1, O_t^k = x}^{T_k} \gamma_t^{(k)}(m)}{\sum_{k=1}^{K} (CP_{X,k}) \, P(O^{(k)}|\lambda) \sum_{t=1}^{T_k-1} \gamma_t^{(k)}(m)} \tag{3.6}$$

3. Initial state probability:

$$\pi = \frac{1}{K} \frac{\sum_{k=1}^{K} (CP_{X,k}) \, P(O^{(k)}|\lambda) \gamma_1^{(k)}(m)}{\sum_{k=1}^{K} (CP_{X,k}) \, P(O^{(k)}|\lambda)} \tag{3.7}$$

It was proved that the generalized training equations will converge in both uniform and non-uniform dependence in [86]. As the constant correlation cooperator represents an uniform dependence, the specialised Eqs. 3.5–3.7 should also converge. The training equations are used in the iterative procedure described in [86]. We begin with random values in the parameters of the HMM, and train it with each observation, until the changes in parameter minimize. After the training, the traditional Viterbi algorithm [98] is used to find the most likely sequence of hidden states and observation sequence. As the predicted $(n + 1)$th observed sequence is a normalized difference between the requests and utilization, we transform the $(n + 1)$th consumer request into a new future utilization using the derivation of Eq. 3.1.

3.4.1.2 HMM-ARIMA Modeling of Seasonal Usage Patterns

The ARIMA method [20] is used to model a single univariate time-series, it could not be used directly for multiple observations. Let us assume, there are n seasonal-trend observations $\{O_1, O_2, \ldots, O_n\}$ for the kth attribute. To predict O_{n+1}, we first aggregate the observations as $AG_n = \sum_{i=1}^{n} O_i$. The aggregated AG_n contains seasonal and trend properties. Hence, we use the Box-Jenkins method [20] to model the AG_n into ARIMA. Prediction errors generated by fitted ARIMA models in different attributes form an error observation matrix, $M(error)$ using Eq. 3.2. We predict the O_{n+1} using the new HMM-ARIMA model combining the aggregated observations and error observation matrix in Eq. 3.8.

$$(1 - \sum_{i=1}^{p} \alpha_i L^i)(1 - L)^d AG_n = (1 + \sum_{i=1}^{q} \theta_i L^i) Multi\_HMM(M(error)) \qquad (3.8)$$

Equation 3.8 consists of three parts. The autoregressive (AR) part depends on the p lagged values of the time-series of aggregated AG_n and α_i is the coefficient constant. The moving average (MA) part depends on the q lagged values of the previous prediction errors and θ_i is the coefficient constant. The third part is the multivariate error reduction attributes where $M(error)$ is the error observation matrix. In ARIMA, a non-stationary time-series needs to be converted into a stationary time-series by a difference operation [20]. Here, d represents the number of times that the difference operation is performed to obtain the stationary time-series. The values of (p,d,q) are determined by the Box-Jenkins method for the aggregated observation[20]. $M(error)$ is determined by aggregating the previous prediction errors generated by univariate ARIMA(p,d,q) process on each observation. As $Multi\_HMM(M(error))$ predicts on error patterns, we reduce possible prediction errors by incorporating it in Eq. 3.8.

3.4.1.3 Selection of Models

We apply the brute-force method for finding the best model. Each prediction model i.e., Multivariate HMM or HMM-ARIMA, is performed on the given history and the performance is measured by the normalized Root Mean Square Error (NRMSE) using Eq. 3.9. A lower NRMSE value indicates the higher prediction accuracy. Hence, we select the model that has lower NRMSE on the given history.

$$NRMSE = \sqrt{\frac{\sum_{i=1}^{n}(\frac{PR(q)-AC(q)}{AC(q)_{max}-AC(q)_{min}})^2}{n}} \qquad (3.9)$$

We assume that there is a history of gap time (lease time—early exit time) for an existing consumer. The normalized gap time sequence is generated by Eq. 3.5 using lease or contract period as a denominator. As it is a single univariate time-series, the univariate HMM model [98] is used to predict the next exit time.

3.4.2 Predicting Runtime Behavior of New Consumers' Requests

New consumers do not have a history. Hence, the above procedure is not applicable to them. In this situation, we devise a bootstrapping technique to predict its heuristics for the new consumer. A community-based bootstrapping technique is used in [91] to establish trust of web services. Similarly, we assume a new consumer belongs to a community and the new consumer's behavior is similar to the community's behavior. For example, the SaaS CRM for universities should behave differently to the SaaS CRM for retail shops.

We assume that a set of communities $\{COM_1, COM_2, .., COM_n\}$ are classified by the IaaS provider. Each community contains either high-frequent or seasonal-trend consumer members. Although the types and number parameters in the member prediction models remain the same (e.g. the number of hidden states in HMM), the parameter values differ from member to member. A multivariate HMM or ARIMA model represented as $(COM_i(x) \mid x \in \{Multi\_HMM, HMM-ARIMA\})$ is generated by aggregating the corresponding models of its members. When a request from a new consumer of a certain community is received, we use its community's most recent aggregated model to transform the requests.

We update the prediction model of a community through an incremental process. Each new user's performance is evaluated, and is then used to update the model. This weighted approach places more emphasis on the new users. Let us assume; the IaaS provider receives a new user's request, q. The predicted usage of the requests using $COM_i(x)$ is $PR(q)$. The actual usage found after the service completion is $AC(q)$. The observation sequence length is n. $AC(q)_{max}$ and $AC(q)_{min}$ are the respective maximum and minimum values in the usage observation receptively. We can evaluate the performance of the prediction using normalized Root Mean Square Error (NRMSE) (Eq. 3.9). The range of NRMSE is [0,1]. A lesser value of NRMSE imposes a less residual variance.

We generate the prediction model $New(x)$ with actual observations using the procedure of Sects. 3.4.1.1 and 3.4.1.2. One important assumption is that these HMMs are similar in structure, i.e. the number of hidden states, and observation symbols are the same in both the new and old communities. Hence, we can use arithmetic to update the communities' HMMs. The $NRMSE$ describes the performance of the community's HMM for the new consumer. We can update the community's HMMs using the NRMSE as a weight in Eq. 3.10.

$$COM_i(x) = w\ COM_i(x) + (1 - w)\ New(x) \tag{3.10}$$

where $x \in \{Multi\_HMM, HMM\text{-}ARIMA\}$, $w = NRMSE$ of new requests.

3.5 An ILP Modeling for Request Optimization

Our target is to select the best set of user requests, U_i that maximizes the long-term profit. The revenue is calculated using the original requests. According to [51], cloud providers have an economic model for setting the price for a service menu. Let us assume the pricing function is represented as $Price(x)$. Hence, the total revenue for N consumer requests at time t, $Revenue_t = \sum_i^N Price(U_i^{(t)})$. The operational cost is calculated on the transformed requests. We get the transformed request of the i_{th} consumer request as $\hat{U}_i^{(t)} = (\hat{c}_i^{(t)}, \hat{s}_i^{(t)}, \hat{nb}_i^{(t)}, \hat{av}_i^{(t)}, \hat{th}_i^{(t)}, \hat{rt}_i^{(t)})$ from the prediction module in Sect. 3.4. According to [51], the operation cost is a function $OP\_Cost(x)$ on the total utilization of composed services. We denote the total resource utilization by N service requests at time t as $Util_t = \sum_i^N \hat{U}_i^{(t)}$. The proposed prediction models transform the requests in a time-series prediction confidence. Hence, we denote the prediction confidence of $Util_t$ as $Pr(Util_t)$. The cost calculation on predicted request behavior should include possible SLA violation costs denoted as SLA_Cost. We formulate the total operation cost at time t using these notations in Eq. 3.11.

$$Cost_t = OP\_Cost(Util_t) + (1 - Pr(Util_t)) \times SLA\_Cost \tag{3.11}$$

The long-term composition period is denoted as T. The composition rules of resources and QoS are summarised in [134, 140]. The constraints on the limited resources are represented as $X_{max}|, X \in \{C, S, NB, AV, TH, RT\}$. As our target is to maximize the profit, we transform the composition problem as a combinatorial ILP optimization problem. B_i is the binary variable that represents whether the i_{th} service request is taken in the composition. The combinatorial ILP optimization problem is formulated in Eq. 3.12 as follows:

$$\text{The objective function: } maximize \sum_{i=1}^{N} \sum_{t=1}^{T} (Revenue_t - Cost_t) B_i \tag{3.12}$$

Subject to,

$$\sum_{i=1}^{N}\sum_{t=1}^{T}\hat{c}_i^{(t)} B_i \leq C_{max}$$

$$\sum_{i=1}^{N}\sum_{t=1}^{T}\hat{s}_i^{(t)} B_i \leq S_{max}$$

$$\sum_{i=1}^{N}\sum_{t=1}^{T}\hat{nb}_i^{(t)} B_i \leq NB_{max}$$

$$max(\hat{av}_i^{(t)} B_i \mid i \in U) \leq AV_{max}$$

$$max(\hat{rt}_i^{(t)} B_i \mid i \in U) \leq TH_{max}$$

$$\sum_{i=1}^{N}\hat{rt}_i^{(t)} B_i \leq RT_{max}$$

$$B_i = \{0, 1\} \mid i \in U$$

The ILP in Eq. 3.12 can be solved using the procedure described in [95]. The solution space gets larger when the length and number of requests increase. We tend to reduce the time length of the requests by finding the critical points. A critical point is a position of time that predicts several points in the sequence with a probability $> \theta$. θ is the threshold for critical point selection. We may get the desired result only by considering the critical points. The time position $\{t_i\}$ is a critical point for $\{t_{i+1}, t_{i+2}, ..., t_{i+p}\}$, if it holds the following property in Eq. 3.13.

$$abs|\Pi_{i=1}^{N}P(\hat{U}_i^{(t_i)}) - \Pi_{i=1}^{N}P(\hat{U}_i^{(t_{i+l})})| < \theta \mid 1 \leq l \leq p \qquad (3.13)$$

We need to find the critical points for the T sequences using $m < T$ sequences. Let us assume that $CT(m) = \{t_i, t_j, ..., t_q\}$ is the set of critical points for the first m sequence using Eq. 3.13. We assume that the critical points are uniformly distributed. Hence, we use the standard deviation of $CT(m)$, sd as the sequence of the critical points for the full sequence, $CT(T) = \{t_i, t_{i+sd}, ..., t_{i+n \times sd}\} \mid n \times sd < T$. We can rewrite the objective function of Eq. 3.12 in Eq. 3.14. We solve the new ILP applying critical points in the procedure described in [95].

The ILP objective function: $maximize \displaystyle\sum_{i=1}^{N}\sum_{t=1}^{CT(T)}(Revenue_t - OP\_Cost_t)R_i$

$$(3.14)$$

3.6 Experiments and Results

A set of experiments have been conducted to evaluate the accuracy of the proposed multivariate HMM-ARIMA for predicting the dynamic behavior of consumer requests in comparison with the univariate HMM, ANN and univariate ARIMA models. Next, we compare the profitability of the proposed heuristic based service composition with a greedy approach and an ILP without heuristics. All the experiments have been conducted on computers with Intel Core i7 CPU (2.13 GHz and 4 GB RAM). The R statistical tool [104] is used to implement the algorithms.

3.6.1 Data Description

We evaluate the proposed method using Google Cluster resource utilization [109], real-world cloud QoS performance [67] and synthetic data. Google Cluster data include CPU and Memory utilization and allocation time-series of 70 jobs over 1 month period. Real-world QoS data includes two time-series (i.e., response time, throughput) for 100 cloud services over 6 months period. The summary of the dataset is given in Table 3.1.

3.6.1.1 Correlation Density Index (CDI) in the Dataset

We randomly pick 70 providers and make one to one mapping with the Google cluster jobs. As the QoS dataset only contains actual service usage, we synthetically generate the service requests using a probabilistic distribution termed *Correlation Density Index (CDI)* (Eq. 3.15). We define CDI as the average of standard deviations among the normalized differences between the request sequences and the actual usage sequences. In Eq. 3.15, $DIFF(i, j, t)$ refers to the normalized difference between the service attribute j's requested value ($PQ(i, j, t)$) and actual usage value ($AQ(i, j, t)$) at time t for service i. $AVG(j, t)$ is the average of normalized difference of $DIFF(i, j, t)$. $SD(j, t)$ refers to the standard deviation of $DIFF(i, j, t)$ over k observations. The $CDI(j)$ is average of $SD(j, t)$ over the time length (m) of the

Table 3.1 Summary of Google Cluster Dataset

Request attribute	Values
Avg response time	337 ms
Avg throughput	3.2 units
Avg availability	55 units
Avg CPU	64 units
Avg memory	49 units
Avg network	52 units
Avg correlation	0.61

history. A higher CDI refers to a lower randomness of the correlations between the service request and the actual service usage in the history. We generate five sets of service requests with five different CDI values (0.5, 0.6, 0.7, 0.8, 0.9) from the given real-world QoS dataset. We manually check the types of the provider and group them in five communities. We randomly select five consumer requests from each community and labelled them as new consumer requests.

$$DIFF(i,j,t) = abs\left|1 - \frac{PQ(i,j,t)}{AQ(i,j,t)}\right|$$

$$AVG(j,t) = \frac{\sum_{i=1}^{k-1} DIFF(i,j,t)}{k-1}$$

$$SD(j,t) = \sqrt{\frac{1}{k-1} \sum_{i=1}^{k-1} (DIFF(i,j,t) - AVG(t))^2} \qquad (3.15)$$

$$CDI(j) = 1 - \frac{\sum_{t=1}^{m} SD(j,t)}{m}$$

3.6.1.2   Setup of Economic Values for Profit Modeling

In this chapter, we assume that the short-term economic model of the provider will remain constant over the long term. The price of resources and QoS are set by following the Rackspace pricing model as ($5/unit per hour for any resource). According to [51], a mapping relationship between operation cost and utilization is devised in Table 3.2. The SLA violation fee is 20% of the revenue credited to consumers. The resource constraints are set by allowing maximum 100 units for each attribute.

Table 3.2 Relationship between resource utilization and operation cost

Resource utilization (%)	Operation cost per hour
5	$110
30	$140
60	$150
90	$160
100	$165

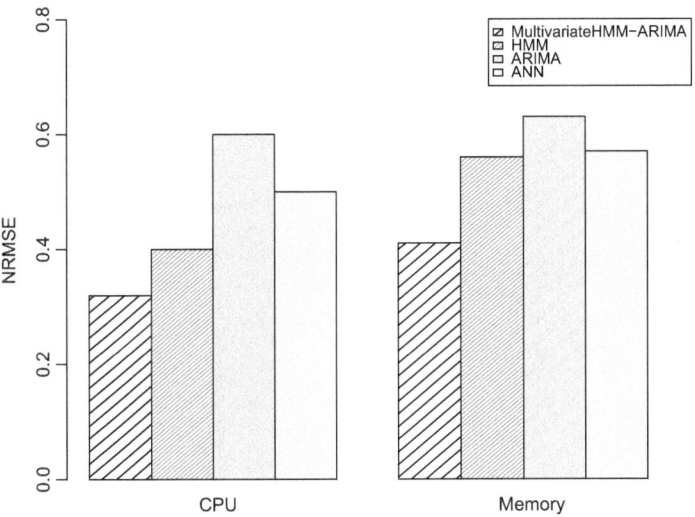

Fig. 3.5 Prediction accuracy on Google Cluster Data

3.6.2 Accuracy in Predicting the Behavior of Consumer Requests

We train the proposed multivariate HMM-ARIMA with the training dataset from Sect. 3.6.1. We use a default 4-state HMM, ARIMA and ANN in R to train each attribute individually. A lower value in the normalized root mean square error (NRMSE) (Eq. 3.9) is used as a performance indicator of the proposed methods. We plot the average NRMSE in prediction models for each attribute (CPU and Memory) in the Google Cluster Dataset in Fig. 3.5. The average NRMSE value of the dataset is enough for comparison as individual discrepancies are accumulated in the comparison. Figure 3.5 depicts that the proposed method predicts more accurately than ANN, univariate HMM, and ARIMA in the real-world dataset with a lower NRMSE value.

As we generate the QoS request sequence synthetically using CDI, we evaluate the effect of CDI on the prediction error (Fig. 3.6). We find that NMRSE reduces when the CDI increases. The proposed method produces lower NRMSE than ANN, HMM, and ARIMA in higher CDI, which is a desired property for the heuristic.

We also evaluate the performance of the community-based prediction for new consumers (Fig. 3.7). Although the prediction using the community's heuristics is not as accurate as the approach for existing consumers, it is still close to the original dataset. The average NRMSE value of the prediction model is 0.43 which is acceptable in real-world applications. Figure 3.8 depicts that a larger community can predict more accurately than a smaller community. There is about a 20% reduction in the average NRMSE when the community grows from 10 consumers to 50 consumers.

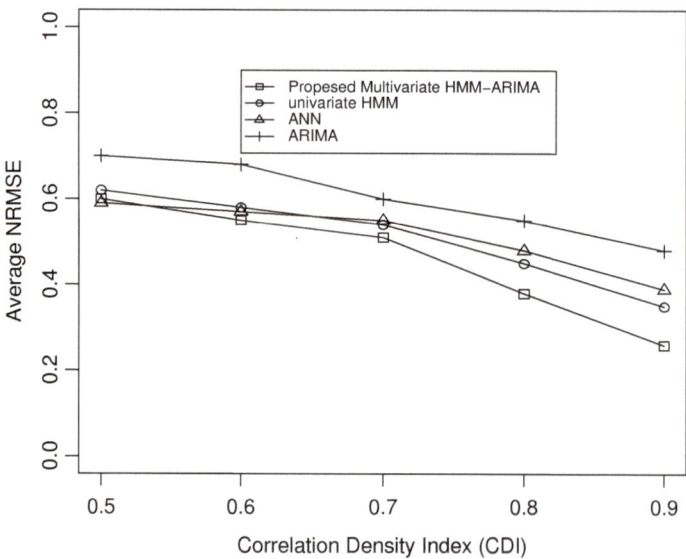

Fig. 3.6 CDI effect on the proposed approach

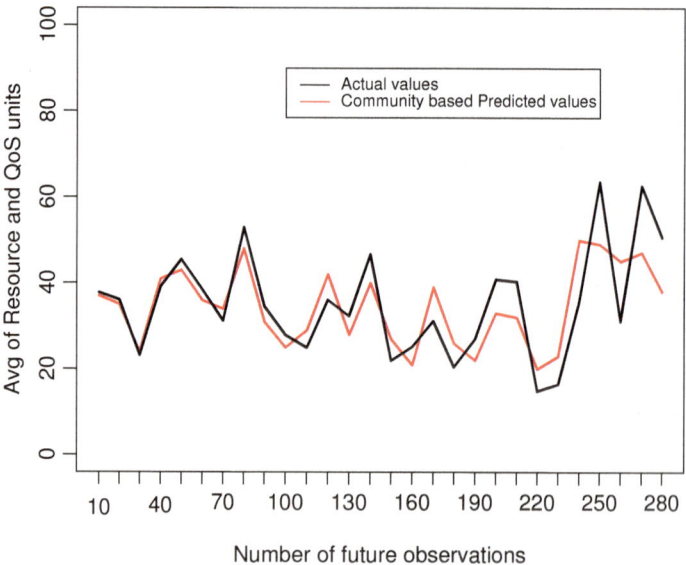

Fig. 3.7 Prediction accuracy of the community heuristic

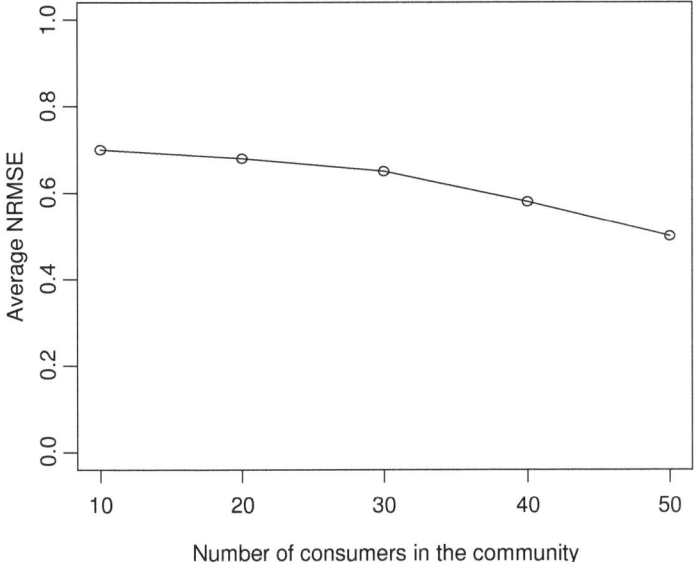

Fig. 3.8   Effect of the community size on prediction

3.6.3   Performance Analysis on Profit Maximization

The performance of the proposed optimization is compared with an ILP without heuristic and a greedy approach [134]. The greedy approach is a short-term composition that admits services on a First In First Served (FIFS) basis. When a new request arrives, it is admitted based on the currently available resources in the greedy approach. Figure 3.9 depicts the cumulative profit over time. Although the proposed approach generates less profit at the beginning, it generates more profit than the greedy and ILP without heuristics (Fig. 3.9) in the long-term.

The monthly resource utilization rate is plotted in Fig. 3.10. The greedy approach only maximizes resource utilization at the beginning while the proposed heuristic-based ILP maximizes resource utilization at a steady rate over the period of composition (Fig. 3.10). More resource utilization creates less operation cost and more profit for the IaaS provider in the long-term.

3.7   Conclusion

In this chapter, we have proposed a novel service composition framework for deter-ministic IaaS requests to maximize the provider's long-term profits. Experimental results show that the proposed multivariate prediction approach performs better than univariate approaches. The real-world applicability of the framework increases by

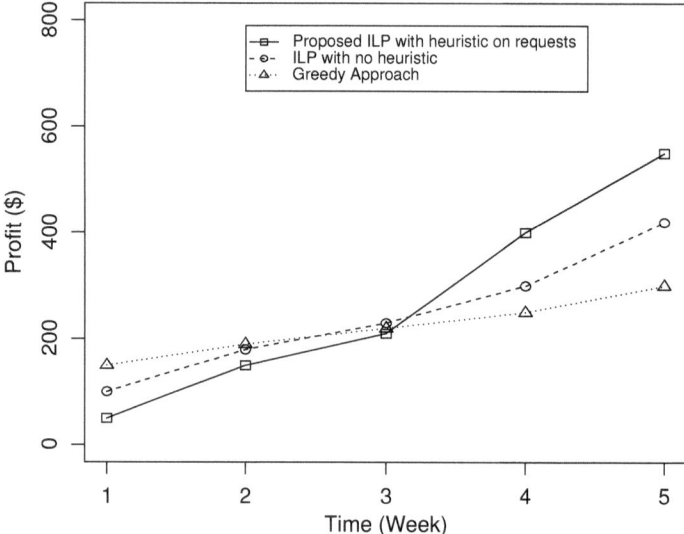

Fig. 3.9 Cumulative profit over time

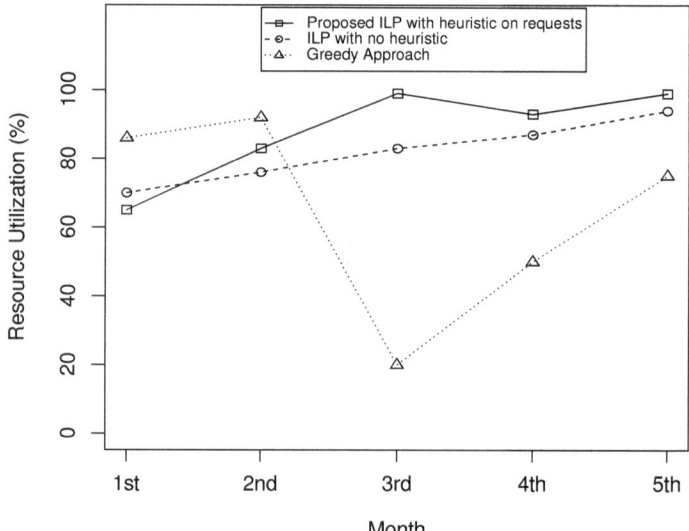

Fig. 3.10 Monthly resource utilization

incorporating a community-based prediction model for new consumer requests. The proposed ILP based optimization approach maximizes both the profit and resource utilization over the longer term. Hence, the proposed framework is more applicable in a real-world environment than the greedy approach. In the next chapter, we will describe the long-term IaaS composition for the stochastic arrival of requests.

Chapter 4
Long-Term IaaS Composition for Stochastic Requests

4.1 Introduction

One of the key characteristic of a cloud service is its *flexibility* [8]. It is a key catalyst for the economic growth of the cloud market. Cloud consumers usually observe three desired properties in a flexible cloud service: (a) *on-demand provision*, (b) *elasticity*, and (c) *flexible pricing* [21]. In the on-demand provision model, computing resources are made available to consumers as needed. Service consumers can use a service at any time irrespective of a short-term or a long-term contract [121]. Cloud elasticity is the ability of an application to automatically adjust the infrastructure resources usage to accommodate varied workloads and priorities [70]. Consumers can extend or shrink the size of services according to their workloads. A flexible pricing model allows consumers to pay only for what they use [8].

The arrival of the service requests to a provider is typically *stochastic* in the flexible cloud environment. New consumer requests may be made at any time and may require the on-demand provision. The composition approach discussed in the previous chapter may not produce an optimal result in the stochastic arrival of requests. The proposed composition approach in Sect. 3.5 of Chap. 3 generates a composition plan considering the *deterministic* arrival of requests. Such composition is carried away for the whole period assuming that new requests will not arrive during the composition interval. However, new requests may be worth considering as they may be more profitable than the current requests. This may trigger periodic updates in the static plan which results in a dynamic composition.

The stochastic arrival of the requests is typically considered in the dynamic economic environments of real-world applications. Dynamic economic operations have practical applications in different research fields, such as supply-chain management, operations research and network optimization [69]. For example, a restaurant management system configures meal menus and prices considering the stochastic arrival model of customers [73]. Similarly, IaaS providers usually perform dynamic operations in the long-term period. For example, service prices often change over

© Springer International Publishing AG 2018
S. Mistry et al., *Economic Models for Managing Cloud Services*,
https://doi.org/10.1007/978-3-319-73876-5_4

a period. Operation costs for the service provisioning also fluctuate over the period due to various external factors such as changes in electricity costs and government regulations [51]. In the previous chapter, deterministic IaaS requests are correlated with a static economic environment. However, such static correlations may not be applicable in a dynamic composition.

Another important aspect of the dynamic IaaS composition is to achieve the multi-objective economic expectations of the provider. Those expectations not only maximize profit but also minimize SLA violations and resource under-utilization. These economic expectations are usually multidimensional [50]. The multidimensional economic expectations may include the provider's expected profit, SLA violations, and resource utilization at different times in the composition period. For example, the provider may set goals to earn $10,000 profit in the first year, $15,000 profit in the second year and $20,000 profit in the third year. Such a periodic goal-driven approach enables the provider to verify the efficiency of the current actions and to change inefficient plans in the middle of a composition interval to achieve the desired profit. To the best of our knowledge, multi-objective economic expectations have yet to be considered in the IaaS composition.

Also to the best of our knowledge, short-term IaaS composition approaches do not presently consider the stochastic arrival of requests and dynamic economic environment [42, 116, 134, 138]. We propose a quantitative long-term economic model for the service composition with a stochastic arrival of service requests. We consider *semantic economic evaluation*. For example, the provider can specify whether it wants "more" profit or "fewer" SLA violations in its economic expectation. The long-term composition model aims to adjust itself to improve request prediction accuracy at runtime. To realize this goal, we propose a Hybrid Adaptive Genetic Algorithm (HAGA) that updates the quality of the composition by detecting runtime changes and incorporating the knowledge of previous optimizations. The key contributions of our proposed model are summarized below.

(a) A long-term economic model that employs a semantic and weighted multidimensional time-series matching approach to compare the long-term economic evaluation of a composition with expectations. The proposed economic model is constructed in the form of a Dynamic Bayesian Network (DBN) [121]. The DBN not only depicts the correlation among resource utilization, QoS provisions, and service pricing but also describes the changes in correlations over time.

(b) A *memory-full* HAGA to generate dynamic solutions for the stochastic arrival of service requests. The *memory-full* feature preserves the global inter-dependency and preference heuristics from the generated composition solutions in previous optimizations. The heuristics are updated based on the changed environment and used in future optimizations to produce computationally efficient solutions. We also perform a local search to check that the solution is not stuck at a local optimum. The infeasible solutions (violating resource constraints) are also repaired by these heuristics. Hence, the hybrid approach provides a directed convergence to the global composition.

This chapter is structured as follows. The dynamic service composition framework, and the long-term economic model are discussed in Sects. 4.2 and 4.3 respectively. The traditional genetic algorithm, hybrid genetic optimization process, experiments and conclusion are presented in Sects. 4.4, 4.5, 4.6, and 4.7 respectively.

4.2   Long-Term Dynamic IaaS Composition Framework

The proposed service composition framework consists of five modules: the stochastic arrival model, the request over-provision module, the economic model of the provider, the optimization module and the composition scheduler (Fig. 4.1). Upon receiving service requests, the stochastic model predicts all future requests. The request over-provision module applies heuristics on the generated requests to predict future QoS tolerance levels and resource utilization. The optimization module calculates the profit of the transformed requests using a long-term economic model of resources and services of the IaaS provider. The composition scheduler creates optimization checkpoints and evaluates the performance of the present composition in the runtime. If there is an update from the prediction module, the scheduler triggers a new optimization process. The following scenario describes the dynamic optimization in a long-term service composition.

Let us assume that the IaaS provider has the following two-dimensional one-year economic expectation: "*maximize profit with minimum SLA violations*". It has maximum 100 units of CPU resources as a constraint. We are not considering QoS or other physical requirements for simplicity. The price of each resource unit is \$5/hour, and the SLA penalty is also \$5/hour. The profitability of the provider is proportional to the resource usage, i.e. the marginal operation cost per node reduces when the resource utilization increases at a node [51]. The provider receives service

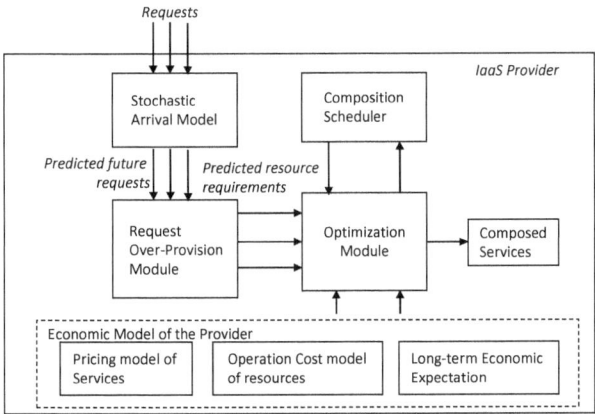

Fig. 4.1 The proposed dynamic service composition framework

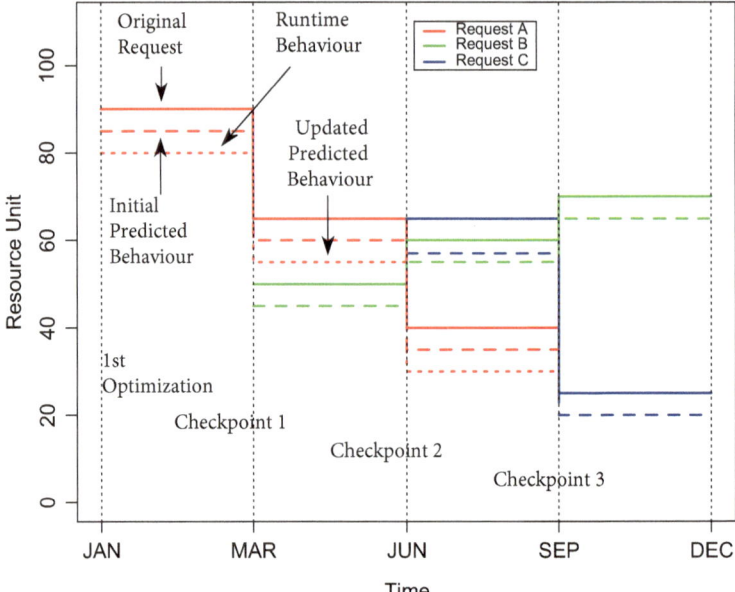

Fig. 4.2 Original and transformed long-term resource requirements

requests over the whole year. It receives Request *A* (the red solid line in Fig. 4.2) from a university in January which spans up to September. Request *B* is generated from a government organization (the green solid line in Fig. 4.2) which will arrive in March and spans up to December. Request *C* is generated from a private company (the solid blue line in Fig. 4.2) which will arrive in June and spans up to December. Table 4.1 describes the quantified resource requirements of these consumers. In traditional greedy business approaches, the provider will commit to Request *A* (University) as it arrives first. However, it cannot accept Request *B* (government) as it does not have enough resources to serve both the requests. Nor can it accept Request *C*, as *A* and *C* generate an SLA violation from June to September. Hence, the greedy approach only generates revenue by serving Request *A* from January to September, and the total profit is $140 (Table 4.2). It needs to be noted that the operation and fixed costs have been removed from all the profits in Table 4.2 for simplification.

The proposed dynamic optimization framework may generate a different composition. The request over-provision module transforms these requests to the predicted runtime behavior (the dashed lines in Fig. 4.2 and Table 4.1).

An optimal composition for the three service requests (Fig. 4.2) can be selected from six combinations. Considering the predicted resource utilisation (over-provisioning approach), we have four combinations with the transformed requests ($\{A\}, \{B\}, \{C\}$ and $\{A, C\}$) that satisfy the constraints (Table 4.2). We find that the combination $\{A, C\}$ is maximising the profit by ($140 + $80) = $220 with a possible future SLA violation of 5 h. However, it is still profitable as the net

Table 4.1 Requested and initially transformed resource usage as well as runtime update

Requests	January–March	March–June	June–September	September–December
Requested resource usage				
A	90	65	42	
B		50	60	70
C			65	25
Initially transformed resource usage				
A	85	60	35	
B		45	55	65
C			60	25
Runtime update on the initial transformation				
A	80	55	30	

Table 4.2 Economic benefits in composition plans

	Net profit ($)		
Combinations	Greedy	Over-provision	Dynamic composition
{A}	140	140	140
{B}	120	120	120
{C}	80	80	80
{A,B}	SLA violation	SLA violation	235
{A,C}	SLA violation	195	195
{B,C}	SLA violation	SLA violation	SLA violation
{A,B,C}	SLA violation	SLA violation	SLA violation
Total	140	195	235

profit after the SLA violation is ($220 − 5 hours × $5/hour) = $195. The SLA violation cost is $5/hour (Table 4.2). In the dynamic optimization approach, the scheduler creates a fixed check point at the beginning of every month. Let us assume that the runtime behavior of A is changed from January to March; then the prediction module updates its future resource utilisation (the dotted line in Fig. 4.2 and Table 4.1). We find a new combination {A, B} that satisfies the resource constraints (with a possible SLA violation of 5 h) and maximizes the profit by ($140 + $120 − 5 hour × $5/hour) = $235 (Table 4.2). As {$C$} is not in a running state until Checkpoint 2, we can update our previous optimization from {A, C} to {A, B} without a penalty. It can be seen that dynamic optimization has a more profitable economic gain in the long term period.

The above case study only considers CPU requirements in the requests. In reality, it consists of CPU, Memory, Network, and QoS requirements. We represent the long-term service requests as a multidimensional time-series by concatenating different short-term service requests. We define the jth short-term service request of the ith consumers as a tuple, $Short_{ij} = \{c, m, nb, av, rt, th, t_s^{ij}, t_e^{ij}\}$, where c, m, nb are the required functional units of CPU, Memory and Network respectively. The QoS requirements av, rt, th specify the required units of Availability, Response time and Throughput respectively. t_s^{ij} and t_e^{ij} specify the respective start and end times of the services, represented in Unix time-stamp. The long-term service requests of the ith consumers are formed using k short-term requests represented as $U_i = (Short_{i1}, \ldots, Short_{ik})$, where $\sum_{j=1}^{k} (t_e^{ij} - t_s^{ij}) = T_{total}$.

We use *Poisson distribution* [58] as the stochastic model. The resource over-provision module is designed in the IaaS composition framework for deterministic requests in Sect. 3.4, Chap. 3. The N long-term requests $\{U_1, U_2, \ldots, U_N\}$ are associated with their arrival times: $\{< U_1, Arrival_1 >, .., < U_N, Arrival_N >\}$. The resource over-provision module predicts the runtime behavior of the requests and transforms it into a time-series denoted as $\{< \hat{U}_1, Arrival_1 >, .., < \hat{U}_N, Arrival_N >\}$. The maximum units of CPU, memory, network, availability, response time and throughput that the provider can supply are denoted as: $(C_{max}, M_{max}, NB_{mx}, AV_{max}, RT_{max}, TH_{max})$. For example, the provider can offer maximum 100% availability, 0.5 throughput, and 2 ms response time in its services. The long-term economic model, the optimization module, and the composition scheduler are described in the following sections.

4.3   Long-Term Economic Model of IaaS Provider

Let us assume that there are k requests (S_k) in the map denoted as $MAP(S_k) = \{< U_1, Arrival_1 >, .., < U_k, Arrival_k >\}$. The task of the economic model is to generate the long-term economic evaluation of the request map. We consider profit (P), the number of SLA violations (NO_SLV), and resource utilization factor (UF) as the key attributes in the economic valuation. The next task is to measure the closeness of the composition to a given long-term economic expectation.

4.3.1   Long-Term Economic Valuation

The first task is to convert the request map $MAP(S_k)$ to the long-term economic valuation denoted as $EVAL(t) = \{P_t, NO\_SLV_t, UF_t \mid t \ \epsilon \ T\}$. We use long-term revenue and operation cost modeling to calculate the profit. As the business models of IaaS providers are similar to business models of utility providers, *demand-driven pricing model* is a common phenomena in a cloud market. For example, the price of a EC2 service fluctuates up to 80% in the Amazon cloud spot market [51]. As DBN successfully models temporal dynamic environments [93], we represent the dynamic pricing behavior as a DBN in Fig. 4.3. The DBN describes the correlations among physical resources (CPU (C), Memory(M) and Network(NB)), QoS values(Availability (AV), Throughput (TH) and Response Time (RT)), demand, and service price. The model calculates the probability (Q) of a service price X at time t for the service request $U^{(t)} = \{C, M, NB, AV, TH, RT\}$ given its previous price at time $(t-1)$ in Eq. 4.1.

$$Q(X, U^{(t)}, t) = P(Price_t = X | U^{(t)}, Price_{t-1}) \qquad (4.1)$$

Fig. 4.3 A DBN of dynamic
pricing

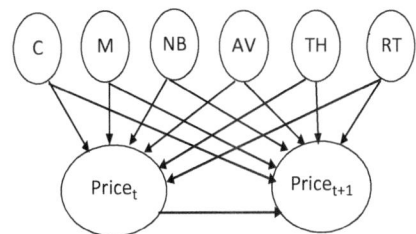

The IaaS provider may serve existing and new requests at the same time. Due
to the pricing model, a service may be priced differently for different consumers.
As long-term requests reserve the resources at current prices, the price is correlated
with the arrival time. For instance, a consumer who arrives at time t always pays
the price advertised at time t. As each request in $MAP(S_k)$ is associated with its
arrival time, we sort them in an ascending order. Let us denote, $Q(X, U^{(t)}, t_0)$ as the
initial probability table for the request U_0. We generate the individual probability
table $Q(X, U^{(t)}, t_i)$ for request U_i using Eq. 4.1. We calculate the revenue time-series
(REV_t) of $MAP(S_k)$ using the Maximum Probable Explanation (MPE) algorithm
[93] on $Q(X, U^{(t)}, t_i)$ in Eq. 4.2.

$$P_i \dots P_0 = arg\ max\ \{Q(X, U^{(t)}, t_i) \mid Y\} \tag{4.2}$$

$$Y = Q(X, U^{(t)}, t_{i-1}), \dots, Q(X, U^{(t)}, t_0)$$

$$REV_t = \sum_i^{|MAP(S_k)|} P_i, \text{ where } U^{(t)} \in U_i$$

The proposed service composition framework transforms the requests to their
runtime behavior. The transformation is performed using multivariate HMM and
ARIMA model discussed in Chap. 3. The original time-series representation of
requests are transformed into new time-series of future runtime behavior denoted
as $\widehat{MAP}(S_k)$. Hence, we can calculate the operation cost of the transformed request
set $\widehat{MAP}(S_k)$. We include three types of costs in the long-term cost modeling: (a) the
power cost of resource utilization (OP_Cost); (b) the fixed cost of initial investment
($Fixed\_Cost$), and (c) SLA violation cost ($SLA\_Penalty$). We apply the following
assumptions to model the long-term cost.

(a) *The fixed costs of the provider are distributed over the servers for the amortisa-
    tion period.* Such costs include data centre building cost, land cost and hardware
    price. Each server i has a capital cost in a time unit t represented as $CAPEX_{it}$.
    Here, t is treated as a month or quarter in a year. If the provider has N physical
    servers, the fixed cost at time t is calculated by Eq. 4.3.

$$Fixed\_Cost_t = CAPEX_{it} \times N \tag{4.3}$$

(b) *The operation cost is determined by the server power consumption.* Although there are other costs, such as maintenance costs, employee salaries and insurance costs, we choose the power consumption cost for simplicity. ARIMA is a popular model to predict the dynamic price of power [51]. In Eq. 4.4, the autoregressive (AR) part depends on the p lagged values of the time-series of aggregated AG_n and α_i is the coefficient constant of the lag operator L. The moving average (MA) part depends on the q lagged values of the previous prediction errors (ϵ_t) and θ_i is the coefficient constant. d represents the number of times that the difference operation is performed to obtain the stationary time-series. The values of (p, d, q) are determined by the Box-Jenkins method for the price history [20].

$$(1 - \sum_{i=1}^{p} \alpha_i L^i)(1 - L)^d Power_t = (1 + \sum_{i=1}^{q} \theta_i L^i)\epsilon_t \qquad (4.4)$$

(c) *Each running physical server should have a predefined threshold (σ) of utility.* For example, the provider may decide that it will not run a physical server unless the server's resources are expected to be used more than 30%. The provider can turn on or off any server(s) at any time. The extra cost is the penalty that the provider pays for SLA violations.

The number of physical servers that will run to satisfy requests depends on the resource allocation module installed in a datacenter [147]. Individual service requests are composed and then used by this resource allocation module in runtime. The composed request time-series, $\{\bar{C}_t, \bar{M}_t, \bar{NB}_t, \bar{AV}_t, \bar{TH}_t, \bar{RT}_t\}$ for $\widehat{MAP}(S_k)$ can be formed using the composition rule of resources [134] and composition rules of the QoSs [140] in Eqs. 4.5 and 4.6:

$$\text{Resource Composition: } \bar{X}_t = \sum_{i}^{|\widehat{MAP}(S_k)|} X_i^{(t)} \text{ where } X = \{C, M, NB\} \qquad (4.5)$$

$$\text{QoS Composition: } \bar{Y}_t = max(y_i^{(t)}); \ | \ y \in \{av, th\} \qquad (4.6)$$

$$\bar{RT}_t = \sum_{i}^{|\widehat{MAP}(S_k)|} (rt_i^{(t)}) \text{ where } i \in \widehat{MAP}(S_k)$$

Our long-term economic model is independent of any particular resource allocation scheme. We assume that the resource allocation scheme installed in the physical servers has a function (F) to convert the composed requests to a utility factor (UF) as in Eq. 4.7.

$$UF_t = F(\bar{C}_t, \bar{M}_t, \bar{NB}_t, \bar{AV}_t, \bar{TH}_t, \bar{RT}_t) \qquad (4.7)$$

Let us assume that a server has a maximum utility factor UF_{max}. Hence, $\lceil \frac{UF_t}{UF_{max}} \rceil$ physical servers are needed to satisfy the composite requests. Each running physical server has two types of power cost units: (a) the fixed power cost unit for the routine operation of the server (fx_unit) and (b) the average variable power cost ($variable\_unit$) to satisfy the utility factor in each server. It is to be noted that the utility factor UF is distributed over all the running physical servers. We can calculate the operation cost at time t using Eq. 4.8.

$$Var\_Cost_t = Power_t \times variable\_unit \times \left\lceil \frac{UF_t}{UF_{max}} \right\rceil \qquad (4.8)$$

$$Routine\_Cost_t = Power_t \times fx\_unit \times \left\lceil \frac{UF_t}{UF_{max}} \right\rceil$$

$$OP\_Cost_t = Routine\_Cost_t + Var\_Cost_t$$

The proposed framework allows SLA violations to occur. The SLA violation cost $SLA\_Cost(t)$ depends on the SLA violation penalty rate ($SLA\_Penalty$) and the number of SLA violations (NO_SLV_t) in a certain time t. We calculate the number of SLA violations and the constrained satisfied utility factor using Algorithm 2. This checks whether a composition satisfies all the constraints. It reduces the number of service requests until all constraints are satisfied. The SLA violation cost (SLA_Cost) is calculated using Eq. 4.9.

$$SLA\_Cost_t = SLA\_Penalty \times NO\_SLV_t \qquad (4.9)$$

The revenue, operation cost and the SLA violation cost are used to calculate the profit of a composition. Algorithm 2 determines the number of SLA violations and the resource utilisation factor. We generate long-term economic valuation of the request map $MAP(S_k)$ using Eqs. 4.2, 4.3, 4.8 and 4.9 to reach Eq. 4.10.

$$P_t = REV_t - Fixed\_Cost_t - OP\_Cost_t - SLA\_Cost_t \qquad (4.10)$$

$$EVAL(t) = \{P_t, NO\_SLV_t, UF_t | \ t \in T\}$$

4.3.2   Semantic Economic Expectation and Fitness of a Composition

The economic evaluation of the optimal composition should closely match the long-term economic expectation. As profit, the number of SLA violations and resource utility factor are the key attributes in the long-term economic valuation of a composition, we include them in the long-term economic expectation. However, the influence of the attributes may not always be equal. For example, SLA violations at peak hours may be more important than the profit when considering business

---

Algorithm 2 Determining the number of SLA violations and utility factor of a composition

---

Require: Request Map: $MAP(S_k)$, Resource and QoS constraints:$(C_{max}, M_{max}, NB_{mx}, AV_{max}, RT_{max}, TH_{max})$, server utility threshold σ and maximum utility factor UF_{max}.

Ensure: the number of SLA violations (NO_SLV_t) and Utility Factor (UF_t) at time t

1: $NO\_SLV_t := -1$
2: **repeat**
3:     $NO\_SLV_t := NO\_SLV_t + 1$
4:     Set $Candidate(|MAP(S_k)|) = \{i \mid$ where, $i \in MAP(S_k)\}$
5:     Generate $X_t := (\bar{C}_t, \bar{M}_t, \bar{NB}_t, \bar{AV}_t, \bar{TH}_t, \bar{RT}_t)$ using $Candidate(|MAP(S_k)|)$ in Eq. 4.5 and 4.6.
6:     Generate $UF_t := F(Y_t)$ using Eq. 4.7.
7:     Server utility threshold $\hat{\sigma} := (UF_{max} \mod UF_t)$
8:     Remove any requests from the $MAP(S_k)$ with a random distribution and update $|MAP(S_k)| := |MAP(S_k)| - 1$
9: **until** $X_t < X_{max} \mid X \in \{C, M, NB, AV, RT, TH\}$ and $\hat{\sigma} < \sigma$
10: Return NO_SLV_t and UF_t

Table 4.3 Distance function for semantic expectations

Semantics (Y)	Distance function
"More" (M)	$M(X, T) = \sum_{t=1}^{T} W_t^X \times (X_t - X_t^E)$
"Less" (L)	$L(X, T) = \sum_{t=1}^{T} W_t^X \times (X_t^E - X_t)$
"Neutral" (N)	$N(X, T) = \sqrt{\sum_{t=1}^{T} \frac{W_t^X}{(X_t^E - X_t)^2}}$

reputation. We incorporate such influence weights in the multidimensional time-series using Eq. 4.11.

$$EXP(t) = \{(P_t^E, W_t^P), (NO\_SLV_t^E, W_t^S), (UF_t^E, W_t^{UF}) \mid t \in T\} \qquad (4.11)$$

We define the fitness of a composition as the time-series distance between the long-term economic evaluation of the composition and the economic expectation. It quantifies how similar the composition time-series is to the expectation time-series. We term it as "neutral" distance measure. In reality, the semantic expectations of the economic attributes are different. For example, "more" profit and "less" SLA violation are expected with a "neutral" utility factor. In point-to-point distance measure, "more" and "less" semantics rely on the positive or negative magnitude of the distance. Hence, we define the set of three semantic distance functions Y ("More (M)", "Less (L)", "Neutral (N)" distance) in the following Table 4.3.

The semantics ("More" (M), "Less" (L) and "Neutral" (N)) are added as $SEM\_EXP(t) = \{(P_t^E, W_t^P, M), (NO\_SLV_t^E, W_t^S, L), (UF_t^E, W_t^{UF}, N)\}$. Figure 4.4 depicts a long-term economic model. As the provider decides the economic expectation

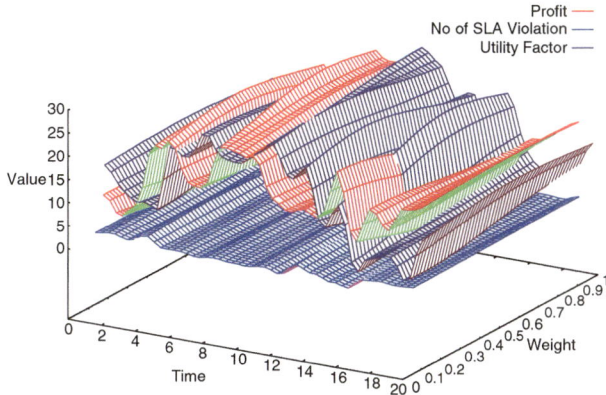

Fig. 4.4 A weighted long-term economic expectation

semantic of a particular attribute, we generalise the long-term semantic economic expectation in Eq. 4.12.

$$SEM\_EXP(t) = \{(X_t^E, W_t^X, Y)\}, \mid X \in \{P, NO\_SLV, UF\} \qquad (4.12)$$

Each attribute in *SEM_EXP(t)* uses the distance function based on its respective semantics. We define the fitness of *EVAL(t)* as the aggregated distance of each attribute in *SEM_EXP(t)*. If the profit, the number of SLA violations, and the utility factor are attributed as "More", "Less", and "Neutral" semantics respectively, we calculate the fitness of the request map in Eq. 4.13.

$$Fitness(MAP(S_k)) = M(P, T) + L(NO\_SLV, T) + N(UF, T) \qquad (4.13)$$

4.4 Genetic Optimization Using IaaS Economic Model

The proposed economic model is non-linear in nature. We design a genetic algorithm (GA) to address the non-linear properties in the IaaS economic model. The task of the optimization process is to find an optimal subset $\{MAP(S_k) \mid k < N\}$ that maximizes the fitness of the composition stated in Eq. 4.13. The GA simulates evolutionary processes by considering an initial *population* of *individuals* and applying genetic operators in each reproduction. In optimization terms, an individual in the population is encoded into a string or *chromosome* that represents a possible solution to a given problem. We use a binary string representation $X[j] = 0$ or 1 to represent the possible solution of $MAP(S_k)$. The jth request is considered in the solution if $X[j] = 1$. For example, a candidate solution $\{B, C\}$ is represented as $\{0110\}$ in the IaaS composition if the incoming requests are $\{A, B, C, D\}$. The fitness of an individual is evaluated based on the fitness function in Eq. 4.13. Highly fit solutions reproduce new "offspring" solutions (i.e., children) by exchanging pieces of their genetic information in a *crossover* procedure. Mutation is often applied after crossover by altering some genes in the strings. The less fit chromosomes in the population are replaced by new children. This process is repeated until a satisfactory solution is found. We use a binary tournament selection method [141] to generate the initial population for the first optimization. The crossover point is set at the midpoint of a chromosome. We set the mutation rate as 2 bits per child. After discarding the duplicated child in crossover operation, the new population replaces the individual chromosomes with the lowest fitness value (steady-state replacement). We continue generating new populations until the solutions are not further improved.

The requests in the long-term IaaS composition are based on their predicted future behavior. However, existing requests in the system may behave differently than predicted. We use fixed interval (ΔT) to check if the existing composition is deviating from the prediction. Other checkpoints are the predicted incoming arrival times of new requests. For example, assume that $\{(A, t_0), (C, t_5)\}$ is the initial IaaS composition. If $\Delta t = 2$, the optimization checkpoints are t_3 and t_5. If Request B arrives at time t_2, we may consider including B if the new predicted behavior of A is different from its initial prediction. Hence, the optimization process should be run again from scratch to update the solution.

4.5 Hybrid Adaptive Genetic Algorithm (HAGA) Based Composition

The economic model described in Sect. 4.3 is non-linear in nature. For example, if Request A and B have operation costs of x and y respectively, the operation cost of the composition AB may be different from the value of $(x + y)$. This is because the two requests may share the same resources in runtime and thus reduce operation costs. Therefore, we require a suitable non-linear combinatorial optimization process to select the optimal composition of requests. Brute-force is a general combinatorial optimization technique that consists of systematically enumerating all possible candidates for the solution and checking whether each candidate satisfies the economic goal [139]. Intuitively, the brute-force approach generates the best solution. However, it has a scalability problem (creating 2^n candidates for n incoming requests) and may not be applicable in the real world. For example, if the provider expects to receive four new incoming requests per month in a year, it has to consider $4 \times 12 = 48$ incoming requests while performing the first optimization at the beginning of the year. If a candidate composition requires 100 ns to evaluate, the brute-force approach requires 325.78 days (2^{48} ns) to find the optimal composition.

We propose HAGA to address the non-linear properties in an IaaS economic model and to solve the scalability issue in real-world applications. Given N requests with arrival times denoted as $MAP(S_N) = \{< U_1, Arrival_1 >, .., < U_N, Arrival_N >\}$, the task of the optimization process is to find the optimal subset $MAP(S_k)$, where $k < N$ that maximizes the fitness of the composition stated in Eq. 4.13.

The HAGA is a hybrid of the Genetic Algorithm (GA) [141] and Ant Colony Optimization (ACO) [147]. In GA, the *crossover* procedure in a highly fitted-population does not guarantee feasible children that satisfy the resource and QoS constraints. For example, $\{C\}$ and $\{A, D\}$ produces the solution $\{A, C\}$ which violates resource constraints (negative fitness) in Fig. 4.5. Hence, we apply a repair operation to the infeasible solution in HAGA. The first task is to *drop* some genes (which are '1' in the chromosome) and then add new genes (reverse the '0' bits to '1'). For example, the solution $\{A, C\}$ is repaired to $\{B, C\}$ by dropping 'A' and adding 'B' in the solution (Fig. 4.5). Randomly chosen bits may not improve the children's fitness. Therefore, we incorporate an ACO-based heuristic operator in HAGA to ensure faster convergence with the global IaaS composition.

4.5.1   Solution Representation in HAGA

We use a binary string representation $X[j] = 0$ or 1 to represent the possible solution of $MAP(S_k)$. The jth request is considered in the solution if $X[j] = 1$. For example, a candidate solution $\{B, C\}$ is represented as $\{0110\}$ in the IaaS composition, if the incoming requests are $\{A, B, C, D\}$ (Fig. 4.5). We use Eq. 4.13 as the fitness function of the solution. For example, we create a request map of $\{B, C\}$ from the solution represented as $\{0110\}$. The proposed model calculates the economic valuation of the request map using Eq. 4.10. As the provider specifies its long-term economic expectation as $SEM\_EXP(t)$, Eq. 4.13 calculates the fitness of the request map of $\{B, C\}$.

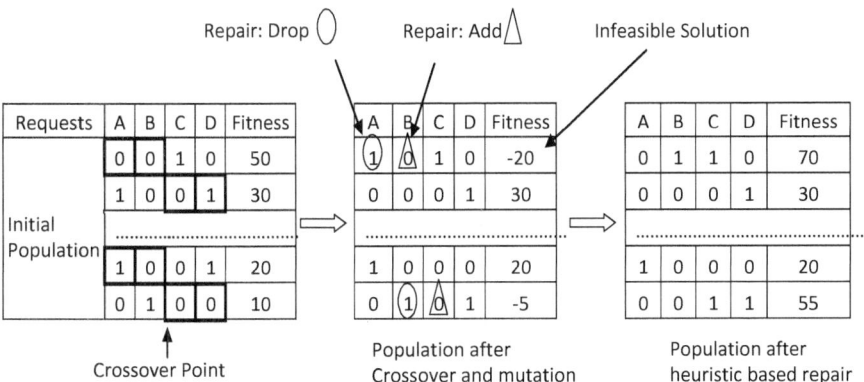

Fig. 4.5 Hybrid genetic optimization in IaaS composition

4.5.2 Initial Population Generation

The size of the population is determined by the number of incoming requests denoted as n. As there could be 2^n candidate solutions, if $2^n \geq 100$, we use a fixed size of $N = 100$ for the population. If $2^n < 100$, we use the size of the population as $N = 2^n$ for the population. As the population is generated randomly, it does not guarantee feasible compositions that satisfy the resource and QoS constraints. For example, consider the solution $\{A, C\}$ which violates resource constraints (negative fitness) in Fig. 4.5. Each of the initial feasible solutions is constructed by a primal heuristic that repeatedly and randomly selects a variable and sets it to '1' if the solution is feasible. The heuristic terminates when the selected variable cannot be added to the solution.

4.5.3 Parent Selection, Crossover, and Mutation

The initial population of feasible compositions is divided into two pools. Each pool has $\frac{N}{2}$ compositions which are randomly selected from the initial population. The compositions are sorted in descending order in each pool. Two individuals with the best fitness, each of which is taken from one of the two tournament pools, are chosen to be the parents. It is one form of binary tournament selection method [141] to select parent chromosomes or compositions before a crossover operation.

As we adopt a binary representation for IaaS service composition, a wide range of the standard GA crossover and mutation operators could be adopted. As the overall performance of GAs for combinatorial optimization problems is often relatively insensitive to the particular choice of crossover operator [33], we set the crossover point as the midpoint of a chromosome. A child is populated by the left half of the first parent and the right half of the second parent (Fig. 4.5). Once a child solution has been generated through a crossover, a procedure mutates randomly selected bits in the child solution, i.e. causing these chosen bits to change from '0' to '1' or vice versa. The rate of mutation is configured as a small value (in the order of 1 or 2 bits per string). As the *crossover* and *mutation* procedure in a highly-fitted population does not guarantee feasible children, a solution repair procedure is required to converge with the global IaaS composition.

4.5.4 Solution Generation with Repair Heuristic

We incorporate the *memory-full* operations in the traditional GA. In such operations, we infer useful knowledge from the generated populations. We store the statistics in two structures: *global inter-dependency matrix* and *global preference heuristic*. These two structures are used to create the repair heuristic operator.

The global inter-dependency matrix (*GIDM*) is the statistical relationship among requests in the generated populations. It has $N \times N$ entries where N is the number of requests. The value $gidm_{ij}$ is the number of times that requests i and j are in a generated feasible solution. For example, if $gidm_{AB} = 0$ and $gidm_{BC} = 1$, a new child solution $\{A, B, C\}$ updates the matrix as $gidm_{AB} = 1$, $gidm_{BC} = 2$, and $gidm_{AC} = 1$. The *GIDM* is a *symmetric* matrix in Eq. 4.14.

$$GIDM = \begin{bmatrix} gidm_{11} & gidm_{12} & . & gidm_{1n} \\ gidm_{21} & gidm_{22} & . & gidm_{2n} \\ . & . & . & . \\ gidm_{n1} & gidm_{n2} & . & gidm_{nn} \end{bmatrix} \tag{4.14}$$

$$gidm_{ij} = gidm_{ji} \text{ and } GIDM = GIDM^T \text{(transpose)}$$

Initially the matrix is empty. While the GA progresses through generating populations, the matrix is updated. According to [141], the children solutions are generated by the best genes of the parents. Hence, a request is eventually grouped with other requests that maximize the fitness. For example, if $\{A, B, C\}$ is the optimal solution from $\{A, B, C, D, E, F\}$; $gidm_{AB}$, $gidm_{BC}$, and $gidm_{AC}$ should have relatively higher values with each other. Although $\{D, E, F\}$ is not the optimal solution, they may be grouped together in the *GIDM*. It states that Request D can maximize the fitness if it is composed with E and F. The inter-dependency of a request i (*IC*) in a solution S is calculated in Eq. 4.15.

$$IC(i) = \sum_{j}^{|S|} gidm_{ji} \tag{4.15}$$

The global preference heuristic (*GPH*) is the probabilistic indicator of a request's influence on the fitness of a solution. It is updated by the fitness of the generated populations containing the particular requests. If $GPH(i) = 0.8$ and $GPH(j) = 0.5$, then request i generates higher fitness than j in the population history. We use ACO [147] to generate the *GPH*. In an ACO, some intelligent ants (agents) deposit *pheromones* and *utilities* on the traversed paths to a solution. The ant selects a path based on the pheromone and utility level of the pre-constructed path. We consider a solution generated by the GA as a path of an individual ant. When the GA generates a population of size n, we consider that n ants generate the solutions. A population is constructed after all ants update their trails with pheromones. In an ACO, the pheromones are evaporated before the update operation to ensure global optima. Similarly, we update the pheromone level of request i ($\tau(i)$) in Eq. 4.16.

$$\tau(i) = (1 - \phi)\tau(i) + \Delta\tau \tag{4.16}$$

Here, ϕ is the evaporation rate and $\Delta\tau$ is a constant pheromone level. In this ACO, we use k-population based pheromone update. We select the top k ants that generate top k fitness in the population. These ants only update the pheromones of their respective requests. Meanwhile, a percentage of existing pheromones in all requests evaporates.

In a typical ACO, the ants return to the source following the same path that it traversed to reach the destination. It ensures the profit of the traversed path. Similarly, we distribute the fitness of the solution to the participating requests. For example, if the composition $\{A, B, C\}$ has the fitness of 100, the average contribution of the requests is 33. The fitness values of the other solutions in the population, i.e. ($\{A, C\}, \{B, D\}$) are 80 and -10. It shows that request 'A' has a positive influence on all the solutions while 'B' has both positive and negative influences. We calculate the fitness influence of the request ($\eta(i)$) by the average fitness per request in Eq. 4.17.

$$\eta(i) = \frac{Fitness(MAP(S_k))}{|MAP(S_k)|} \mid i \in MAP(S_k) \tag{4.17}$$

We calculate the pheromone level (τ) and fitness influence (η) of all elements in a request map when a new population is generated. As the *GPH* is the probabilistic indicator of a request's influence, the relative performance of the requests can be calculated in Eq. 4.18. Here, α and β are positive numbers to control pheromones and the influence of fitness of candidate requests respectively.

$$GPH(i) = \frac{[\tau(i)]^\alpha \times [\eta(i)]^\beta}{\sum_{j=1}^{N} [\tau(i)]^\alpha \times [\eta(i)]^\beta} \tag{4.18}$$

After determining the *IC* and *GPH* of a population, a repair operator can be designed which considers the inclusion and exclusion of each variable in the child solution. At first, we drop (changing variable from '1' to '0') a request from the composition which is less inter-dependent with other requests and has a lower influence on the fitness of the previous solutions globally. In the *ADD* phase, we change the variable from '0' to '1' which is more inter-dependent and has a higher influence on the fitness of the previous solutions. The aim of the DROP phase is to obtain a feasible solution from an infeasible solution, while the ADD phase aims to improve the fitness of a feasible solution. Algorithm 3 describes the repair operation.

4.5.5 Runtime Optimization Scheduling

The requests in the long-term IaaS composition are based on their predicted future behavior. However, existing requests in the system may behave differently to that predicted. We use a fixed interval (ΔT) to check whether or not the current composition is deviating from the prediction. Other checkpoints are the predicted incoming arrival times of the new requests. For example, assume that $\{(A, t_0), (C, t_5)\}$ is the

---

Algorithm 3 Repair operation in an infeasible solution

Require: Binary representation X of infeasible Request Map: $MAP(S_k)$, IC, and
   GPH
Ensure: The feasible new binary representation X
 1: **for** i:=1 **to** N **do**
 2:   $Y[i] \leftarrow IC(i) \times GPH(i)$
 3: **end for**
 4: Rearrange X based on $min(Y)$ /* Drop Phase */
 5: **for** $i := 1$ **to** N **do**
 6:   **if** $X[i] = 1$ **then**
 7:     $Z \leftarrow Fitness(X)$ and $\hat{Z} \leftarrow Fitness(\hat{X})$ where, $\hat{X}[i] = 0$ using Equation 4.13.
 8:     **if** $(\hat{Z} > Z$ and $\hat{Z} > 0)$ **then**
 9:       $X[i] \leftarrow 0$
10:     **end if**
11:   **end if**
12: **end for**
13: Rearrange X based on $max(Y)$ /* Add Phase */
14: **for** $i := 1$ **to** N **do**
15:   **if** $X[i] = 0$ **then**
16:     $Z \leftarrow Fitness(X)$ and $\hat{Z} \leftarrow Fitness(\hat{X})$ where, $\hat{X}[i] = 1$ using Equation 4.13.
17:     **if** $(\hat{Z} > Z$ and $\hat{Z} > 0)$ **then**
18:       $X[i] \leftarrow 1$
19:     **end if**
20:   **end if**
21: **end for**
22: Return X

---

initial IaaS composition. If $\Delta t = 2$, the optimization checkpoints are t_3 and t_5. If Request B arrives at time t_2, we may consider the inclusion of B if the new predicted behavior of A is different from its initial prediction. We can run the optimization process from scratch in the traditional way. However, it does not take advantage of the *memory-full* properties of the hybrid GA. We use the *IC* and *GPH* generated in previous heuristics to create the initial population of the new optimization. As the *GIDM* of the previous optimization groups the requests based on their inter-dependency, we generate a complete directed-influence graph where the edge $E(i,j)$ represents the relative influence of i on j compared to the other requests. The $E(i,j)$ is calculated using the *GIDM* and *IC* in Eq. 4.19.

$$E(i,j) = \frac{GIDM[i,j]}{IC(i)} \tag{4.19}$$

Figure 4.6 depicts the *GIDM* and influence graph of four requests (A, B, C and D). Here, A is inter-connected with B, and C is inter-connected with D. Let us assume that the request i is deviated to $\hat{i}$ in runtime. Hence, the composition that includes

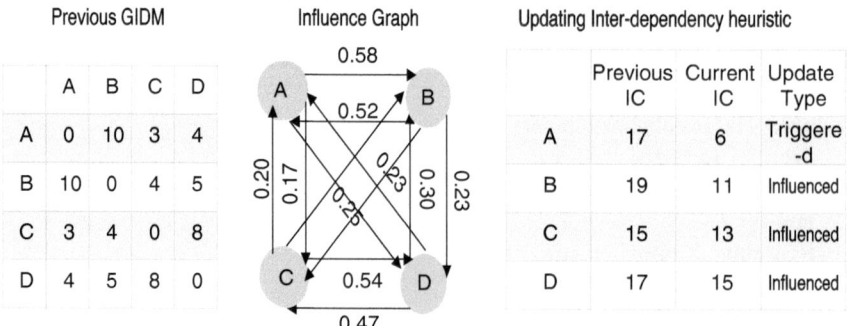

Fig. 4.6 Runtime modification of the inter-dependency heuristic

i will not perform as it is predicted. As *IC* and *GPH* control the solution repair operation in the proposed hybrid GA, the deviation of i should be reflected on them. The deviation, $d = \sqrt{\sum_{t=0}^{T}(\hat{i}_t - i_t)^2}$ reduces the *IC* and *GPH* of the request with the constant factor c in Eq. 4.20.

$$IC(i) = IC(i) - d \times c \qquad (4.20)$$
$$GPH(i) = GPH(i) - d \times c$$

Note that this update is *triggered* and should only influence the inter-connected requests of i. Figure 4.6 depicts that the deviation in Request A has a greater influence on the Request B than the other requests. The $E(i, j)$ is used to reflect the deviation d in j with the constant c in Eq. 4.21.

$$IC(j) = IC(i) - E(i, j) \times d \times c \qquad (4.21)$$
$$GPH(j) = GPH(i) - E(i, j) \times d \times c$$

We generate the new population based on the descending order of $MAX(IC \times GPH)$. Algorithm 3 and the GA procedures are repeated with the new population to address the runtime behavior.

4.6   Experiments and Results

A set of experiments have been conducted to evaluate the efficiency of the proposed approach. First, we evaluate the prediction accuracy of the economic model. The fitness of the economic model based composition is compared with a greedy approach, the traditional GA, Ant Colony Optimization (ACO) approaches, and a brute force approach. In the greedy approach, the provider does not consider the future arrival and evaluation of the requests. It accepts the requests that do not violate the SLA at the time of arrival [135]. The brute-force approach is also based on the fitness function (Eq. 4.13). It will consider all the possible compositions (2^N for N requests) to choose the optimal composition. The efficiency of HAGA is compared with the traditional GA and ACO approaches. All the experiments have been conducted on computers with Intel Core i7 CPU (2.13 GHz and 4 GB RAM). The R statistical tool [104] is used to implement the algorithms.

4.6.1 Data Description

We evaluate the proposed method using a mixture of Google Cluster resource utilisation [109], real-world cloud QoS performance [67] described in Sect. 3.6.1 in Chap. 3. We randomly pick 70 Google Cluster jobs and make one-to-one mapping with the 100 sets of QoS data. We randomly generate 70 arrival time points and attach them to the requests to create a stochastic map of 70 long-term requests. We synthetically generate the runtime behavior of the service requests using a probabilistic distribution termed the *Correlation Density Index (CDI)* (Eq. 3.15). We generate five sets of service runtime requests with five different CDI values (0.5, 0.6, 0.7, 0.8, 0.9) from the map of 70 long-term requests. The long-term economic expectation is also synthetically created. The mean and standard deviations of the attributes in economic expectation are as follows: profit (mean: $100, sd: $20, and weight: 0.5), number of SLA violations (mean: $3, sd: $2, and weight: 0.3), and utility factor (mean: 80%, sd: 30%, and weight: 0.2).

4.6.2 Setup of Long-Term Economic Model

The proposed model incorporates a change of service price and operation cost. We use the time-series of electricity price (E_t) from the Australian Bureau of Statistics [41] to generate the change in the service price and operation cost. The price of resources and QoS are set by following a weighted Google Compute Engine pricing model as ($5 \times E_t$/unit per hour for any types of resources) [52]. A short-term mapping relationship is established between operation cost and utilization [51]. We generate the long-term behavior between operation cost and utilization using the dynamic electricity price in Table 4.4. The SLA violation fee is 20% of the revenue credited to consumers. The resource constraints are set by allowing a maximum 100 units for each attribute. We use the resource allocation algorithm in [135] as the utility factor in Eq. 4.7.

Table 4.4 Long-term
relationship between utility
factor and operation cost

UF (%)	Cost/hour
5	$110 \times E_t$
20	$120 \times E_t$
30	$140 \times E_t$
60	$150 \times E_t$
100	$165 \times E_t$

Table 4.5 HAGA, GA, and
ACO parameter values

Parameters	Values
Crossover point	Middle
Mutation rate	2 bits per child
Initial pheromone level, τ	10
Pheromone evaporation rate, ϕ	0.3
Pheromone update, $\Delta\tau$	5
Pheromone control operator, α	0.5
Fitness control operator, β	0.5
IC update constant, C	5
GPH update constant, c	2

4.6.3   Setup of HAGA, GA, and ACO Parameters

The proposed HAGA inherits parameters from traditional GA and ACO. As our
target is not so much about finding the fine-tuned values of the parameters, e.g.
cross-over point and mutation rate, we use same parameter values in HAGA,
GA, and ACO so that the comparison is not influenced by the selection operator.
Table 4.5 summarises the values of the parameters used in the experiments. These
parameter values are commonly preferred settings for GA and ACO.

4.6.4   Efficiency of the HAGA-Based Composition

At first, we evaluate the performance of the proposed DBN in the economic model.
We model the 18-month (Jan 2012–Sep 2013) electricity prices with the proposed
DBN. The price history is represented in time-series denoted as $(AC(q))$ and the
predicted price from the DBN is represented in time-series denoted as $(PR(q))$. The
prediction accuracy i.e. distance between $(AC(q))$ and $(PR(q))$ are calculated using
normalized Root Mean Square Error (NRMSE) defined in Eq. 3.9. Figure 4.7 depicts
the closeness of the prediction to the actual behavior. The NRMSE of the DBN is
0.3 which is acceptable in prediction accuracy.

We evaluate the efficiency of the proposed method. To achieve that, we simulate
a 1-year IaaS composition with 12 checkpoints (one for each month). All the
incoming requests are selected from the 70 request map. The arrival times of the
requests follow a Poisson distribution with the mean value λ which ranges from 1 to

10 (Unit requests per month). Figure 4.8 depicts the required convergence time for the proposed HAGA, traditional GA, ACO, Greedy, and brute-force methods with increasing λ values. The brute-force approach increases exponentially and requires 2010 min (34 h) to converge for a small λ value (3.2). As a service provider usually

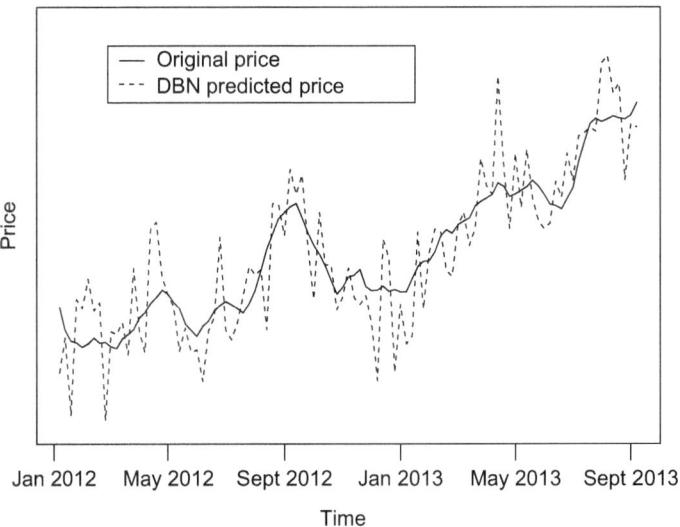

Fig. 4.7 Prediction accuracy of DBN

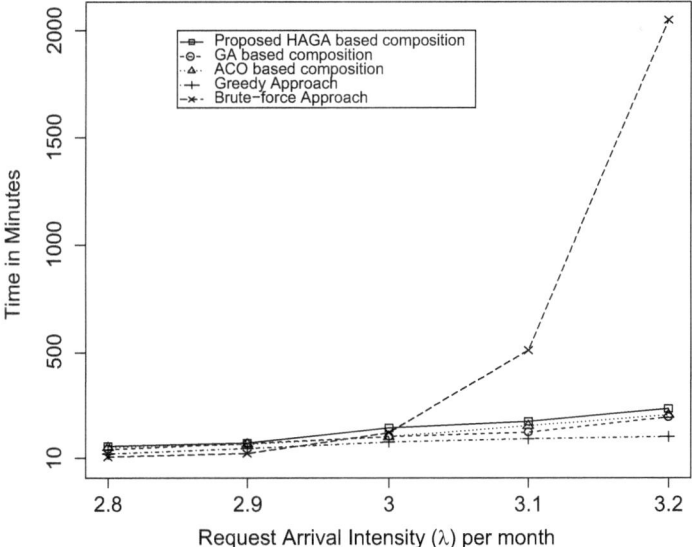

Fig. 4.8 Effect of request arrival intensity in solution convergence

receives a high number of requests and needs to make prompt decisions, the brute-force approach is not applicable in the real-world situation, compared to the other approaches (Fig. 4.8).

To evaluate the quality of the solution, we test the expectation fitness of the proposed HAGA, traditional GA, ACO, Greedy, and brute-force methods using a 35 request map (Fig. 4.9). We observe that the greedy approach only maximizes the economic fitness at the beginning, while the proposed heuristic-based service composition approach maximizes the fitness in steady rates over the period of composition. The proposed HAGA based approach outperforms the traditional GA-based method and ACO in the 18-month period, with an extra cumulative fitness of 25%. Although the brute-force approach outputs the best result, it is not a practical choice due to its exponential runtime complexity.

As all the types of combinations are compared with the brute-force method, we use the result of that method as a baseline and normalize the fitness values as $\frac{Evolutionary_t}{Brute\_Force_t}$. We exclude comparing the greedy approach in further experiments due to its poor fitness value in the long-term (Fig. 4.9). Next, we compare the effect of the solution space size on the proposed algorithm. Figure 4.10 depicts that HAGA performs better when the solution space is relatively larger. The key reason for this is that the HAGA stores the knowledge from the previous optimization, which directs choosing suitable candidates in a large solution space. The GA and ACO approaches select candidates randomly, and it causes local optimum solutions (Fig. 4.11).

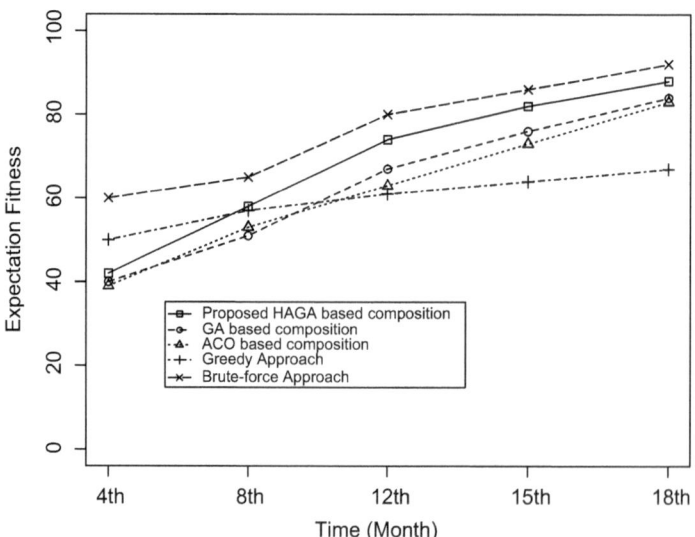

Fig. 4.9 Comparison of HAGA-based long-term composition with other approaches

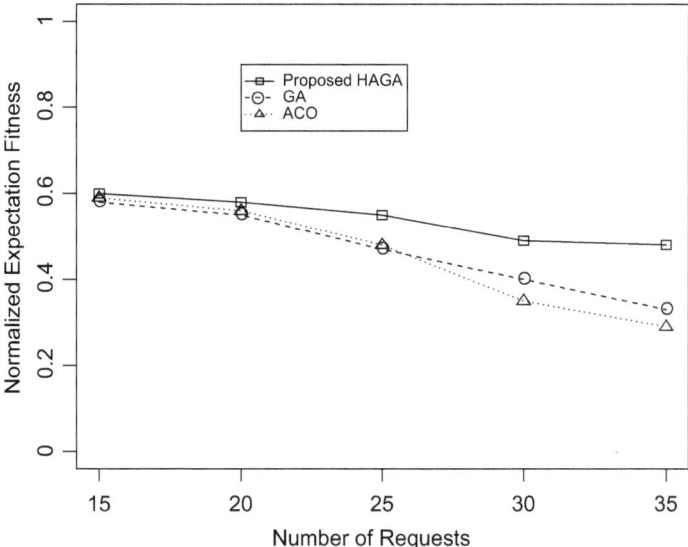

Fig. 4.10 Effect of the solution space size

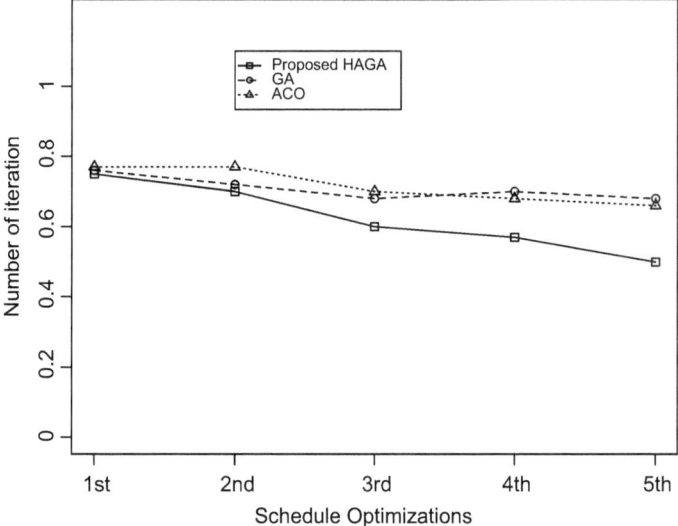

Fig. 4.11 Number of iterations in dynamic environment

4.6.5   Time Complexity Analysis

The proposed HAGA approach converges using the *GPH*. It selects more suitable candidates in the composition than do GA and ACO do when generating a population. Figure 4.12 depicts that HAGA converges faster than the GA and

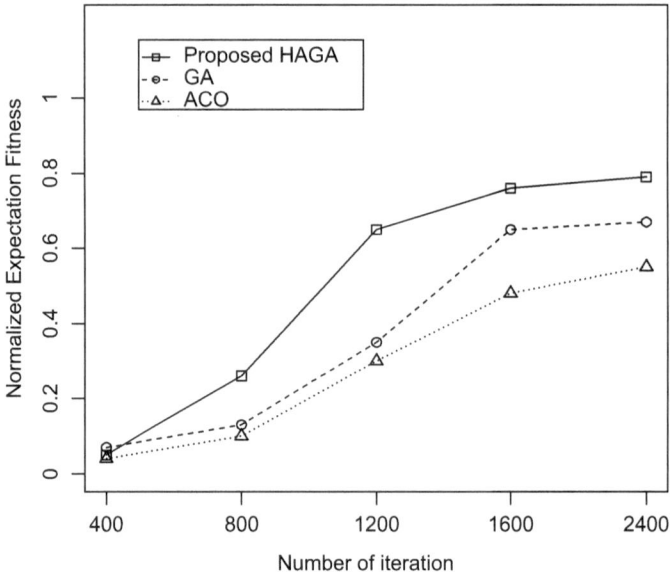

Fig. 4.12 Global solution convergence time

ACO approaches in a single optimization. While HAGA achieves approximate convergence in 1200 iterations, GA and ACO take about 1600 iterations to reach the convergence.

As HAGA is *memory-full*, successive optimization in the changed environment generates a lower number of iterations than GA and ACO to update the previous composition (Fig. 4.11). GA and ACO do not store information from the previous optimization. Thus, it requires the almost same amount of iterations for GA and ACO to converge in each checkpoint (Fig. 4.11). In contrast, HAGA reduces the number of iterations in the successive optimization as shown in Fig. 4.11.

4.7 Conclusion

In this chapter, we have proposed an advanced hybrid genetic optimization process that updates the quality of a cloud service request composition by detecting the runtime changes and incorporating the knowledge transfer among optimization processes at multiple checkpoints in the long-term period. It enables providers to express semantic long-term economic exceptions. Such preferences are mostly applicable in the real-world business model. Experimental results show that the proposed hybrid genetic approach is more profitable than the GA, ACO, and greedy approaches. It reduces the optimization time at the runtime and increases its applicability in the real-world than do the GA and ACO approaches. In the next chapter, we will develop the qualitative IaaS composition framework.

Chapter 5
Long-Term Qualitative IaaS Composition

5.1 Introduction

User preferences are one of the key research subjects in developing personalized applications [126]. In many real life service composition scenarios, the target is to achieve the desired *functional* goal while ensuring *user-provided preferences*. For example, a travel planner usually composes services from different transportation and accommodation services. The functional goal of the planner is to find a trip from a source to a destination for its users. However, such a composition usually takes into account user preferences such as total costs, journey times and modes of transportation. A user may specify that he/she is flexible on tour dates but wishes to travel on business class or on a flight with a lower price.

User preferences are usually considered in the cloud service composition from the *consumer's* perspective [127]. According to [139], the functional and QoS attributes in a long-term consumer request are variable over a period, qualitative in nature and closely related to the price. For example, a university may require higher availability in IaaS services when the semester commences but with lower availability during semester breaks (to save the money).

The long-term business strategies of the provider are often *qualitative* in nature. For example, mobile carrier companies normally create various plans for different types of consumers [87]. Sometimes they offer mobile phones at low prices as a business strategy. Similarly, in the cloud market, if a provider finds its CPU units are more fault-tolerant than hard disks, it may prefer CPU-intensive service requests more than memory-intensive requests to avoid probable Service Level Agreement (SLA) violations. Although we have studied quantitative economic models in Chaps. 3 and 4, a provider's qualitative preferences are not considered in IaaS compositions.

The providers' preferences usually appear in the form of a *decision variable* while considering IaaS composition as a decision-support system [122]. The decision variable distinguishes different types of consumers. For example, the duration

© Springer International Publishing AG 2018
S. Mistry et al., *Economic Models for Managing Cloud Services*,
https://doi.org/10.1007/978-3-319-73876-5_5

of a consumer request can be treated as a decision variable as it separates short-term and long-term consumers. Different business strategies are created according to a decision variable. For example, the provider may offer discounts on service prices only for long-term consumers.

The *qualitative preferences* play an important role in development of *service menus*. Given the available initial capacity of resources (e.g. CPU resources, network resources and storage resources) the first important decision for an IaaS provider is to define the menu of services [4] to offer to consumers. Creating a menu of products is vital to address revenue management issues [36]. The task of setting a different price schema per service menu is computationally intensive and hard to implement. Hence, service providers usually relate prices to resources and QoS qualitatively. For example, higher QoS are often labeled with higher prices, and lower QoS are labeled with lower prices.

To the best of our knowledge, existing qualitative service composition approaches are performed from the consumers' perspectives [111, 126, 139]. As objectives of IaaS providers are different from service consumers, the qualitative preferences of the consumers are not *similar* to the preferences of providers. Besides, the *semantics* of preferences may not be static during the whole period of composition. For example, higher QoS in the first year may be treated as average QoS in the second year due to technological advances. We propose a qualitative economic model by incorporating decision variables such as the length of requests and the reputation of customers. We represent the economic model as the Temporal CP-Net (TempCP-Net) which is a collection of dynamic CP-nets [18] spanning the composition time segments. We transform the TempCP-net into a k-d tree as nodes in the preference graph could be considered as points. The k-d tree enables an efficient multidimensional point query [5] which is required in qualitative composition. We assume the provider operates with a fixed amount of resources [51]. *We focus on the deterministic arrivals of the incoming requests, i.e. all the requests are known at the start of the qualitative composition.*

The k-d tree is used to compute the global preference ranking of a composition. Hence, we transform the IaaS composition as a preference maximization optimization problem. We consider both the global and local optimization approaches to select the optimal composition considering the k-d tree represented TempCP-net as the economic model. Firstly, *we assume the provider has no knowledge-base of historical request patterns*. We formalize a Dynamic Programming (DP)-based [74] approach that considers all requests at the time of optimization. As this approach also considers all requests at the beginning of the composition, it is indifferent to the flow rate of incoming requests, i.e. the temporal distribution of the requests. This may pose a scalability issue in the runtime due to comparisons among a large number of candidate solutions. On the other hand, we devise a heuristic-based local optimization approach to accept or reject requests in each segment so that the overall decision over the segments converge collectively into an acceptable approximate global optimal composition.

Next, *we assume the provider has access to historical requests*. A set of incoming requests can have different distributions of historical requests in the runtime of a composition. We need to find the best sequence of local selection of requests in the runtime. As the distributions are dynamic, we use a model-free reinforcement learning approach called *Q-learning* [129] to find the best sequence of request selections. The traditional two-dimensional Q-learning algorithm calculates the expected global ranking, i.e. *Q-values* of the composition for each local selection of requests in the composition period [128]. We propose a three-dimensional Q-learning approach that considers the execution order of the local section in the time segments to find the best sequence of selecting incoming requests. We use the Kolmogorov-Smirnov test (K-S test) [44] as a statistical distribution matching algorithm to find correlations between incoming requests and the set of historical requests. We propose a model to use the learned Q-values, using the statistical correlations for the composition in runtime. We propose a heuristic-based approach using the aggregated learned Q-values to compose the new or non-matched request patterns. The novelty of the proposed framework is summarized as follows.

(a) The use of decision variables in a TempCP-Net to represent qualitative preferences of an IaaS provider.
(b) The use of reinforcement learning to find the best order of sequential local optimizations from historical request patterns.
(c) The use of statistical analysis to find an optimal composition in runtime.

The chapter is structured as follows. Motivation, the Temporal CP-Net and optimization algorithms are discussed in Sects. 5.2, 5.3, and 5.4 respectively. The reinforcement learning approach, experiments and the conclusion are presented in Sects. 5.5, 5.6 and 5.7 respectively.

5.2 Motivation: A Qualitative IaaS Economic Model with Decision Variables

Let us assume; a new IaaS provider starts offering virtual CPU services associated with QoS of availability for simplicity. It can provide a maximum 100 CPU units and 100% availability. The provider's qualitative preferences on CPU, availability, and price can be interpreted into three semantic levels: high, moderate, and low, as shown in Fig. 5.1a. The interpretation of semantic levels is dynamic and adjusted according to cloud market performance and economic conditions. In the first year, more than $1000 is treated as a higher price (Fig. 5.1a). Due to predicted inflation, more than $1300 is anticipated and is treated as a higher price in the second and third years. The provider now has different preference rankings based on its annual goals over a 3-year period. For the first year, the provider prefers to provide high-quality services at relatively lower prices, to build its reputation in the market. Hence, the provider decides that "availability" of a service is the most important attribute, followed by "CPU" and "price". For the second year, the provider expects to provide services with higher prices and relatively fewer resources and QoS to

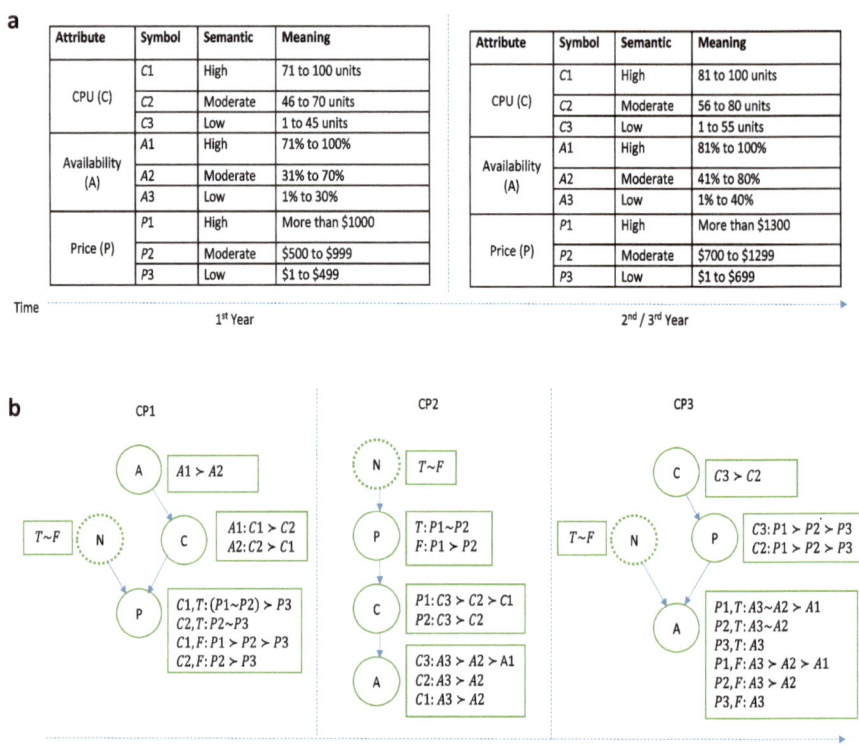

Fig. 5.1 (**a**) Semantic representation of preferred service attributes, and (**b**) a TempCP-Net

maximize profits. Thus "price" decides "CPU" and "availability". For the third year, the provider predicts that high-speed CPU units may be more error-prone due to an aging infrastructure. Therefore, the provider's preference is that providing relatively lower "CPU" has a higher priority than relatively higher "price" and lower "availability". The provider prefers to incentivize long-term contracts by offering discounts on service prices. The short-term and long-term requests are distinguished by a decision variable, labeled N. A true (T) value of N means the request spans over the next period (long-term requests) and a false (F) value of N means the request ends in the current period (short-term requests). In the first and second years, N decides the "price" levels for both long-term and short-term requests. The higher and moderate "price" are treated indifferently for long-term requests but differently for short-term requests in the first and second years. The decision variable, N, decides "availability" in the third year. The preference is to provide relatively higher "availability" to long-term requests than to short-term requests with the same moderate "price".

The CP-Net can elegantly represent these qualitative preferences. For example, an arc from "CPU" to "availability" means the preference of "availability" depends on the preference of "CPU" units. *Decision variables are distinguished using dashed circles.* The economic preferences are captured in a temporal CP-Net denoted as TempCP-Net, which is a collection of period-based CP-Nets. As the provider has annual preferences, the 3-year TempCP-Net is a set of {(CP1, Year 1),(CP2, Year 2), (CP3, Year 3)}, in which each sub-component corresponds to an annual preference (Fig. 5.1b).

CP1 captures the first-year reputation building strategy in Fig. 5.1b. Hence, the "high" availability has a higher priority than the "moderate" availability, i.e. $A1 \succ A2$. Note that the "low" availability ($A3$) is not in the provider's preference in CP1. The choice of availability determines the preference of CPU units. If the "high" availability ($A1$) is chosen, the provider prefers to supply the "high" CPU units rather than the "moderate" CPU units ($A1 : C1 \succ C2$). However, if the "moderate" availability ($A2$) is chosen, the provider prefers to supply the "moderate" CPU units rather than the "high" CPU units ($A2 : C2 \succ C1$). This is because a moderate QoS may not increase the provider's reputation as expected, thus packaging it with lower CPU units may increase the probability of reducing SLA violations rather than packaging with higher CPU units. Finally, the price of the service is chosen based on the selection of the levels of availability, CPU units and the decision variable N. As this is a reputation-building phase, the provider will not charge "high" price ($P1$) while providing "moderate" CPU units ($C2, T : P2 \sim P3$ and $C2, F : P2 \succ P3$). As the decision variable (N) prefers to provide a discount to long-term requests, the "lower" price has the same preference level of "moderate" price while supplying "moderate" CPU units for long-term requests ($C2, T : P2 \sim P3$). However, "moderate" price is preferred than "lower" price while providing "moderate" CPU units for short-term requests ($C2, F : P2 \succ P3$). In CP1, the most preferred service provision is ($A1, C1, P1$) for short-term requests and both ($A1, C1, P1$) and ($A1, C1, P2$) are the most preferred service provisions for long-term requests. In CP1, the least preferred choice is ($A2, C1, P3$) for both short-term and long-term requests. CP2 and CP3 capture the profit maximization and risk management strategies in the second and third years respectively. In CP2, the most preferred service provision is ($P1, C3, A3$) for short-term requests and both ($P1, C3, A3$) and ($P2, C3, A3$) are the most preferred service provisions for long-term requests. In CP2, the least preferred service is ($P2, C2, A2$) for both long-term and short-term requests expressing the preference for the higher price. In the third year, the most preferred service provision is ($C3, P1, A3$) for short-term requests while both ($C3, P1, A3$) and ($C3, P1, A2$) are the most preferred service provisions for long-term requests. In CP3, the least preferred service is ($C2, P3, A3$).

Let us assume four requests, {$R1$}, {$R2$}, {$R3$}, and {$R4$} arrive at the beginning of the composition (Fig. 5.2a). For simplicity, a request is specified in annual segments. In Fig. 5.2a, ($C : 80, A : 90, P : \$800$) is the first year segment of {$R1$}, which means that the consumer requires a VM with 80 CPU units and 90% availability and can pay \$800 for this service in the first year. The annual requirements of {$R2$}, {$R3$} and {$R4$} are described in the same way. As there are four requests, the optimal composition will be selected from $2^4 = 16$ combinations of the requests in the brute-force approach. The TempCP-Net (Fig. 5.1b) provides

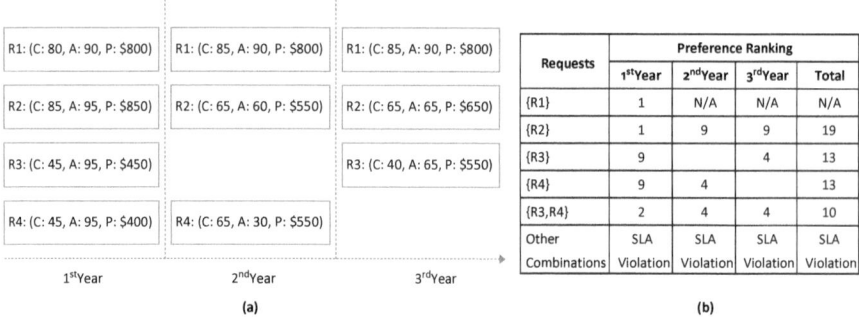

R1: (C: 80, A: 90, P: $800)	R1: (C: 85, A: 90, P: $800)	R1: (C: 85, A: 90, P: $800)
R2: (C: 85, A: 95, P: $850)	R2: (C: 65, A: 60, P: $550)	R2: (C: 65, A: 65, P: $650)
R3: (C: 45, A: 95, P: $450)		R3: (C: 40, A: 65, P: $550)
R4: (C: 45, A: 95, P: $400)	R4: (C: 65, A: 30, P: $550)	
1stYear	2ndYear	3rdYear

Requests	Preference Ranking			
	1stYear	2ndYear	3rdYear	Total
{R1}	1	N/A	N/A	N/A
{R2}	1	9	9	19
{R3}	9		4	13
{R4}	9	4		13
{R3,R4}	2	4	4	10
Other Combinations	SLA Violation	SLA Violation	SLA Violation	SLA Violation

(a)   (b)

Fig. 5.2 (a) Incoming requests, and (b) the preference ranking table

the objective function for the optimal IaaS composition selection. The preference ranking (lower values indicate higher ranking) of the combinations of the requests is retrieved through matching the TempCP-Net with the combinations of the requests. For example, the first year segment of $\{R1\}$ falls into the "high" CPU units ($C1$), "high" availability ($A1$) and "moderate" price ($P2$) in Fig. 5.1a. As $\{R1\}$ spans all segments, the true (T) value of decision variable (N) is applied on $\{R1\}$. The request ($R1 : A1, C1, P2$) is the 1st ranked preference in the first year. However, the second year segment of $\{R1\}$ requires a "high" CPU in the "moderate" cost range, which is out of the preference (N/A) for long-term requests in CP2. The total preference ranking of each request is tabulated under "Total" in Fig. 5.2b. As two segments of $\{R1\}$ are out of the preference ranking, its total ranking is N/A. $\{R3\}$ and $\{R4\}$ are combined into a request $\{R3, R4\}$. We cannot consider other combinations due to a constraint of maximum 100 CPU units. The combined $\{R3, R4\}$ are treated as long-term requests ($N = true$) as $\{R3, R4\}$ spans from the 1st year to the 3rd year. According to the total qualitative rankings, $\{R3, R4\}$ is the optimal composition.

A sequential optimization process may produce a global solution in a smaller number of comparisons. Let us assume, the sequential optimization operates in a right to left year sequence (3rd, 2nd and 1st). In the 3rd year $2^3 = 8$ comparisons are performed and only the highest ranked $R3$ is accepted (see Fig. 5.2b). As $R1$ (N/A ranking) and $R2$ are already rejected, they are not considered in any subsequent optimization. The local optimizations in the 2nd and 1st year accept the remaining $R4$ in the solution. Hence, the optimal solution $\{R3, R4\}$ is produced in ten comparisons. However, the sequence of local optimizations is important. Given a left-to-right sequence (1st, 2nd and 3rd), $2^4 = 16$ comparisons are performed and only the highest-ranked $R1$ is accepted in the in the first year. However, as $R1$ has "N/A" ranking in the following years, the optimization generates an unacceptable solution. Hence, we require machine-learning techniques to find the best sequence of local optimizations.

5.3   The Temporal CP-Net Based Qualitative Economic Model

We require not only an intuitive tool for structuring a provider's preferences, but also a support for an efficient optimization process. The set of functional and non-functional attributes is $V = \{X_1, \ldots, X_n\}$ with finite domains $\{D(X_1), \ldots, D(X_n)\}$ and semantic domains $\{S(X_1), \ldots, S(X_n)\}$. CPU($C$), Network bandwidth($NB$) and Memory($M$) are typical functional attributes, while QoS attributes are Availability (A), Response Time (RT), Throughput (TP) and Price (P). The numerical value x_n in $D(X_n)$ is mapped into a semantic value s_n in $S(X_n)$ using a mapping table, $s_n = Sem\_Table(X_n, x_n)$. Figure 5.1a is such a semantic table that maps 70–100 units of CPU as a "high" CPU value. In the long-term, the preference order and related semantics of V remain constant for a certain time, but they may vary in the next period. We assume a set of decision variables $DN = \{N_1, N_2, \ldots, N_d\}$. Typical decision variables are duration of the requests and reputation of consumers. For simplicity, we consider the decision variable as a binary variable, i.e. it can only take true or false $\{T, F\}$ values. For example, if a request spans over the next time interval, the corresponding decision variable is set as true. Similarly, if a consumer is trusted, the corresponding decision variable is also set as true.

First, the total composition time, T, is divided into m intervals $\{I_1, I_2, \ldots, I_m\}$ where, $T = \sum_{i=1}^{m} I_i$. In an interval I_k, the IaaS provider can specify a preference ranking of service configurations over complete assignments on V and DN with the semantic domain $Sem\_D^{I_k}(V)$. The set of all service configurations is denoted as O^{I_k} for the interval I_k. A preference ranking is a total order ($\succeq$) over the set of service configurations: $o_1 \succeq o_2$ means that a configuration o_1 is equally or more preferred than o_2. We use $o_1 \succ o_2$ to denote the fact that provisioning service o_1 is more preferred than o_2 (i.e., $o_1 \succeq o_2$ and $o_2 \not\succeq o_1$), while $o_1 \sim o_2$ denotes that the provider has no preference between the configurations o_1 and o_2 (i.e. $o_1 \not\succeq o_2$ and $o_2 \not\succeq o_1$). Similarly, $T \sim F$ denotes that the provider's preference is indifferent between the true and false values of a decision variable.

Direct assessment of a long-term preference relation is generally infeasible due to the exponential size of $O^{I_k} \mid \forall k \in [1, m]$. We represent the long-term economic model in a temporal CP-Net (TempCP-Net), which is a set of CP-Nets and semantic mapping tables over different intervals defined as TempCP-Net = $\{(CP^{I_k}, Sem\_Table^{I_k}, I_k) \mid \forall k \in [1, m]\}$. A CP-Net can concisely specify a preference relation in a graphical structure. A CP-Net in the interval I_k, CP^{I_k} is a directed graph G over V and DN whose nodes are annotated with conditional preference tables $CPT(X_i)$ for each $X_i \in V$. We use a dashed circle to represent a node of DN and a solid circle to represent a node of V. In this book, we focus on only acyclic CP-Nets. Each conditional preference table $CPT(X_i)$ associates a total order $\succ_u^i$ with each instantiating u of X_i's parents $Pa(X_i) = U$ [111]. For example, in $CP1$, $A = Pa(C)$ and the $CPT(C)$ contains $\{A1, A2\}$ while preferences are made over $\{C1, C2\}$ (Fig. 5.1b).

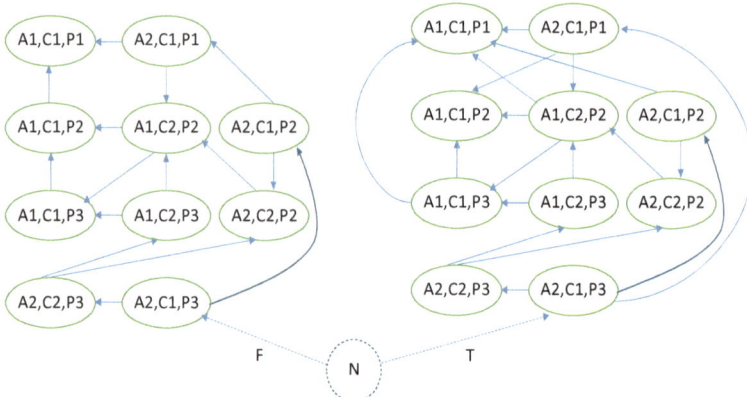

Fig. 5.3 The induced preference graph of CP1

The preference $o \succ \acute{o}$ is a *consequence* of TempCP-Net, iff $o \succ \acute{o}$ holds in all preference orderings consistent with the *ceteris paribus* preference statements ("all else being equal") encoded by the CPTs of the TempCP-Net [127]. The set of consequences $o \succ \acute{o}$ of an acyclic TempCP-Net constitutes a partial order over the service configuration. This partial order can be represented by an acyclic directed graph, referred to as the *induced preference graph*. The nodes of the induced preference graph correspond to the complete assignments of the variables in the network. There is an edge from node $\acute{o}$ to node o iff the assignments at $\acute{o}$ and o differ only in the value of a single variable X. Given the values assigned by $\acute{o}$ and o to $Pa(X)$, the value assigned by o to X is preferable to the value assigned by $\acute{o}$ to X. The induced preference graphs are produced from each decision variable. As decision variables create different preference configurations for different types of consumers, the induced preference graphs are embedded in a decision tree.

Figure 5.3 depicts the induced preference graphs of *CP*1. Two induced preference graphs are embedded in a decision tree for short-term and long-term requests respectively (Fig. 5.3). For short-term requests, there is no outgoing edge from $(A1, C1, P1)$ as it is the most-preferred request configuration. Similarly, there is no incoming edge to $(A2, C1, P3)$ as it is the least-preferred configuration. As the $CPT(CP1)$ states $A1 \succ A2$, there is an edge from $(A2, C1, P1)$ to $(A1, C1, P1)$ considering the *ceteris paribus* preference statements. For the long-term request, there is no outgoing edge from either $(A1, C1, P1)$ or $(A1, C1, P2)$ as they are the most-preferred configuration (Fig. 5.3). The induced preference graph (total ordering of all configurations) is created using pairwise comparison (ordering queries) of the configurations [111]. If n and d are the numbers of attributes and decision variables respectively in the TempCP-Net and q is the number of output configurations in an interval, the time complexity for ordering queries in an interval is $O(ndq^2)$.

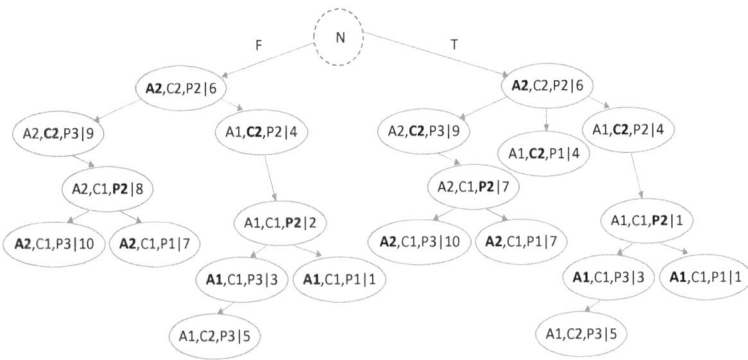

Fig. 5.4 *The k-d tree indexing of the induced preference graph*

5.3.1   The k-d Tree Indexing of the Induced Preference Graph

Given a semantic request configuration $Sem\_Req = (s_1, \ldots, s_n) \mid$ where $s_i \in S(X_i)$, and $X_i \in V$, the induced preference graph enables a search for the preference ranking of $(s_1, \ldots, s_n)$. Such a graph-based searching approach requires linearly traversing over the graph (time complexity $O(n)$) [111]. Considering the tuple $(s_1, \ldots, s_n)$ as a multidimensional vector, we improve the search process using the k-d tree [5]. The k-d tree is a binary tree in which every node is a k-dimensional point (Fig. 5.4). Every non-leaf node can be considered as implicitly generating a splitting hyperplane that divides the space into two, known as half-spaces. Points on the left and right sides of this hyperplane are represented by the left and right subtrees of that node respectively. We use the canonical method to construct the k-d tree [13]:

- The selection of splitting planes follows a cycle as the construction algorithm moves down the tree. For example, in Fig. 5.4 the root is an "Availability-aligned" plane: both the root's children have "CPU-aligned planes," the root's grandchildren have "Price-aligned" planes, the root's great-grandchildren have again "Availability-aligned" planes, and so on.
- As all the n points are available from the induced preference graph, we insert points by selecting the median of the points being put into the subtree, with respect to their coordinates in the axes being used to create the splitting plane. This would result in a balanced k-d tree construction in $O(n\ log(n))$ times [13]. Each node in the k-d tree is annotated with its respective preference order from the induced graph. For example, the root node of both the k-d trees $(A2, C2, P2)$ is annotated with the preference ranking 6 in Fig. 5.4.

The k-d tree indexing is performed for each of induced preference graphs by the decision variables. For example, we create two separate k-d tree indices for short-term and long-term requests respectively in Fig. 5.4. The same ranking values are annotated for indifferent preferences. For example, both $(A1, C2, P1)$ and

$(A1, C2, P2)$ are annotated with the preference ranking 4 for long-term requests in Fig. 5.4. Starting with the root node, the searching algorithm moves down the tree recursively, in the same way, that it would if the search point was being inserted. If the search point is matched with a node, it returns the annotated ranking value. For example, the search for the short-term request $(A2, C1, P3)$ returns ranking 10 using only four comparisons. A non-matched search point is discarded in the composition. The time complexity in k-d tree searching an interval for a particular decision variable is $O(log(n))$.

5.3.2 Ranking the Consumers' Requests Using the TempCP-Net

Let us assume a consumer divides its service usage time in n intervals and service requirements in the intervals vary from one to another. We define the request of consumer u over the composition time T as $R_u = \{(x_i, I_j) \mid x_i \in D(X_i), X_i \in V, \text{and } T = \sum_{j=1}^{m} I_j\}$. A set of N requests is represented as $\bar{R} = \{R_1, \ldots, R_N\}$. We combine the requests in $\bar{R}$ using the aggregation rules in Eq. 5.1.

$$\text{Summation rule: } \bar{x}_i = \sum_{i=1}^{N} x_i, \text{where } X_i \in \{C, M, NB, RT, P\} \quad (5.1)$$

$$\text{maximization rule: } \bar{y}_i = max(y_i), \forall i \in [1, N] \text{where } Y_i \in \{A, TP\}$$

For example, the combined first year request $\{R1 : (C : 80, A : 90, P : \$800), R2 : (C : 85, A : 95, P : \$850)\}$ in Fig. 5.1c is $(C : 165, A : 95, P : 1650)$.

Note that, the intervals in consumer requests may differ from the intervals in the provider's TempCP-Net. In the first case, the start and the end times of an *inclusive* request segment are from the same temporal segment of the TempCP-Net. For example, if a CP-Net in TempCP-net operates between 1st and 31st January, a request spanning from 4th January to 25th January is an inclusive segment. As a single CP-Net is operating over the request, the request could be directly matched with the induced k-d tree from Sect. 5.3.1. In the second case, the start and end times of an *overlapping* request segment are from different temporal segments of the TempCP-Net. As more than one CP-Net is operating over the request, we divide an overlapping request, R (interval $[T_0, T_m]$) into smaller inclusive segments. In Fig. 5.5a, a request R is divided into R_1 and R_2 to match the corresponding $CP1$ and $CP2$. Note that only attributes with *temporal semantics* require such a segmentation. For example, "Price" has *temporal semantics* in the consumer requests. If the consumer requires 100 units of CPU for 12 months for $120, it still requires 100 units of CPU each month but the monthly cost will be $10. If the attribute X in R has *temporal semantics* and the segmentation is applied in $[T_j, T_k]$, the new value for the attribute X is calculated in Eq. 5.2.

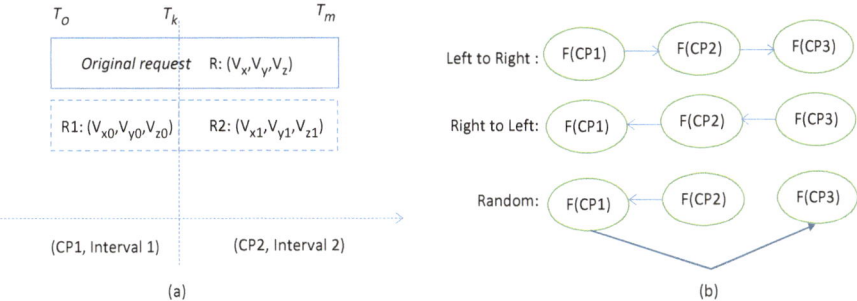

Fig. 5.5 (**a**) Temporal semantic segmentation of a request, and (**b**) some sequential orders for local optimization

$$x_i^{[T_j, T_k]} = x_i^{[T_0, T_m]} \times \frac{|T_k - T_j|}{|T_m - T_0|} \tag{5.2}$$

We define $Pref(\text{TempCP-Net}, \bar{R}) : V \to [1, n]$ as the ranking function that finds the preference order of $\bar{R}$ in the k-d trees of the TempCP-Net. As the TempCP-Net is constructed in semantic domains, we transform $\bar{R}$ into the semantic $\acute{R} = \{(s_i, I_j) \mid s_i \in S(X_i), X_i \in V, \text{ and } T = \sum_{j=1}^{m} I_j\}$ using the *Sem_Table* in the TempCP-Net. Each temporal segments in $\acute{R}$ is matched with the corresponding temporal k-d tree using the matching process in Sect. 5.3.1. We denote the matching process in interval i as $M^i(s_i)$. Hence, the global preference function can be defined in Eq. 5.3.

$$Pref(\text{TempCP-Net}, \bar{R}) = M^1(s_1) + \ldots + M^i(s_i) + \ldots + M^m(s_n) \tag{5.3}$$

5.4   Optimization Algorithms for Qualitative IaaS Composition

Given a set of N long-term requests $\bar{R}$ and the IaaS provider's TempCP-Net, the IaaS composition is to find an optimal set $\bar{r} \subseteq \bar{R}$ that minimizes the ranking output $Pref(\text{TempCP-Net}, \bar{r})$ in Eq. 5.3 (a lower value means a higher rank). There are two approaches to solve the temporal optimization problems: (a) global optimization, and (b) sequential local optimization [74]. The global approach considers the entire period and the input set at the time of composition. A common method for global optimization is the brute-force approach, which attempts all combinations of requests over the entire composition period and finds the minimum one. The time complexity of this approach is exponential (2^N) which is not applicable in real-time applications. We formulate a dynamic programming (DP) approach that solves the optimization in super-polynomial time ($N^{O(N)}$) [74]. As the size of the input requests is in proportion to the length of the composition time, the global

DP approach may not be feasible for a long-term composition. We propose a sequential local approach that divides the total time into segments according to the corresponding time intervals and each segment optimizes only the requests which operate in that interval [125]. This approach has a sequential effect for overlapping requests. Two local optimizations in different intervals may have different accept or reject opinions for the same overlapping request. As the quality of the final composition is dependent on the sequence order, we devise a heuristic-based approach to approximate the optimal solution.

5.4.1 Dynamic Programming-Based IaaS Composition

We propose a dynamic programming framework to weigh the benefits of accepting or rejecting a request. Accepting a request will lead to immediate revenue, but this acceptance might diminish future resource utilization for other requests. Dynamic Programming (DP) is an algorithmic paradigm that solves a given complex problem by breaking it into sub-problems (overlapping sub-problems) and stores the results of sub-problems to avoid repeated computations (optimal substructure) [74]. We denote $\bar{R}(N)$ as a set of N requests and $i \in [1, N]$ as the ith request. If $C(\bar{R}(N), k)$ returns the optimal subset of requests of size k, it either accepts the Nth request (the kth place is already filled) or rejects it (reduces $\bar{R}(N)$ to $\bar{R}(N-1)$). We formulate the DP in Eq. 5.4.

$$\bar{R}_1 = \{N \cup C(\bar{R}(N-1), k-1)\} \tag{5.4}$$

$$\bar{R}_2 = C(\bar{R}(N-1), k)$$

$$C(\bar{R}(N), k) = \begin{cases} \bar{R}_1, \text{ if } Pref(\text{TempCP-Net}, \bar{R}_1) < Pref(\text{TempCP-Net}, \bar{R}_2) \\ \bar{R}_2, \text{ if } Pref(\text{TempCP-Net}, \bar{R}_1) \geq Pref(\text{TempCP-Net}, \bar{R}_2) \\ \{i\} \text{ if } k = 1 \text{ and } Pref(\text{TempCP-Net}, \{i\}) \text{ is minimum} \\ \emptyset \text{ if } k = 0 \end{cases}$$

In Eq. 5.4, $\bar{R}_1$ refers to the set that accepts the Nth request and $\bar{R}_2$ refers to the set that rejects the Nth request. The base case is defined on $K = 1$ (only one request output) that performs a linear search to find the highest ranked request i. The DP can reduce the recomputations of same sub-problems by constructing a temporary array in the bottom-up manner [74]. The complexity of finding $C(\bar{R}(N), k)$ is $O(N^k)$. The final optimal subset can have at most N requests. Hence, we can find the optimal solution (Sol) through the iterative operation in Eq. 5.5. The final complexity of the DP based solution is $O(N^{O(N)})$.

$$Sol = C(\bar{R}(N), i), \text{ where } Pref(\text{TempCP-Net}, C(\bar{R}(N), i)) \text{ is minimum} \tag{5.5}$$

5.4.2   Heuristic-Based Sequential IaaS Composition

We use a heuristic-based sequential aggregation of local optimizations to approximate the global optimization in reduced time complexity. Each interval in TempCP-Net only considers the request segments within its range and performs DP-based optimizations by using its CP-Net as TempCP-Net (TempCP-Net = CP_i) in Eq. 5.4. These local optimizations in the intervals can run in parallel if there are no overlapping requests. However, the decision to accept or reject overlapping requests cannot be taken in parallel. Hence, different sequences of optimization order are performed to produce the optimal composition. For example, the left-to-right sequence first conducts optimization from the left-intervals to the right-intervals in Fig. 5.5b. Finding the best sequence in sequential optimization is NP-Complete [74]. We build our heuristics by exploring several key composition scenarios, described below.

- Almost Disjoint Pattern: Here, the requests in an interval are mostly disjoint and evenly cover that interval (Fig. 5.6a). An interval that contains such a pattern can be assumed that rejecting an overlapping request may not affect the global ranking, as the overlapped request can be replaced by one or more disjoint requests with high possibility.
- Almost Overlapping Pattern: The requests in an interval are mostly long-overlapping in this pattern (Fig. 5.6b). The local optimization at a specified interval of a sequence may not be changed in other sequences as the acceptance and rejection of most of the requests are decided in the first interval.
- Chain Pattern: In this pattern, the requests are short-overlapped and almost evenly distributed over the intervals (Fig. 5.6c). Several sequences of local optimizations need to be applied to achieve the optimal result.
- Hybrid Pattern: Both the long-overlapping and short-overlapping requests are almost evenly distributed in this pattern (Fig. 5.6d). The final result should also maintain the ratio of different types of requests.

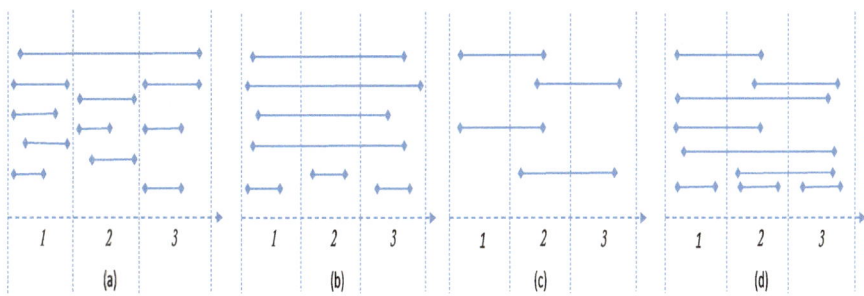

Fig. 5.6 The key composition scenarios (**a**) almost disjoint, (**b**) almost overlapping, (**c**) chain, and (**d**) hybrid patterns

We formulate the following generic heuristics to find out the optimal sequences of local optimizations for different patterns. We define the overlapping ratio of a request N in Eq. 5.6.

$$O\_Ratio(N) = \frac{\text{Number of operating intervals of } N}{\text{Total number of intervals}} \tag{5.6}$$

- **Heuristic 1:** If most local optimizations reject a long-overlapping request, the final output should also reject it. If most local optimizations separately accept the request, the final output should also accept it. This heuristic is common in collective decision processes.
- **Heuristic 2:** If two set of requests $\{1, 2, \ldots, i, .., n\}$ and $\{1, 2, \ldots, j, \ldots, n\}$ produce the final ranking x and y respectively in an interval, a local optimization prefers accepting the request i to the request j if $O\_Ratio(j) < O\_Ratio(i)$ and $|x - y| < \tau$. τ is the highest acceptable difference in the ranking set by the provider. The heuristic prefers disjoint requests to the overlapping requests when optimizing an interval. It reduces the effect of sequencing by replacing overlapping requests with disjoint requests without affecting the ranking in an individual optimization.

We devise a two-phase based approach (Algorithm 4) to incorporate these heuristics. In the first phase, we filter long-overlapping requests for acceptance or rejection (heuristic 1). The first phase is described in Steps 1–3 in Algorithm 4. It sets the final solution with a set of long overlapping requests which are voted by the intervals independently. In the second phase, we add new requests in the final solution using heuristic 2 (Steps 4–8). At least three different sequences are generated, and the final solution is updated only when the ranking of the solution is improved. The random generation of sequences is stopped when no improvements are made in the final ranking in Algorithm 4.

5.5 Reinforcement Learning for Long-Term IaaS Requests Composition

The approach in Algorithm 4 could be improved by finding the *best sequence* of local optimizations. Hence, we devise a machine-learning approach to find the best local service provision policy using historical request patterns.

Algorithm 4 The heuristic-based sequential optimization

Require: The Request set($\bar{R}$), Acceptance window(l) and Maximum additive ranking (p)

Ensure: The optimal composition

1: final solution = $\emptyset$
2: Run local dynamic programming based optimization in each of the n intervals in parallel. Store the cumulative appearance frequency of a request in the first l ranking (the acceptance window will be set by the provider). For example, if $l = 5$ and A appears in both 1st rank and 3rd rank, the frequency of A is 2. By default, the frequency is 0. Rank the requests based on their frequencies.
3: Add the rankings of a request from each interval. Accept the request and add to the final solution if its additive ranking is less than p (set by the provider).
4: temporary solution = final solution
5: Generate the left to right sequence of intervals $(I_1, I_2, \ldots, I_m)$.
6: Start dynamic programming-based optimization in the first interval. Add new requests in the temporary solution by following heuristic 2. Only add requests if there are available resources. After finishing optimization in an interval, continue adding new requests in the following intervals of the sequence. If the ranking of the temporary solution is greater than the final solution, set final solution = initial solution (update operation).
7: Generate the right to left sequence of intervals $(I_m, I_{n-1}, \ldots, I_1)$ and try to update the final solution by following Step 6.
8: Generate a new random sequence of intervals $(I_k, I_{n-1}, \ldots, I_l)$ and try to update the final solution by following Step 6. If the ranking of the final solution is improved, start Step 8 again. Otherwise, return the final solution.

5.5.1 A MDP Model for Long-Term Composition

We model the local sequential optimizations in an IaaS composition as a Markov Decision Process (MDP) [128]. A MDP is usually models a sequential decision process in an uncertain environment [112]. According to [128], reinforcement learning is applied in MDP models to optimize the quality of a service composition in dynamic environments. The goal of an MDP is to provide an optimal policy which is a decision strategy to optimize a particular criterion such as maximising a total reward of the actions [115]. We consider the choice of service provisions, i.e. a node of the k-d tree in a CP-Net as an action in IaaS service compositions. We model the MPD for an IaaS composition as a 6-tuple $IaaS\_M = < S, A_s, s_0, F, P(.,.), R(.,.) >$ where:

- $S = \{I_1, I_2, \ldots, I_m\}$ is a finite set of intervals or segments in the TempCP-Net. There are three states in Fig. 5.7.
- A_{I_s} is the finite set of actions available from segment I_s. If CP_s is the corresponding CP-Net in interval I_s, the multidimensional nodes of the induced k-d tree are

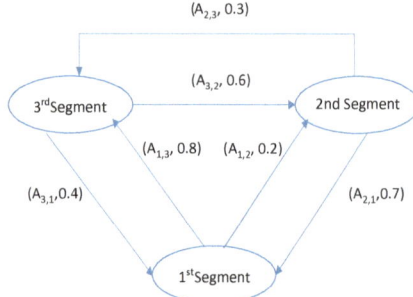

Action	CP-Net	Service Provision	Preference Ranking or Reward
A$_{1,2}$	CP1	(C1,A1,P1)	1
A$_{1,3}$	CP1	(C1,A1,P2)	2
A$_{2,1}$	CP2	(C2, A2, P2)	4
A$_{2,3}$	CP2	(C2, A2, P1)	2
A$_{3,1}$	CP3	(C3, A3, P1)	1
A$_{3,2}$	CP3	(C2, A2, P2)	4

Fig. 5.7 A MDP model for IaaS request composition

considered to be actions. A decision maker can select requests according to the provider's preferences, i.e. CP-Nets.

- s_0 is the starting state, i.e., the first segment of local optimizations.
- F is the counter of number of state or segment transitions. The local optimizations of IaaS composition stop when F reaches a certain value determined by the decision maker.
- $P_a(I_s, \acute{I}_s)$ is the probability that choosing a particular service configuration a in Interval I_s at time t will lead to Interval $\acute{I}_s$.
- $R_a(I_s, \acute{I}_s)$ is the immediate preference ranking that service configuration a in Interval I_s produces after transitioning to Interval $\acute{I}_s$. We calculate the preference ranking using Eq. 5.3.

The MDP for an IaaS composition with a TempCP-Net can be visualized as a transition graph. In Fig. 5.7, we construct a MDP using the TempCP-Net described in Fig. 5.1c. For simplicity, we use two service provisions or actions in each segment. The probabilities of state transitions are labeled with the weighted directed edges. In Fig. 5.7, if the action $A_{1,2}$ is taken, i.e. the service $(C1, A1, P1)$ is provisioned in the first interval according to CP1, there is a 20% probability of providing highly ranked services in the second interval according to CP2. The MDP produces an optimal policy based on the starting state. The optimal policy is constructed by taking actions with the highest probability. In Fig. 5.7, if the third segment is the starting segment, the optimal policy is $\{A_{3,2} : (C2, A2, P2), A_{2,1} : (C2, A2, P2), A_{1,3} : (C1, A1, P2)\}$ as the probabilities of state transitions are 0.6, 0.7 and 0.4 respectively. The requests are composed based on the optimal policy. For example, the optimal policy most closely matches with the combination of incoming requests $\{R3, R4\}$ from Fig. 5.2a. If the optimal policy does not match with any request composition, the next best optimal policy is constructed. The process stops when a policy is matched with a request composition.

5.5.2   Q-learning Approach for IaaS Composition

The MDP model (above) may create multiple alternative composition strategies or policies due to different starting segments. We may not have sufficient knowledge about the reward functions or preference ranking of the overlapping incoming requests in runtime. Hence, the transition probabilities of the MDP should be learned through experiences in runtime. We apply a reinforcement learning approach called Q-learning [129]. There are six key elements of a reinforcement learning system: (a) environment, (b) state, (c) action, (d) policy, (e) reward function and (f) value function [38]. We map these elements in an IaaS composition as follows.

- *Environment*: In the standard reinforcement model, an environment is where the decision maker takes actions [38]. The set of N long-term requests $\bar{R}$ and the IaaS provider's TempCP-Net creates the environment for the composer.
- *State (s)*: In the standard reinforcement model, the state refers to a specific condition of the environment [38]. We consider the segments in the TempCP-net as states. Each state performs local IaaS composition, i.e. selecting requests based on the segment's CP-Net.
- *Action (a)*: In the standard reinforcement model, an action follows a specific decision [38]. In an IaaS composition, the qualitative service preferences, i.e. nodes in the k-d tree are regarded as "actions". Hence, an "action" refers to accepting or rejecting a request in the context of composition. The TempCP-Net describes all possible "actions". However, given a set of incoming requests, we may only perform a specific set of actions. For example, if consumers want lower-priced services, the composer cannot provision higher-priced services. In Fig. 5.7, we describe a subset of possible actions in the first interval according to CP1.
- *Policy (π)*: In the standard reinforcement model, a policy defines the decision maker's way of behaving at a given time. A policy is a state-action pair, i.e. choosing an action according to the state of the environment [38]. We define a policy as a set of sequential actions. In Fig. 5.7, a composer's policy is taking actions $\{A_{3,2} : (C2, A2, P2), A_{2,1} : (C2, A2, P2), A_{1,3} : (C1, A1, P2)\}$ from Segment 3 to Segment 1.
- *Reward function (R)*: In the standard reinforcement model, the reward function defines the goal in a reinforcement learning problem. It maps each state-action pair to a reward, indicating the intrinsic desirability of that state [38]. In an IaaS composition, the preference ranking of a provisioned service is considered as a reward. In Fig. 5.7, the composer gets a Reward 4 when the Action $A_{2,1}$ is performed, i.e., requests are composed based on $(C2, A2, P2)$ in Segment 2. Note, the composer's objective is to minimize the total reward: a lower reward value means a higher ranking.
- *Value function (V)*: In the IaaS composition, a value function predicts the preference rankings over all the segments by accepting requests following a random policy $(π)$.

Q-learning is a popular reinforcement learning: the optimal policy is learned through the history of interactions with the environment [129]. We treat this history of interactions as a sequence of *experiences*. An *experience* is a tuple $< s, a, r, \acute{s} >$ which means the decision maker got Reward r when it moved from State s to $\acute{s}$ by performing Action a. A history of state-action-reward can be represented as $< s_0, a_0, r_1, s_1, a_1, r_2, \ldots >$. We use local optimizations in each segment to generate the history of state-action-rewards for an IaaS composition.

5.5.2.1 Generating Preference Rankings (Rewards)

We use Dynamic Programming (DP) [74] to find the optimal subset of requests in a segment of TempCP-Net. The DP generates all the possible subsets efficiently by avoiding repeated computations in the process of finding the optimal subset [74]. We denote $\bar{R}(N)$ as a set of N requests in a segment and $i \in [1, N]$ as the ith request. If $C(\bar{R}(N), k)$ returns the optimal subset of requests of size k, it either accepts the Nth request (the kth place is already filled) or rejects it (reduces $\bar{R}(N)$ to $\bar{R}(N-1)$). In Eq. 5.4, $\bar{R}_1$ refers to the set that accepts the Nth request and $\bar{R}_2$ refers to the set that rejects the Nth request. The base case is defined on $K = 1$ (only one request output) that performs a linear search to find the highest ranked request i. The DP can reduce the recomputations of the same sub-problems by constructing a temporary array in bottom-up manner [74]. The array stores all the possible actions ($A(s)$) and related preference rankings or rewards (R(s)) of a segment (state) in Eq. 5.7.

$$\text{Action set, } A(s) = \{C(\bar{R}(N), k) \mid \forall k \in [1, N] \text{ and } \bar{R}(N) \text{ belongs to segment } s\}$$
(5.7)

$$\text{Reward set, } R(s) = \{Pref(CP(s), C(\bar{R}(N), k)) \mid \forall k \in [1, N]\}$$
(5.8)

5.5.2.2 Two-dimensional Q-values for Composition Sequences

Given a history of sequences, the target of the composer is to find the optimal policy ($\pi*$) that minimizes the total preference rankings (rewards). The cumulative reward starting from an arbitrary state or segment s_t and following a policy π of n sequential actions are defined in Eq. 5.9. Here γ is the discounted factor in the range $[0, 1)$. It decides the decision maker's weighted preference on future rankings or rewards. If $\gamma = 1$, this would be same as the total reward. If $\gamma = 0$, the composer ignores all future rewards.

$$V^{\pi}(s_t) = r_t + \gamma r_{t+1} + \gamma^2 r_{t+2} + \ldots + \gamma^n r_{t+n} = \sum_{i=0}^{n} \gamma^n r_{t+n}$$
(5.9)

Based on Eq. 5.9, the optimal policy ($\pi*$) is the policy that maximizes $V^{\pi}(s_t)$ for all s_t (Eq. 5.10). As mentioned earlier, the state transition function and reward function of a MDP may not be known. Thus, $\pi*$ cannot be calculated directly. It has to be learned through a trial-and-error process.

$$\pi^* = argmax_\pi V^\pi(s_t) \mid \forall s_t \in S \tag{5.10}$$

The Q-learning process [129] uses a recursive Q function denoted as $Q^\pi(s,a)$ to simulate the cumulative reward following a policy π. $Q^\pi(s,a)$ is the expected global preference ranking (cumulative reward) of performing Action a (provisioning a service configuration to requests) in State s and then following the policy π. In Eq. 5.11, $P(\acute{s}|s,a)$ is the probability to move from Segment s to Segment $\acute{s}$ with Action a, $R(s,a,\acute{s})$ is the current preference ranking for the transition and $V^\pi(\acute{s})$ denotes the future global preference ranking from Segment $\acute{s}$.

$$Q^\pi(s,a) = \sum_{\acute{s}} P(\acute{s}|s,a)(R(s,a,\acute{s}) + \gamma V^\pi(\acute{s})) \tag{5.11}$$

Q-learning uses temporal differences to estimate the value of $Q^\pi(s,a)$ [129]. Similar to the Q-learning process [129], we maintain a table of $Q[S,A]$, where S is the set of segments or states and A is the set of actions. $Q[s,a]$ represents its current estimate of $Q^\pi(s,a)$. For each state-action pair (s,a), the initial $Q[s,a]$ is set to 0. The process starts with an arbitrary state (s), executes an action (a), receives a reward (r) and observes all possible next states. The composer uses temporal differences [128] to update the state of $Q[s,a]$ using Eq. 5.12. In Eq. 5.12, α is the learning rate. Intuitively, higher values of α give higher weights to the current estimates than the previously learned Q-values. The process is terminated when no updates on Q values are possible (a convergence is achieved).

$$Q[s,a] = (1-\alpha)Q[s,a] + \alpha(r + \gamma max_{\acute{a}}Q[\acute{s},\acute{a}]) \tag{5.12}$$

The learned $Q[S,A]$ is used to produce the optimal policy for each state or segment using Eq. 5.13. The optimal policy is found in a greedy fashion, i.e. tracing the best sequences of segments is as simple as following the links with the highest rankings at each segment. Figure 5.8a illustrates a two-dimensional $Q[S,A]$ with five segments and ten actions. According to Fig. 5.8a, if we start from state 5, the optimal action (provisioning service) should be $A5$ or $A10$ as it produces higher ranked Q-values.

$$\pi^*(s) = argmax_a Q[s,a] \mid \forall a \in A(s) \tag{5.13}$$

5.5.2.3 Three-dimensional Q-values for Composition Sequences

The Q-learning process described above allows *model-free* state transitions as the generic MDP has no initial and terminal states [115]. Although the learned $Q[S,A]$

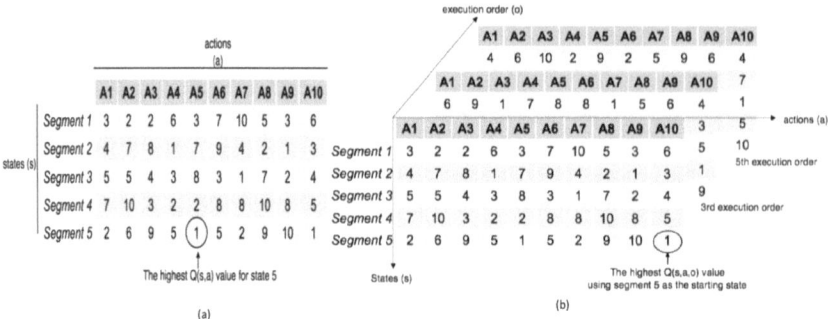

Fig. 5.8 (**a**) 2d Q-values in a $Q[S, A]$, and (**b**) 3d Q-values in a $Q[S, A, O]$

indicates the long-term effect of the sequential order, the execution order of the states is missing. For example, a transition policy, {*Segment 1, Segment 2, Segment 1, Segment 3, Segment 5, Segment 4, Segment 1*} are allowed in Fig. 5.8a. Note that *Segment 1* is executed multiple times in the policy. Hence, the $Q[s = Segment\ 1, A]$ does not contain the Q-values based on the execution order of *Segment 1* in Fig. 5.8a.

We maintain a three-dimensional table $Q[S, A, 0]$, where S is the set of segments or states, A is the set of actions, and O is the set of execution orders. The actions may be better selected by using the execution orders as the third dimension. A state-action pair will have Q-values in different execution orders. In Fig. 5.8b, if Segment 5 is executed first, $Q(s = segment\ 5, a = A10)$ is 1. If Segment 5 is executed last, the $Q(s = segment\ 5, a = A10)$ is 10. Figure 5.8b depicts that action $A10$ is less desirable in segment 5 when being executed last, but more desirable when being executed first.

We extend Eq. 5.12 to facilitate the execution order. The process starts with an arbitrary state (s), executes an action (a), receives a reward (r) and observes all possible next states with different orders. The update process in three-dimensional Q-values are explained in Eq. 5.14. Here, $ó$ is the next order after o in a sequence. α is the learning rate of the process.

$$Q[s, a, o] = (1 - \alpha)Q[s, a, o] + \alpha(r + \gamma max_{(á, ó)} Q[ś, á, ó]) \qquad (5.14)$$

Three-dimensional Q-values usually require more training and learning time to learn than two-dimensional Q-values if the traditional model-free MDP is used. However, we apply constraints on state transitions to speed up the learning convergence. The rejected requests in a local IaaS optimizations are not considered in subsequent segments. Hence, multiple execution orders of same states are unnecessary in a policy π. We consider the following constraints on the Q-learning process:

Algorithm 5 The three-dimensional Q-learning process for IaaS composition

---

1: Initialise Q(s,a,o) to 0
2: **for** each episode **do**
3:     $s \leftarrow s_0$
4:     execution order, $o \leftarrow 1$
5:     **while** $o \neq$ total number of states **do**
6:         Choose action a from s in o using ϵ-greedy policy
7:         Execute a, observe reward r and next state $\acute{s}$
8:         $Q[s, a, o] \leftarrow (1 - \alpha)Q[s, a, o] + \alpha(r + \gamma max_{(\acute{a},\acute{o})}Q[\acute{s}, \acute{a}, \acute{o}])$
9:         $o \leftarrow o + 1$
10:    **end while**
11: **end for**

- *Unique state policy*: A policy π should only contain unique states. If we perform a local optimization in a segment, the same state should not be considered in a different execution order for a policy.
- *Policy termination condition*: The policy should stop the transition once all the states are executed in order. Hence, in Fig. 5.8b, a policy of local optimizations cannot have more than five tuples of $\langle state, action, execution\ order \rangle$.

The three-dimensional Q-values are learned in multiple episodes or rounds. In each round, the Q-values are updated using Eq. 5.14. Algorithm 5 uses a ϵ-greedy policy for executing the MDP during the learning. The ϵ-greedy policy chooses to execute the optimal action (i.e., $argmax_{(a,o)}Q(s, a, o)$) with a probability of $(1 - \epsilon)$. the ϵ-greedy policy ensures that $Q(s, a, o)$ is being optimized continuously. It also guarantees that all the available actions are given chances to be tried out by the composer. The optimal policy is generated with the highest rankings at each segment using Eq. 5.15 which is similar to the process in the two-dimensional Q-learning [128].

$$\pi^*(s) = argmax_{(a,o)}Q[s, a, o] \mid \forall a \in A(s) \text{ and } o \in [1, |A(s)|] \tag{5.15}$$

5.5.3 Determining Initial Q-values Using Statistical Analysis

A set of incoming requests in an IaaS composition may have different distributions for each requested attribute, such as normal, left-skewed and right-skewed distributions [108]. If a significant number of consumers require median values of an attribute, the attribute follows a normal distribution. For example, the CPU requirements follow a normal distribution in Fig. 5.9a. If a significant number of consumers require high range values of an attribute, the attribute follows a right-skewed distribution. For example, the availability requirements follow a right-skewed distribution in Fig. 5.9b. If a significant number of the consumers require low range values of an attribute, the attribute follows a left-skewed distribution. For

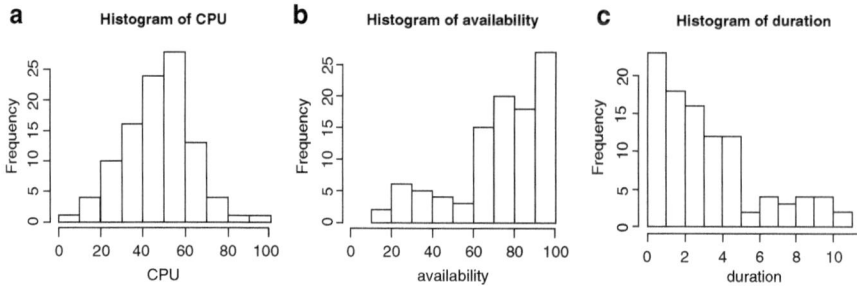

Fig. 5.9 Different types of distributions: (**a**) Normal, (**b**) right-skewed, and (**c**) left-skewed

example, the duration of requests follows a right-skewed distribution in Fig. 5.9c. Other distribution types are uniform, plateau, and multi-modal [108]. We denote H as the set of distributions, i.e. $H = \{$normal, uniform, right-skewed, left-skewed$\}$. For a set of requests R and a set of X attributes, the meta-information of distributions on the attributes is represented as $Dist(R)$, where $Dist(R) = \{h_i \mid \forall i \in [1, n], h_i \in H, x_i \in X\}$.

In the standard reinforcement learning, the learned Q-values and the corresponding environment have high correlations [129]. Algorithm 5 starts learning from scratch as initial Q-values are set to zero. According to [83], the Q-learning algorithm produces similar patterns of Q-values in related environments. We develop the following heuristic on initializing Q-values:

Heuristic on initialising Q-values for similar patterns: As the Q-learning algorithm produces similar patterns of Q-values in related environments, the learned Q-values for a particular set of incoming requests (R_1) can be used as the initial Q-values for a set of incoming requests (R_2) if $Dist(R_1) \sim Dist(R_2)$. Such initialization should produce a faster learning convergence to an optimal policy.

Let us assume the provider has access to a history of N different sets of requests $\{R_1, R_2, ..., R_N\}$. The corresponding three-dimensional learned Q-Matrices are represented as $\{Q_1[S, A, O], Q_2[S, A, O], ..., Q_N[S, A, O]\}$. Upon receiving a new set of requests R_{N+1}, we select the $Q_i[S, A, O]$ as initial Q-values in Algorithm 5 if $Dist(R_{N+1}) \sim Dist(R_i) \mid i \in [1, N]$.

We use the Kolmogorov-Smirnov test (K-S test) [44] to find the similarity among the distributions of two sets of requests, i.e. R_i and R_j. Let us assume that the first histogram of the attribute X_a in R_i has m observations in the cumulative distribution $F(x)$ and the second histogram of the attribute X_a in R_j has n observations in the cumulative distribution $G(x)$. We define cumulative distribution functions in Eq. 5.16:

$$F(x) = F(x-1) + \frac{\text{no. of observations at the level } x}{\text{Total } m \text{ observations}}, \quad F(0) = 0 \qquad (5.16)$$

$$G(x) = G(x-1) + \frac{\text{no. of observations at the level } x}{\text{Total } n \text{ observations}}, \quad G(0) = 0$$

The null hypothesis is that both observations are generated by the same distribution. The null hypothesis is tested in the K-S test with two values $L_{m,n}$ and $L_{m,n,\alpha}$ defined in Eq. 5.17. Here $L_{m,n}$ is the maximum difference in the cumulative distribution functions and $L_{m,n,\alpha}$ is the critical value from Kolmorogov distribution functions [44]. α is the confidence level to reject the null hypothesis. According to the recommendation in [38], we reject the null hypothesis (at significance level α) if $L_{m,n} > L_{m,n,\alpha}$. For example, $\alpha = 0.05$ gives 95% confidence to reject the null hypothesis. We can conclude that two distributions are similar if $L_{m,n} < L_{m,n,\alpha}$ for all attributes. If $Dist(R_{N+1}) \sim Dist(R_i)$, the $[Q_i[S, A, O]]$ is used as the initial Q-values in Algorithm 5.

$$L_{m,n} = max_x |\, F(x) - G(x)| \tag{5.17}$$

$$L_{m,n,\alpha} = c(\alpha) \sqrt{\frac{m+n}{mn}}$$

$$c(\alpha) = \text{the inverse of the Kolmorogov distribution at } \alpha$$

We used aggregation bootstrapping heuristic in Chap. 3 to initialise the Q-values when $Dist(R_{N+1}) \neq Dist(R_i)$, i.e. K-S test is failed to find the similarity of a new set of incoming requests in the history. According to Sect. 3.4.2, the aggregation of large historical patterns are used to predict the pattern of a new set of requests. We develop the following heuristic for dissimilar patterns:

Heuristic on initialising Q-values for dissimilar patterns: When there are a large number of historical Q-values, the aggregated historical Q-values may improve the learning process in a new environment. We use the following averaged aggregation function to generate the initial Q-values for the new request pattern R_{N+1} in Eq. 5.18:

$$\acute{Q}_{N+1}[S, A, O] = \frac{1}{N}(Q_1[S, A, 0] + Q_2[S, A, 0] + \ldots\ldots + Q_N[S, A, 0]) \tag{5.18}$$

5.6 Experiments and Results

A set of experiments have been conducted to evaluate the accuracy and runtime efficiency of the proposed Q-learning based long-term IaaS composition. We compare the proposed approach with a global DP-based approach and the heuristic-based sequential optimization approach. The DP-based approach generates all the combinations in a recursive manner and reduces the regenerations of combinations by constructing a temporary array in a bottom-up manner. The heuristic based sequential optimization approach generates random sequences of local optimizations in an iterative process. It prefers short-term requests over long-term requests in local optimizations. It accepts long-term requests in the final composition through collaborative decisions of local optimizations. All the experiments have been conducted on computers with Intel Core i7 CPU (2.13 GHz and 4 GB RAM). Java is used to implement the algorithms.

5.6.1 Simulation Setup

As it is difficult to find a real-world IaaS provider's business strategies, we synthetically create 10 different yearly temporal CP-Nets with 12 intervals in each TempCP-Net. Each TempCP-Net has six attributes, i.e. CPU, Memory, Availability, Response time, Throughput, Price and Request length, as a decision variable. The dependencies among the attributes are randomly generated. The values of an attribute are divided into ten semantic levels (from higher to lower values). The conditional preference tables in a TempCP-Net are filled with random conditional preferences, each of which is a random order of semantic values. We create user requests as a mixture of Google Cluster resource utilization [109], real-world cloud QoS performance [67] and randomly generated availability and prices. Google Cluster data include CPU and Memory utilization and allocation time-series of 70 jobs over a 1 month period. The real-world QoS data [67] include two time-series (i.e. response time and throughput) for 100 cloud services over a 6 month period. We randomly pick 70 Google Cluster jobs and make one-to-one mapping with the 100 sets of QoS data. A 6 month request is extended to a 12 month request using random duplication of segments.

We use request lengths as decision variables in the TempCP-Net. We randomly select requests from Google Cluster jobs and create four different distributions: (a) normal distribution; (b) right-skewed distribution; (c) left-skewed distribution, and (d) random distribution. We create five sets of requests for each of the distributions. The sets (first to fifth) have 30, 40, 50, 60 and 70 requests respectively. We follow Table 5.1 to create the sets in each distribution. For example, to create the first set of 30 requests in the normal distribution, 18 random requests (60%) are segmented into requests of 4–8 months, 6 random requests (20%) are segmented into requests of 1–3 months and 6 random requests (20%) are segmented into requests of 9–12 months. The request length and the number of requests are randomly created in a random distribution. We use Poisson distribution to generate the start time of requests. If a

Table 5.1 Four distributions according to the request length

	Request length (in months)		
Distribution type	1–3	4–8	9–12
Normal	20%	60%	20%
Right-skewed	20%	20%	60%
Left-skewed	20%	60%	20%
Random	Random	Random	Random

request exceeds 12 months from the start time, we manually shift the start time to an earlier time segment to keep the request within 12 months.

We create four different patterns of the input requests: (a) disjoint pattern: 80% of the request set is segmented into requests of 1–2 month period; (b) overlapping pattern: 80% of the request set is segmented into requests of 8–12 month period; (c) chain pattern: 80% of the request set is segmented into requests of 2–8 month period, and (d) hybrid pattern: it is a collection of 35% disjoint requests, 35% overlapping requests and 30% of requests which spans in 2–8 month period. In each pattern, other types of requests are randomly distributed with different intervals.

5.6.2 Efficiency of the Heuristic-Based Sequential Optimization

In the first experiment, we analyze the efficiency of the proposed heuristic based sequential optimization. As the proposed Algorithm 4 needs an acceptance window (l) and additive ranking (p) in its first phase (accepting long-overlapping requests), we use 3 different configurations of acceptance window: (a) conservative ($l = 3, p = 15$), (b) moderate ($l = 7, p = 30$) and liberal ($l = 10, p = 45$). Each request pattern (disjoint, overlapping, chain and hybrid) is filled with different numbers of requests ranging from 30 to 70. A request pattern filled with a certain number of requests is executed in ten different TempCP-Nets using the proposed heuristic approach (with three different acceptance windows) and the global DP approach. The outputs are averaged and normalised as ($\frac{1}{ranking}$) (higher values mean top rankings, lower values mean low rankings).

Figures 5.10, 5.11, 5.12 and 5.13 depict the performance of the approaches in the disjoint, overlapping, chain and hybrid patterns respectively. In all figures, the quality of the output is increased when the number of requests is increased. At least one of the acceptance windows produces close outputs to the DP-based approach in a higher number of requests. All three acceptance window configurations of the heuristic-based approach perform close to the DP-based approach in the disjoint and hybrid patterns (Figs. 5.10 and 5.13). Of the three, only the output of conservative ($l = 3, p = 15$) configuration is not performing close to the DP-based approach in the overlapping pattern (Fig. 5.11). It may refuse many possible overlapping requests in the final output composition. In Fig. 5.12, only the output of the moderate ($l = 7, p = 30$) configuration is acceptable and close to the DP approach in higher numbers of requests (Fig. 5.12).

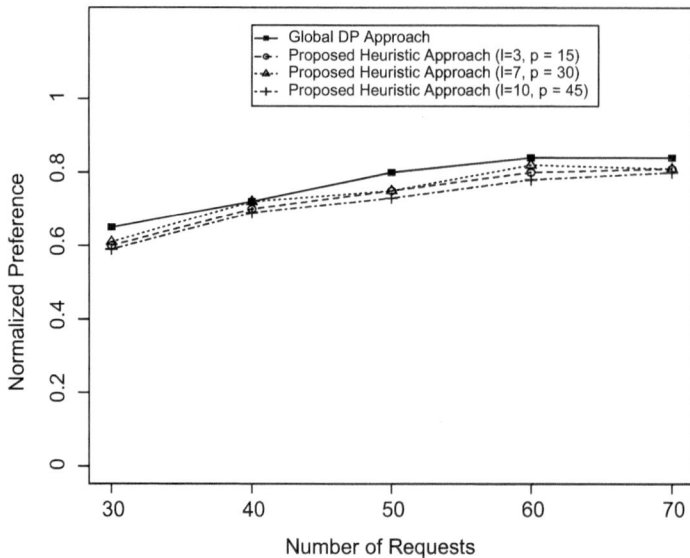

Fig. 5.10 Accuracy of the heuristic-based sequential approach in the disjoint pattern

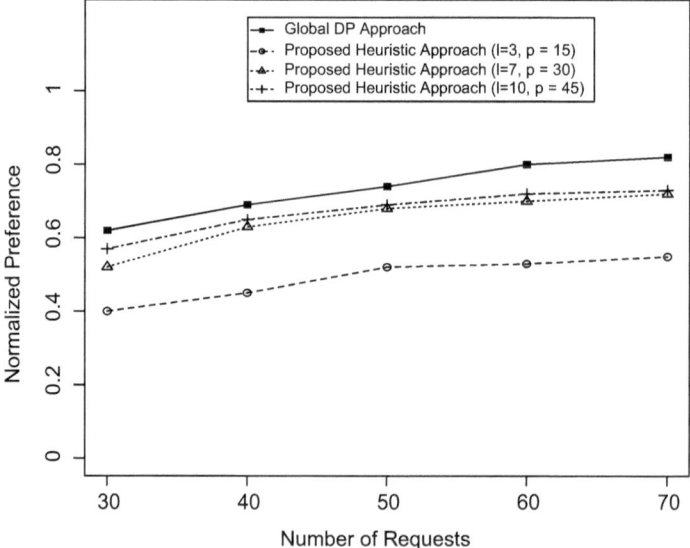

Fig. 5.11 Accuracy of the heuristic-based sequential approach in the overlapping pattern

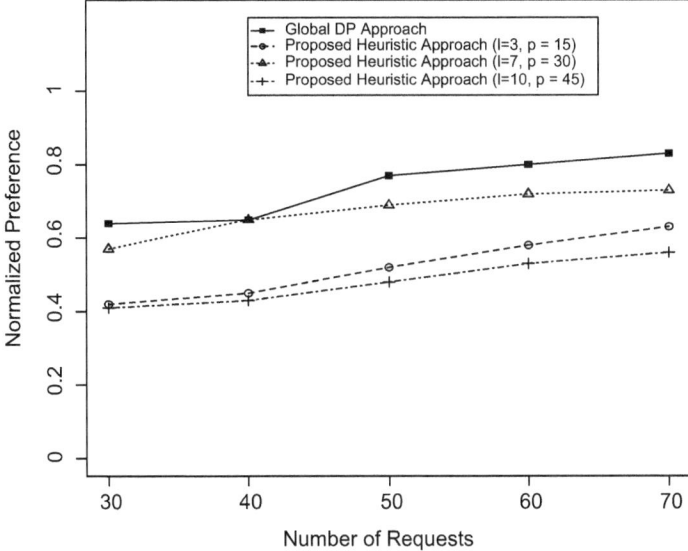

Fig. 5.12 Accuracy of the heuristic-based sequential approach in the chain pattern

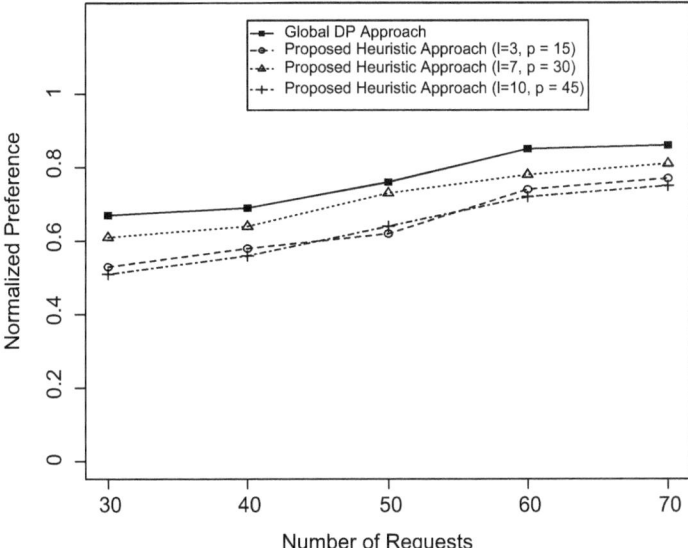

Fig. 5.13 Accuracy of the heuristic-based sequential approach in the hybrid pattern

5.6.3 Time Complexity Analysis of the Sequential Optimization

Although the global DP based approach produces better results than the proposed approach, it is not applicable in runtime. The convergence time of the global

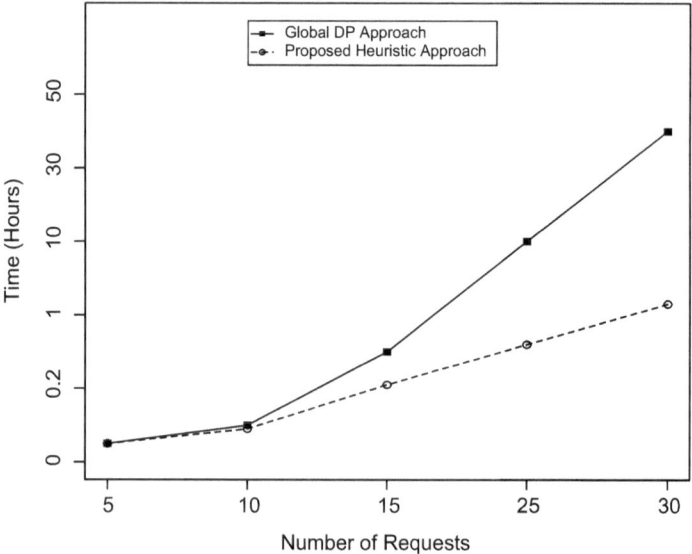

Fig. 5.14 The global vs sequential optimization time complexity

approach and the proposed approach are close for fewer requests in Fig. 5.14. However, the convergence time of the proposed approach is significantly lower than the global approach for a higher number of requests (Fig. 5.14).

5.6.4 Efficiency of the Q-learning Based IaaS Composition

Next, we analyze the efficiency of the proposed three-dimensional Q-learning approach. We use three different learning rates: (a) low ($\alpha = 0.2$), (b) moderate ($\alpha = 0.5$), and (c) high ($\alpha = 0.8$) to learn three-dimensional Q-matrices in Algorithm 5. All five sets of requests in each of the distributions (normal, right-skewed, left-skewed and random) are executed in ten different TempCP-Nets using the proposed three-dimensional Q-learning approach, the two-dimensional Q-learning approach, the dynamic programming and the heuristic based sequential optimization approach. The outputs are averaged and normalized as ($\frac{1}{ranking}$) (higher values mean higher rankings, lower values mean lower rankings).

Figures 5.15, 5.16, 5.17 and 5.18 depict the performances of the approaches in the normal, left-skewed, right-skewed and random distributions respectively. In all distributions (Figs. 5.15, 5.16, 5.17 and 5.18), the proposed three-dimensional Q-learning approach performs closest to the DP-based approach and performs significantly better than the two-dimensional Q-learning and heuristic based approaches using moderate ($\alpha = 0.5$) and low ($\alpha = 0.2$) learning rates. In all distributions (Figs. 5.15, 5.16, 5.17 and 5.18), the performances of the two-

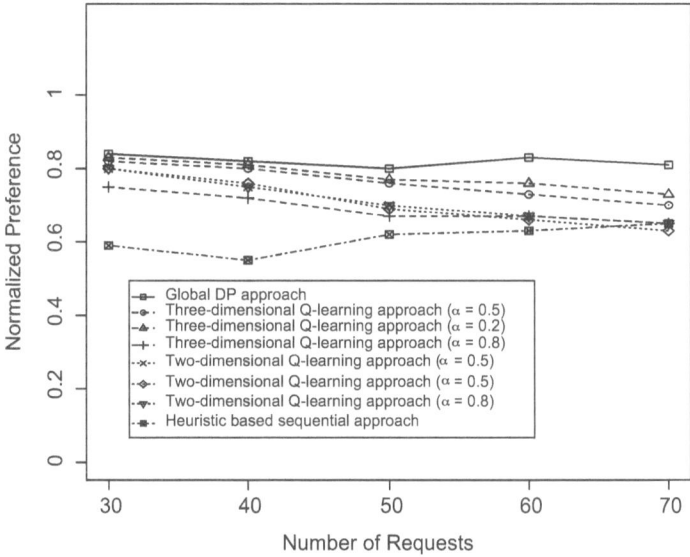

Fig. 5.15 Accuracy of the Q-learning approach in the normal distribution

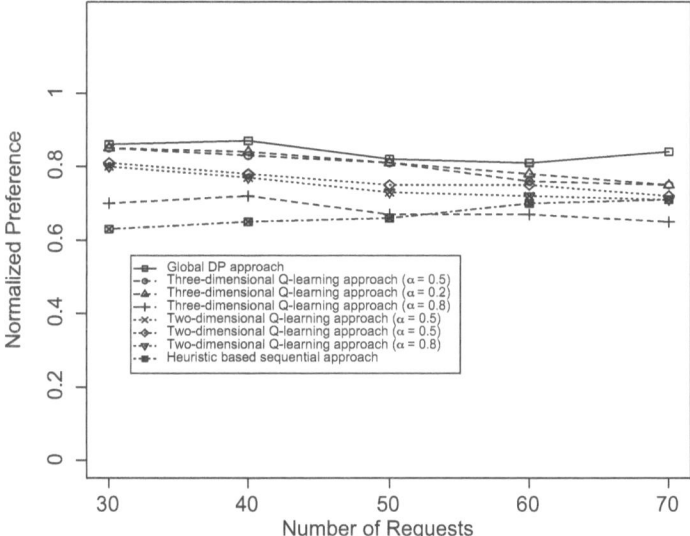

Fig. 5.16 Accuracy of the Q-learning approach in the right-skewed distribution

dimensional Q-learning approach and the three-dimensional Q-learning approach using a high learning rate ($\alpha = 0.8$) are almost similar and are better than the performances of the heuristic based sequential optimization approach for fewer requests, i.e. 30, 40 and 50 requests. We observe that the quality of the output

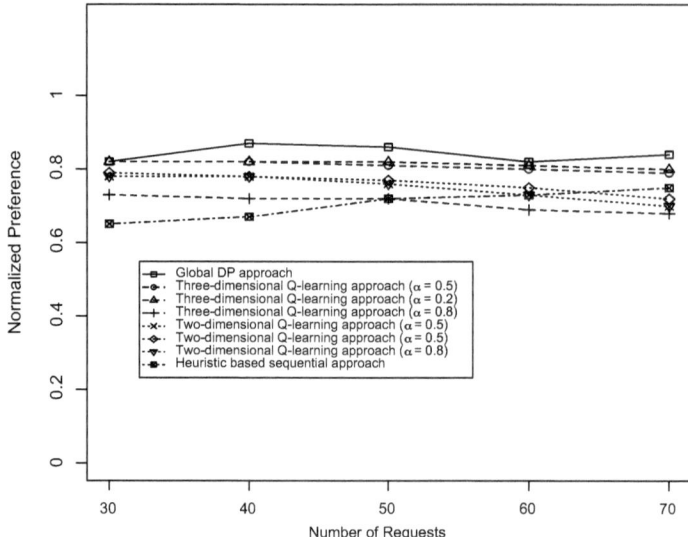

Fig. 5.17 Accuracy of the Q-learning approach in the left-skewed distribution

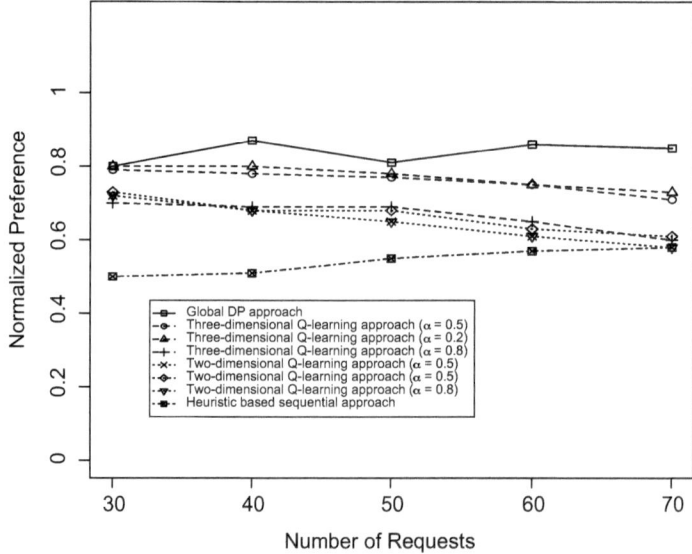

Fig. 5.18 Accuracy of the Q-learning approach in the random distribution

in the proposed Q-learning approach decreases when the number of requests is
increased in all distributions. This is due to larger transition probabilities in state-
action sequences of Q-values for larger numbers of requests. On the other hand, the
quality of the output in the heuristic based approach is increased when the number of

requests is increased. However, the heuristic-based approach performs similarly to the Q-learning approach for higher numbers of requests (60 and 70) only in the right-skewed and left-skewed distributions (Figs. 5.16 and 5.17). Only the performance of the proposed three-dimensional Q-learning approach is acceptable for the normal and random distributions using moderate ($\alpha = 0.5$) and low ($\alpha = 0.2$) learning rates (Figs. 5.15 and 5.18). The proposed Q-learning approach overestimates the Q-values using a high learning rate ($\alpha = 0.8$) and has a lower performance than the Q-learning approach using low and moderate learning rates.

5.6.5 Runtime Efficiency of the Heuristic-Based Learned Q-matrices

Next, we randomly choose 12 of learned Q-matrices which are created in the first experiment (no Q-matrices of the random distributions) as history. The corresponding requests of the remaining four learned Q-matrices are treated as new incoming requests. As the distributions of incoming requests are known (similar patterns), we apply the K-S test and initialize Q-values using the corresponding Q-values from the history according to Sect. 5.5.3. We compare the runtime accuracy of the K-S test based Q-learning approach with the Q-values learned from scratches in Fig. 5.19.

Figure 5.19 depicts that the Q-learning approach using the K-S test generates results close to the Q-learning approach when starting from scratch. The Q-learning

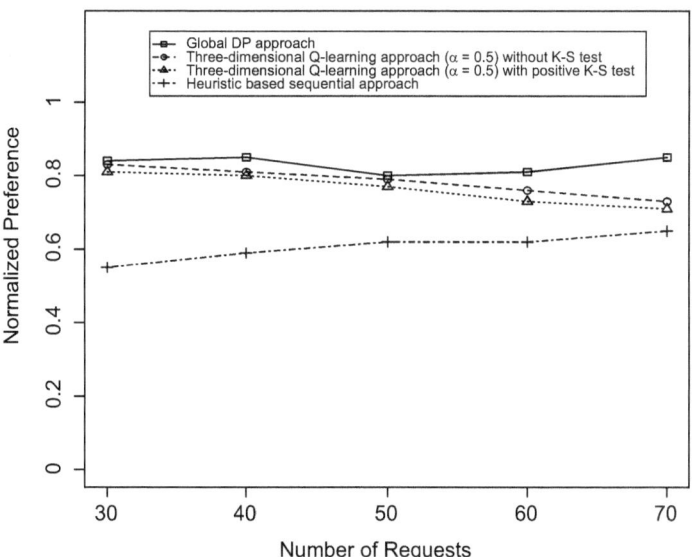

Fig. 5.19 Runtime accuracy of the proposed approach for similar pattern

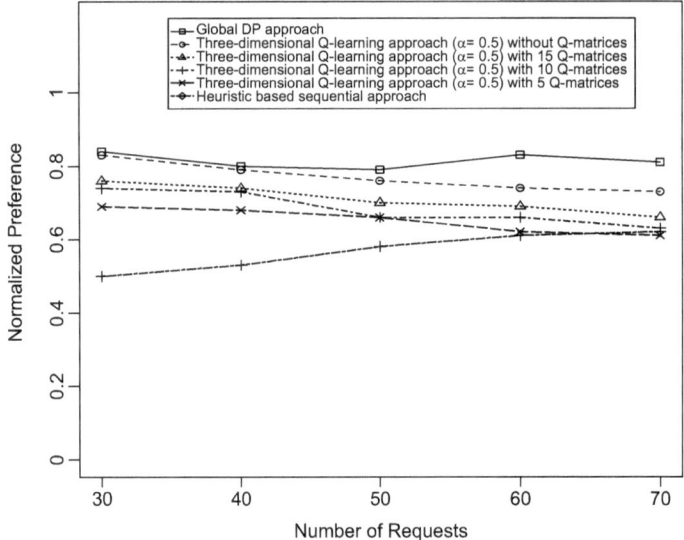

Fig. 5.20 Runtime accuracy of the proposed approach for dissimilar pattern

approach using the K-S test performs better than the heuristic based sequential approach. Five sets of the random distributions (Sect. 5.6.1) are treated as new incoming requests. As distributions of the incoming requests are unknown (i.e. a dissimilar pattern), we aggregate the historical Q-values according to Sect. 5.5.3. Figure 5.20 depicts that the aggregation of a higher number of Q-matrices (e.g. 15) generates results close to the Q-learning approach when started from scratch.

Although the global DP-based approach produces better results than proposed approach, it is not applicable in runtime (time complexity $O(N^{O(N)})$). The convergence time of the DP-based approach, the proposed three-dimensional Q-learning approach with and without K-S test and the heuristic-based optimization approach are similar to smaller numbers of requests in Fig. 5.21. The convergence time of the proposed approach without K-S test is lower than the DP-based approach but significantly higher than the proposed approach with K-S test and the heuristic approach for a high number of requests in Fig. 5.21. Although the proposed approach with K-S test converges slowly than the heuristic based approach, the convergence time of the proposed approach is practical in runtime according to Fig. 5.21. Figure 5.22 depicts the time complexity of the proposed approach in different distributions. It takes a relatively higher time to converge in the random distributions than the other distributions in Fig. 5.22. As the left-skewed distribution has higher short-term requests, local optimizations have lower inter-dependencies in a random sequence. It drives a faster convergence for the proposed approach in a left-skewed distribution (Fig. 5.22).

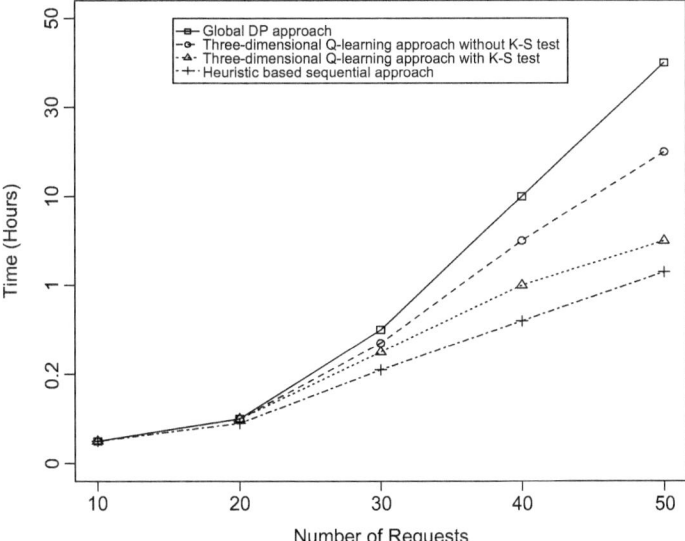

Fig. 5.21 Runtime performance in different distributions

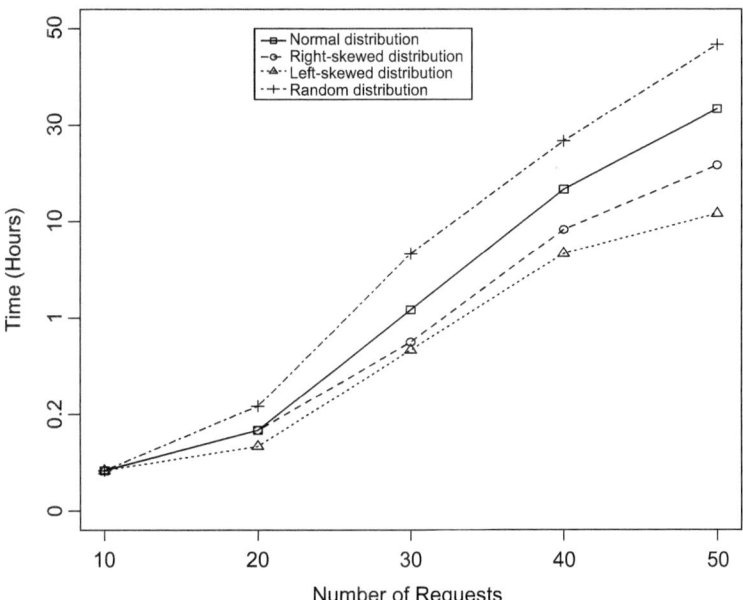

Fig. 5.22 Time complexity in different distributions

5.7   Conclusion

An IaaS provider can create its long-term qualitative business preferences using the proposed TempCP-Net framework with decision variables. We have proposed a three-dimensional Q-learning approach to compose an optimal set of long-term requests according to the provider's qualitative preferences. Experimental results show that the proposed three-dimensional Q-learning approach generates more accurate results than the heuristic based sequential optimization approach in different distributions. The proposed approach converges slowly to build a history of Q-matrices. However, the proposed approach is efficient in runtime as its convergence time is similar to the heuristic based sequential optimization approach given a history of Q-matrices. We will analyze the runtime performance of the IaaS provider in the next chapter.

Chapter 6
Service Providers' Long-Term QoS Prediction Model

6.1 Introduction

It is natural for different providers to compete in the cloud market to maximize their profits using their individual economic models. The *performance index* of a provider can be calculated using the information of resource utilization, price fairness, consumers' satisfactions and providers' profits [71]. It is necessary for a provider to compare its performances with the overall performance of the cloud market. For example, a higher performance index of the market indicates that most providers are making profits while maintaining service level agreements. Conversely, a lower performance index of a provider may suggest the provider should find some alternative solutions to become competitive and profitable in the market.

The future performance of peer IaaS providers may play an important role to construct an effective long-term economic model. For example, if it is predicted that the cloud service prices will be reduced in near future, the provider may place an emphasis on new service configurations with added functionality to attract new consumers and to increase its revenue. The quantitative and qualitative composition approaches described in Chaps. 3–5 assume that the provider sets its economic expectations and preferences before the composition. In the real world, these preferences are influenced by the market performance [34]. For example, in 2015 Rackspace Hosting reduced its rates towards the levels charged by other global cloud providers, such as Amazon Web Services (AWS), Microsoft Azure and Google [114].

The future QoS performance of the provider is also important in the long-term composition from the consumers' perspective. The long-term QoS by a service provider may vary for various reasons, e.g. a change in resource allocation policy, resource sharing, multi-tenancy or economic models [68]. Hence, the long-term QoS guarantees from a service provider may not always be available. For

© Springer International Publishing AG 2018

S. Mistry et al., *Economic Models for Managing Cloud Services*,

https://doi.org/10.1007/978-3-319-73876-5_6

example, in Amazon EC2, only the long-term QoS "availability" is advertised
[3]. In Windows Azure, the I/O performance is advertised for short-term periods
only in comparative terms such as high, moderate and low [92]. A QoS prediction model is thus needed to obtain long-term QoS values before creating the
composition.

We propose a *multivariate* prediction model for QoS values. Existing QoS
prediction models do not usually consider existing correlations among the QoS
attributes in performance history [84, 98, 144, 148, 151, 152]. However, these
correlations are prevalent in cloud service composition where a QoS attribute is
correlated with one or many other QoS attributes. For example, response times and
throughput usually have a strong negative correlation. Hence, when predicting the
time-series for a particular QoS attribute, we need to consider the historical time-
series of the QoS attribute and any correlated QoS attributes. For example, the
predicted values of response times would decrease while the predicted values of
throughput increase. Each cloud service provider will generate a series of predicted
QoS values for its cloud service through this prediction model, based on the history
and the short-term advertisement. *We assume that the past QoS history is provided
by the service provider or by any trusted third party that monitors the providers QoS
performances over a period.*

The chapter is structured as follows. The QoS prediction framework and the
multivariate prediction model are discussed in Sects. 6.2 and 6.3 respectively. The
forecasting model, experiments and conclusion are presented in Sects. 6.4, 6.5,
and 6.6 respectively.

6.2   The Multivariate QoS Forecasting Framework

The QoS forecasting problem is formulated as follows. Let a cloud composition plan
SC consist of k service providers $\{S_i \mid i = 1, 2, .., k\}$. Each service provider supplies
QoS history and short-term advertisements in time-series. The QoS model consists
of n attributes and corresponding attribute values where Q_{j_t} refers to the value of
the QoS attribute j at the time t. Thus, the QoS history of the service provider S_i is
defined in a vector $HIS(S_i) = \{ (Q_{1_t}, Q_{2_t}, \ldots, Q_{n_t}) \mid t \in [1, m] \}$ and the short-
term advertisement is defined in a vector $ADV(S_i) = \{(Q_{1_t}, Q_{2_t}, \ldots, Q_{n_t}) \mid t \in
(m, s]$ and $m < s\}$. The problem is to predict the long-term QoS performance of the
composition $PRD(SC) = \{ (Q_{1_t}, Q_{2_t}, \ldots\ldots, Q_{n_t}) \mid t \in (m, z]$ and $m < s \ll z\}$.

The multivariate QoS prediction model (Fig. 6.1) has three main parts: prediction
model, forecasting, and the aggregator. The multivariate prediction model takes
a QoS history as an input from the service providers. The model is then fed to
a prediction module to predict QoS values up to a time specified by end users.
Necessary adjustments need to be performed based on the difference between the
predicted values and the short-term advertisements published by service providers.
In the aggregator, the predicted QoS values of all service providers in the service

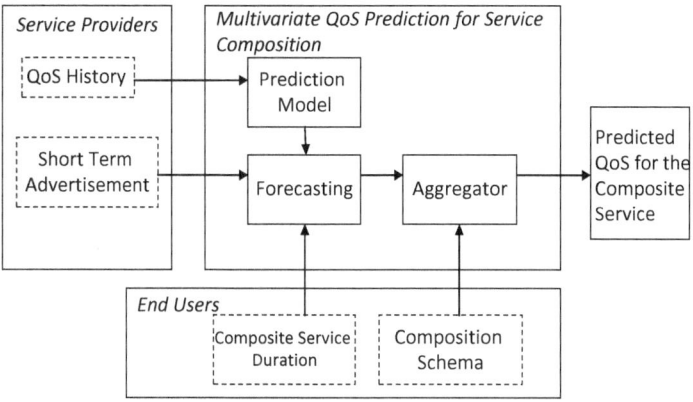

Fig. 6.1 The multivariate QoS prediction framework

composition are aggregated, based on the composition schema. The aggregation rules rely on the QoS attributes. *We only focus on the prediction and forecasting module in the following sections.*

6.3 Multivariate QoS Prediction Model (MQPM)

Given the history of a time-series, a model is required to identify the pattern of the time-series based on observed values [19]. ARIMA and Holt-Winters are widely used to model univariate time-series [35, 75]. ARIMA is an improved form of linear regression and Holt-Winters is an enhanced form of exponential smoothing. If we decompose the multivariate QoS history into individual univariate time-series, each time-series can be fitted into a univariate model. For example, the multivariate QoS history *History(Responsetime$_t$, Throughput$_t$)* is decomposed into two individual univariate time-series, *Responsetime$_t$* and *Throughput$_t$* in Fig. 6.2. *Responsetime$_t$* best fits the ARIMA model and *Throughput$_t$* best fits the Holt-Winters model. There are errors between the predicted and observed values (Fig. 6.2). We believe these errors can be further minimized using the correlations among the QoS attributes.

Response time and *Throughput* have a strong negative correlation in Fig. 6.2. An increase in *Response time* is followed by a decrease in *Throughput* and vice-versa. Thus the predicted *Throughput* values obtained from the univariate models can be further decreased if an increasing trend in *Response time* is observed. Another multivariate time-series prediction model, the Vector Autoregressive (VAR) model, assumes constant correlations among QoS attributes. This fails to predict QoS values effectively if there are random changes in trend or seasonality in the QoS history. Therefore we devise a new multivariate QoS prediction model named MQPM.

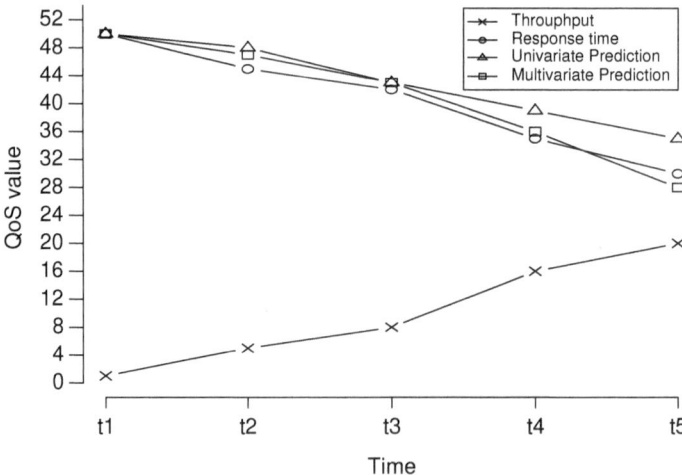

Fig. 6.2 Prediction error reduction using a multivariate analysis

We define some terms related to this model before its formal presentation.

- **Backshift Operator** (B): In time-series analysis, a backshift operator operates on an element of a time-series to produce previous elements. For example, given a time-series of a QoS attribute as $x = \{ Q_{x_1}, Q_{x_2}, .., Q_{x_t}, .., Q_{x_{t+m}} \}$; the backshift operator is B when $BQ_{x_t} = Q_{x_{t-1}}$ or $B^{-1}Q_{x_t} = Q_{x_{t+1}}$ and $B^k Q_{x_t} = Q_{x_{t-k}}$.
- **Cross Backshift Operator** ($CB_{x,y}$): The cross backshift operator operates on an element of a time-series to produce the previous elements of another time-series. For example, given a time-series of a QoS attribute x as $x = \{ Q_{x_1}, Q_{x_2}, \ldots, Q_{x_t}, \ldots, Q_{x_{t+m}} \}$ and a time series of another QoS attribute y as $y = \{ Q_{y_1}, Q_{y_2}, \ldots, Q_{y_t}, \ldots Q_{y_{t+m}} \}$; the cross backshift operator is $CB_{x,y}$ when $CB_{x,y}Q_{x_t} = Q_{y_{t-1}}$ or $CB_{x,y}^{-1}Q_{x_t} = Q_{y_{t+1}}$ and $CB_{x,y}^k Q_{x_t} = Q_{y_{t-k}}$.
- **Correlation Operator** ($CP_{x,y}$): Given $\bar{Q}_x$ and $\bar{Q}_y$ as the mean of time-series x and y, and S_{Q_x} and S_{Q_y} as their standard deviations; the correlation operator between the time-series x and y is a Pearson Correlation:

$$CP_{x,y} = \frac{1}{m-1} \sum_{i=1}^{m} \left(\frac{Q_{x_i} - \bar{Q}_x}{S_{Q_x}} \right) \left(\frac{Q_{y_i} - \bar{Q}_y}{S_{Q_y}} \right) \qquad (6.1)$$

- **Root Mean Square Error** (RMSE): RMSE is used to evaluate the performance of a prediction model. Let us assume the time-series of an individual QoS attribute in the QoS history fits many prediction models. If the predicted time-series are $(\hat{Q}_{1_t}, \hat{Q}_{2_t}, \ldots, \hat{Q}_{n_t})$, the prediction error is calculated using Eq. 6.2. A lesser value of RMSE imposes a better prediction model.

$$RMSE(i) = \sqrt{\frac{\sum_{i=1}^{m} (\hat{Q}_{i_t} - Q_{i_t})^2}{m}} \qquad (6.2)$$

MQPM uses the cross backshift operator and the correlation operator to reduce RMSE in individual univariate models in two phases. In the first phase, we transform ARIMA and Holt-Winters into the MQPM as stated in Sects. 6.3.1 and 6.3.2 respectively. In the second phase, we devise an algorithm for adaptive prediction error reduction in the MQPM as stated in Sect. 6.3.3.

6.3.1 Transforming ARIMA into the MQPM

Using the cross backshift operator and the correlation operator, we extend the univariate ARIMA(p,d,q) model into a multivariate model in Eq. 6.3. Three parts are integrated in this equation. In the *first* part, the *autoregressive (AR)* depends on the p_n lagged values of the time-series of n_{th} QoS attributes and φ_{n_p} is the coefficient constant. In the *second* part, The *moving average (MA)* depends on the q_n lagged values of the previous prediction errors and θ_{n_p} is the coefficient constant. B_n is a backshift operator for the n_{th} QoS attribute. The *third* part is the multivariate error reduction attributes where k_n is the lagged values of the $\{1, 2, \ldots, n - 1\}$ QoS attributes, $CP_{n,i}$ is the correlation operator of the QoS attribute i relative to the QoS attribute n; and $\alpha_{n,i,j}$ is the constant coefficient of the time-series value of the QoS attributes i relative to the time-series value of the QoS attributes n at the j_{th} time slot. In ARIMA, a non-stationary time-series needs to be converted into a stationary time-series by a difference operation. Here, d_n represents the number of times that the difference operation is performed to obtain the stationary time-series.

$$(\sum_{i=1,i\neq 1}^{n} \sum_{j=1}^{k_1} \alpha_{1,i,j}(CP_{1,i})(CB^{j}_{1,i}))\hat{Q}_{1_t} + ((1 - \sum_{i=1}^{p_1} \varphi_{1_i}B^{i}_1)(1 - B_1)^{d_1})\hat{Q}_{1_t} = (1 + \sum_{i=1}^{q_1} \theta_{1_i}B^{i}_1)\varepsilon_{1_t}$$

$$\ldots$$

$$\ldots \tag{6.3}$$

$$(\sum_{i=1,i\neq n}^{n} \sum_{j=1}^{k_n} \alpha_{n,i,j}(CP_{n,i})(CB^{j}_{n,i}))\hat{Q}_{n_t} + ((1 - \sum_{i=1}^{p_n} \varphi_{n_i}B^{i}_n)(1 - B_n)^{d_n})\hat{Q}_{1_t} = (1 + \sum_{i=1}^{q_n} \theta_{n_i}B^{i}_n)\varepsilon_{n_t}$$

6.3.2 Transforming Holt-Winters into the MQPM

It is uncertain that attributes in multivariate QoS time-series will always fit in ARIMA individually. For example, in the dataset [67], 80 service providers' QoS history among 94 service providers best fitted in the ARIMA model. The remainder best fitted in Holt-Winters. To reduce the error in Holt-Winters, the multivariate error reduction part in Eq. 6.3 is also used to extend the Holt-Winters model to multivariate models in Eq. 6.4. Here, $\hat{Q}_{n_{t+1}}$ is the predicted value at $t + 1$ time slot. At time t, m_{n_t} describes the level, b_{n_t} describes trend and $c_{n_{t-s}}$ describes seasonality where s specifies the seasonal period. x_{n_t} is the multivariate error reduction factor as described in Eq. 6.3. η_n, β_n and γ_n are the constant coefficients for calculating the level, trend and seasonality respectively.

$$\hat{Q}_{1_{t+1}} = m_{1_t} + b_{1_t} + c_{1_{t-s}} + x_{1_t}$$
$$\hat{Q}_{2_{t+1}} = m_{2_t} + b_{2_t} + c_{2_{t-s}} + x_{2_t}$$
$$\dots\dots$$
$$\dots\dots$$
$$\hat{Q}_{n_{t+1}} = m_{n_t} + b_{n_t} + c_{n_{t-s}} + x_{n_t}$$

where,   (6.4)

$$m_{n_t} = \eta_n(Q_{n_t} - c_{n_{t-s}}) + (1 - \eta_n)(m_{n_{t-1}} + b_{n_{t-1}})$$
$$b_{n_t} = \beta_n(m_{n_t} - m_{n_{t-1}}) + (1 - \beta_n)b_{n_{t-1}}$$
$$c_{n_t} = \gamma_n(Q_{n_t} - m_{n_t}) + (1 - \gamma_n)c_{n_{t-s}}$$
$$x_{n_t} = \sum_{i=1, i\neq n}^{n} \sum_{j=1}^{k_n} \alpha_{n,i,j}(CP_{n,i})(CB_{n,i}^{j})$$

6.3.3 Prediction Error Reduction Algorithm in the MQPM

Given a multivariate QoS history, we first decompose the time-series into individual univariate time-series. Then we fit each time series into an ARIMA model using the Box-Jenkins method [19] and into a Holt-Winters model [29]. If the RMSE of ARIMA is less than the RMSE of Holt-Winters, we will choose Eq. 6.3, otherwise we choose Eq. 6.4. In Eq. 6.3, the optimal values of AR and MA parts are calculated by the Box-Jenkins method. If Eq. 6.4 is used, the optimal values of coefficients are calculated by the Holt-Winters method. To have a reduced RMSE in either the Box-Jenkins or the Holt-Winters method, we need to find the optimal values of k_n and $\alpha_{n,i,j}$ of the multivariate error reduction factor in either equation for the n_{th} QoS attribute of the QoS history.

6.3.3.1 Calculating k_n for the n_{th} QoS Attribute

Let us assume that $n = \{Q_{n_1}, Q_{n_2}, Q_{n_3} \dots\dots Q_{n_m}\}$ and $i = \{Q_{i_1}, Q_{i_2}, Q_{i_3} \dots\dots Q_{i_m}\}$ are two time-series of the n_{th} and i_{th} QoS attributes in the history respectively. To calculate a k lagged coefficient of i for n, we first transform n and i into

$n_{m-k} = \{Q_{n_t} \mid k < t \le m\}$ and $i_{m-k} = \{Q_{i_t} \mid 1 \le t < (m-k)\}$ respectively, and then calculate the correlation operator $CP_{n_{m-k},i_{m-k}}$ using Eq. 6.1. As it is a Pearson correlation, values above 0.40 can be treated as candidate lagged values. In this process we calculate all the lagged values (k) for QoS attributes 1 to $n-1$ for the n_{th} QoS attribute.

6.3.3.2 $\alpha_{n,i,j}$ for the n_{th} QoS Attribute

The values of $\alpha_{n,i,j}$ should be sufficiently adaptable to reduce the RMSE from the first phase of ARIMA and Holt-Winters for the n_{th} attribute of the QoS history. Let us assume the i_{th} attribute is the only correlated attribute to the n_{th} QoS attribute and there is a first lagged operation of i to n. Using Eq. 6.3 or 6.4 in the second phase, the predicted values of the n_{th} QoS attribute can be written as:

$$Q_{n_t}^2 = Q_{n_t}^1 + \alpha_t(CP_{n,i})Q_{i_{t-1}} \tag{6.5}$$

As α_t is used to reduce the RMSE in the second phase; we should find optimal values of α_t and also predict the time-series of α_t. We first calculate α_t from the observed values. To do so, let us assume there is no prediction error in Eq. 6.5. Thus, in the second phase, the predicted values become the observed values $Q_{n_t}^2 = Q_{n_t}$. Substituting Q_{n_t} in Eq. 6.5, we get values for α from Eq. 6.6.

$$\alpha_t = \frac{Q_{n_t} - Q_{n_t}^1}{(CP_{n,i})Q_{i_{t-1}}} \quad \mid 1 \le t \le m \tag{6.6}$$

As α_t can be considered as a time-series, we can model α_t prediction $\hat{\alpha}_t$ using the univariate ARMIA or Holt-Winters model in Eq. 6.7.

$$\hat{\alpha}_t = \begin{cases} \text{ARIMA}(\,p,d,q) \text{ on } \alpha_t \text{ , where} \\ \text{RMSE(ARIMA}(\,p,d,q)(\alpha_t)) < \text{RMSE(Holt-Winters}(\alpha_t)) \\ \text{Holt-Winters}(\alpha_t) \text{ , where} \\ \text{RMSE(ARIMA}(\,p,d,q)(\alpha_t)) \ge \text{RMSE(Holt-Winters}(\alpha_t)) \end{cases} \tag{6.7}$$

To find the prediction pattern of α coefficients for all correlated attributes, we devise an iteration on sorted QoS attributes as described in Algorithm 6.

6.4   Forecasting from the MQPM

We need the long-term forecast using the QoS history. Using the proposed multi-variate analysis, the QoS history is modelled as $\{\hat{Q}_{1_t}, \hat{Q}_{2_t}, \ldots, \hat{Q}_{n_t}\}$. As the model uses observed values, we can only forecast one step ahead, i.e. $\hat{Q}_{n_{t+1}}$. End users

---

Algorithm 6 Finding $\hat{\alpha}_t$ for all the co-related attributes of the n_{th} QoS attribute

---

Require: The multivariate time-series of n QoS attributes $(Q_{1_t}, Q_{2_t}, \ldots, Q_{n_t})$ and
   the set of correlation operators between the n_{th} and other QoS operators
   $\{CP(n, 1), CP(n, 2), \ldots, CP(n, n-1)\}$
Ensure: The set of predicted adaptive coefficient $\hat{\alpha}_t$ for the n_{th} QoS attribute from
   $\{1, 2, .., n-1\}$ QoS attributes
1: a[n-1] is the descending-order-sorted array of attributes based on $CP(n, i)$
2: $Q_{n_t}^1$ is the first-phase prediction on the n_{th} QoS attribute
3: **for** $i := 1$ **to** $n-1$ **do**
4:    Get α_t using Equation 6.6
5:    Store predicted $\hat{\alpha}_t$ for attribute i using Equation 6.7
6:    $Q_{n_t}^1 = Q_{n_t}^1 + \alpha_t(CP_{n,i})Q_{i_{t-1}}$
7: **end for**

---

require a long-term forecast, i.e. l-step forecast. If the QoS history is modelled with
Eq. 6.3, we formulate the l-step forecast for the n_{th} QoS attribute using the recursive
procedure [47] in Eq. 6.8.

$$\hat{Q}_{n_{t+l}} = \sum_{i=1}^{p_n} \varphi_{n_i} \hat{Q}_{n_{t+l-i}} + \sum_{i=1, i \neq n}^{n} \sum_{j=1}^{k_n} (\hat{\alpha}_{n,i,t+l-j}) \hat{Q}_{i_{t+l-j}} CP(n, i) \tag{6.8}$$

The l-step forecast of the coefficient adaptive factor $(\hat{\alpha}_{n,i,t+l-j})$ is calculated using
the prediction procedure in Sect. 6.3.3.2. The prediction of the correlated attributes
also uses Eq. 6.8. All the QoS attributes are predicted in parallel operations. Thus
the predicted values of $(\hat{Q}_{1_{t+l}}, \hat{Q}_{2_{t+l}}, \ldots, \hat{Q}_{n_{t+l}})$ are only computed when $(\hat{Q}_{1_{t+l-1}}, \hat{Q}_{2_{t+l-1}}, \ldots, \hat{Q}_{n_{t+l-1}})$ have already been computed. A similar procedure is followed
in Eq. 6.4. As Eq. 6.4 uses recursive values of previous forecasts, they can be treated
as the observations in the l-step forecast.

The short-term advertisements of a service provider may change the behavior
of forecasting. Let us assume that $(\hat{Q}_{1_{t+s}}, \hat{Q}_{2_{t+s}}, \ldots, \hat{Q}_{n_{t+s}})$ is a s-step ahead short-
term forecast and $(Q_{1_{t+s}}, Q_{2_{t+s}}, \ldots, Q_{n_{t+s}})$ is the short-term advertisement from
the service provider. If the difference between the RMSE of the predicted forecast
and the short-term advertisement is unacceptable, there could well be a change in
the service provider's delivery system. In fact advertisements often tends to show
improved QoS. If a user believes that the RMSE difference is acceptable, the user
can use Eq. 6.8 for forecasting; otherwise, the user may adjust the forecast with a
level-adjusting factor. The resulting l-step QoS forecast adjusted by a short-term
advertisement is presented in Eq. 6.9.

$$\hat{Q}_{n_{t+l}} = \sum_{i=1, i \neq n}^{n} \sum_{j=1}^{k_n} (\hat{\alpha}_{n,i,t+l-j}) \hat{Q}_{i_{t+l-j}} CP(n, i) + \gamma$$

$$\gamma = \sum_{i=1}^{p_n} \varphi_{n_i} \hat{Q}_{n_{t+l-i}} + \frac{\sum_{i=1}^{s} |Q_{n_{t+i}} - \hat{Q}_{n_{t+i}}|}{s} \tag{6.9}$$

Table 6.1 Summary of the real-world QoS dataset

QoS attribute	Values
Min response time (r_{min})	13 ms
Max response time (r_{max})	1538 ms
Avg response time (r_{avg})	337 ms
Min throughput (th_{min})	0.0
Max throughput (th_{max})	5.0
Avg throughput (th_{avg})	3.2
Avg correlation operator $CP(r, th)$	0.62

6.5 Experiments and Results

A set of experiments have been conducted to assess the performance of the proposed prediction model. We compare the proposed multivariate prediction model with MQPM, ARIMA, Holt-Winters, and VAR. All experiments have been conducted on computers with Intel Core i7 CPU (2.13 GHz and 4 GB RAM).

6.5.1 Data Description

We evaluate the proposed approach using real cloud service data [67]. These real data include two time-series data (i.e. response time and throughput) for 100 cloud services. In each service, the QoS history is 6 months old (28 time slots). We discard six service providers' data as there are zero throughput and zero response times for most of the time in the time-series. The summary of the dataset is given in Table 6.1.

The response time and the throughput have a strong correlation in the dataset. To support the decision-making, we add the attribute of cost into the dataset which has no correlation with response time or throughput. The costs of services stay at a stable level for a time interval and reduce over the period based on the market situation [45]. We generate the cost with random distribution and reduce it over random time periods.

6.5.2 Comparison Among the Prediction Models

In this experiment, we compare the performance of the proposed multivariate model (MQPM) with ARIMA, Holt-Winters, and VAR. We use the statistical package R to generate the predicted values of the models. Using Eq. 6.2, the RMSE is calculated based on the observed and predicted values. Our target is to improve the prediction, i.e. a reduction in the RMSE. The results of the RMSE in *throughput* and *response time* for the services are presented in Figs. 6.3 and 6.4 respectively. We

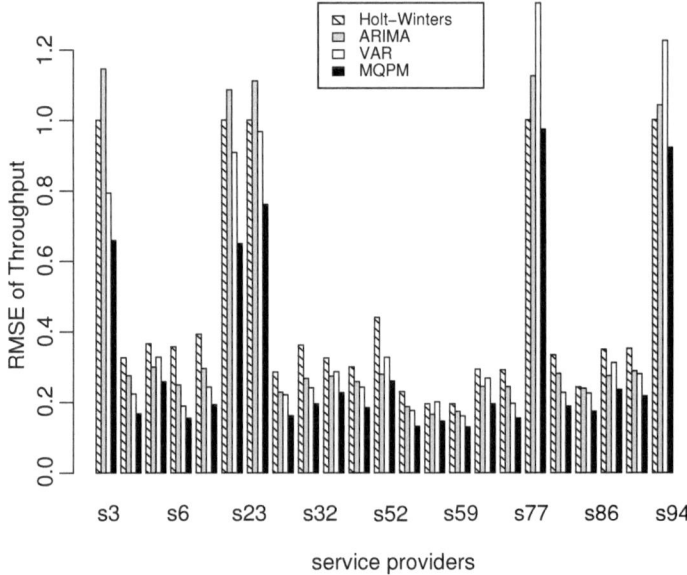

Fig. 6.3 RMSE of throughput in different service providers

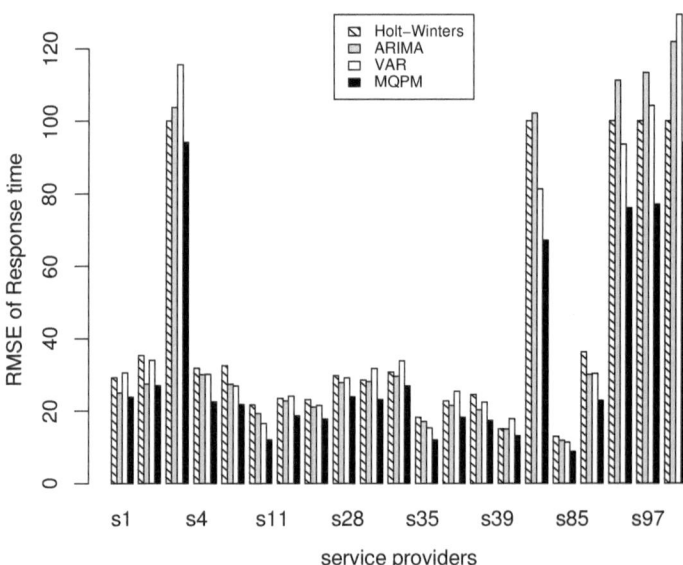

Fig. 6.4 RMSE of response time in different service providers

Table 6.2 Summary of the performance of prediction models

Prediction model	RMSE		
	Avg. throughput	Avg. response time	Avg. cost
MQPM	0.32	59	236
ARIMA	0.43	89	245
Holt_winters	0.55	75	265
VAR	0.53	82	257
RMSE reduction by MQPM	26%	21.3%	0.04%

randomly select 40 service providers and show the RMSEs of the prediction models on those providers in Figs. 6.3 and 6.4. We find that the proposed model, MQPM has lower RMSEs than the other models for each service provider. The average RMSEs for the prediction models are depicted in Table 6.2. We see that the MQPM reduces RMSEs significantly in *throughput* and *response time*. As the cost is not correlated with other attributes, the proposed model performs as a univariate model here.

6.5.3 Effect of the Time-Series Length on MQPM

In this experiment, we discuss the effect of QoS history length on the proposed multivariate prediction model. The performance of the proposed model relies on the adjusting correlation factor α. The more accurately α is predicted, the more accurate the prediction model is. To assess the effect of QoS history length on MQPM, we need to generate different time-series that vary in length but retain similar correlations among the QoS attributes. There are two variation methods: we may either extend or divide the QoS history. As our multivariate time-series dataset is comprised only of 28 real readings, the lengths of the divided time-series are too small to affect the prediction. On the other hand, the correlations among the QoS attributes may not exist if the dataset is extended at random. Therefore, we generate a new set of time-series with varying lengths by extending a random original QoS history ten times, using the ARIMA model. This is because ARIMA can retain the correlations in the simulated dataset. In each extension, we perform the RMSE of MQPM and plot them in Fig. 6.5. We observe that the RMSE of the original time series reduces in each extension. In Fig. 6.5, the RMSE is reduced by about 50% after the original time series is extended by ten times. From this experiment, we conclude that MQPM performs better when the number of time slots in the QoS history becomes larger.

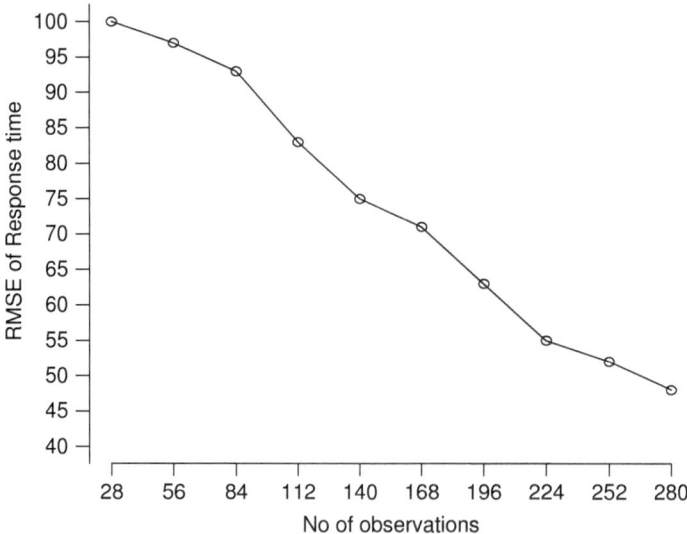

Fig. 6.5 Effect of time-series length on RMSE

6.6   Conclusion

We have used QoS history and short-term advertisements to predict the long-term QoS behavior of service providers. Correlations among the QoS attributes are used to improve the prediction error rate. In this chapter, we do not consider the trust issues in the QoS history and the short-term advertisements. Incorporating the trust issue into the proposed model is a subject for possible future work.

Chapter 7
Conclusion

Check for updates

Numerous reports predict that global cloud services will increase from $180B in 2015 to $390B in 2020, attaining a Compound Annual Growth Rate (CAGR) of 17%. SaaS-based applications are predicted to grow at 18% CAGR, and IaaS or PaaS is predicted to grow at 27% CAGR [114]. To further build and capitalize on this trend, further innovations in the cloud market are required. For example, a solid theoretical framework and architecture for an economically viable cloud service infrastructure may boost the confidence of investors on their Return on Investments (ROI). In this respect, we propose an IaaS service composition framework to maximize long-term profits using quantitative and qualitative economic models.

The proposed economic models in this book have the potential to provide the necessary impetus for wider investment and adoption of the cloud on a greater scale and at a faster pace. For any solution to be deployable, it needs to be congruent with what users and providers would naturally regard as a primary reason to adopt the cloud approach. Business economics is critical to informing business decisions. Therefore, the use of economic models as optimization tools for the selection of service requests fits almost intuitively in the way business is usually done.

We have considered the long-term IaaS composition from a single IaaS provider's perspective. The composition framework is the key component to the cloud service management. Due to the limitation of resource availability, the provider requires a sound, theoretical tool that enables it to plan and optimize resource utilization over time. Figure 7.1 summarizes the concepts (presented in the book) in the context of the long-term IaaS service composition. We have identified five key elements in the composition: (a) service request representation, (b) arrival models of the requests, (c) runtime behavior of the requests, (d) the long-term economic models, and (e) the optimization approach. We have identified the correlations among these elements in designing an effective IaaS composition framework. For example, the quantitative economic model could not be applied when the requests are modeled qualitatively (i.e. using CP-Nets). Upon receiving incoming requests, we have applied request transformations using novel prediction models in the runtime behavior of the

© Springer International Publishing AG 2018
S. Mistry et al., *Economic Models for Managing Cloud Services*,
https://doi.org/10.1007/978-3-319-73876-5_7

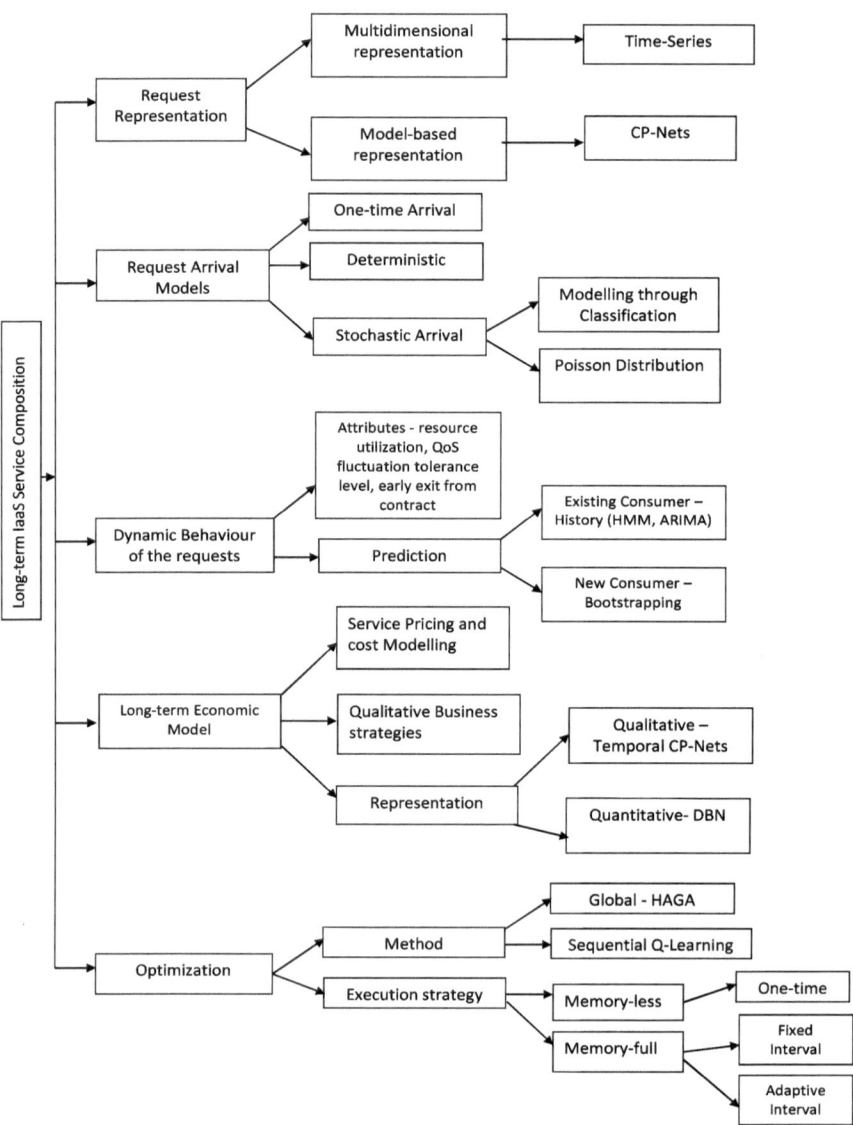

Fig. 7.1 Key elements in the long-term IaaS composition

consumers. We have proposed a new HMM-ARIMA model to predict the runtime behavior of existing consumers using historical data. A bootstrapping prediction model has been proposed for new consumers without historical data. The transformed requests have been used by the economic models. We have designed the quantitative economic model using Dynamic Bayesian Network (DBN) to compose long-term requests which are represented in multidimensional time-series. We have designed the qualitative economic model using Temporal CP-Nets to represent the business strategies of the provider. The design of an effective optimization approach depends on the type of economic model and the arrival models of the requests. We have designed a global memory-full optimization approach to compose stochastic requests according to the quantitative economic model. It periodically updates the quality of the composition by predicting the future changes. We have also designed a reinforcement learning based sequential optimization approach to compose the deterministic requests (represented in CP-Nets) according to the provider's long-term business strategies (i.e. the qualitative economic model). Our contributions and their significance in each chapter are summarized below.

In Chap. 2, we discussed existing works relating to service composition approaches from both the consumers' and providers' perspectives. We found that existing composition approaches do not consider long-term aspects such as dynamic consumer behavior or the stochastic arrival of requests. We considered computing resources to be higher-level abstractions or services. Hence, economic models are natural solutions to the long-term IaaS composition. Also in Chap. 2, we discussed existing economic models in operations research and the cloud environment. We found that modeling long-term relationships among composite QoS, resource utilization, and operation costs have not yet been analyzed. Such modeling ensures resource optimization and should provide a quantitative method to measure the quality of a set of requests. Resource utilization is a lower-level approach to maximize profits by cost minimization over a longer term. On the other hand, business strategies are higher-level techniques to maximize profit by considering the market competition. Service menu creation, setting prices and enabling different service delivery options are examples of higher-level business strategies. Long-term business strategies are often represented in qualitative economic models. Hence, in the IaaS composition, qualitative economic models are complementary to quantitative economic models. In Chap. 2, we discussed existing qualitative economic models from the consumers' perspectives. However, we found that the qualitative preferences of the consumers are not analogous to the long-term business strategies of providers.

Developing a quantitative economic model is a key research challenge for the IaaS composition. In Chap. 1, we mentioned three key research issues in respect of the quantitative economic model: predicting dynamic consumer behavior; transforming consumer requests to SLA violations and operation costs, and finding an effective optimization process for the stochastic arrival of the incoming requests.

In Chap. 3, we addressed an important research issue on consumers' runtime behavior, and found a solution to the research question—*"How efficiently can we predict the dynamic runtime behavior of the service requests?"* We found that consumers' service requests are influenced by their dynamic behavior. Here, we considered heuristics on resource utilization level, QoS fluctuation tolerance levels and early exit from a contract in the long-term composition. At first, we predicted the behavior from historical request patterns. In the real world, consumers' resource usage patterns usually possess the feature of high frequency with seasonal trends. Existing univariate models (e.g. HMM, ARIMA, ANN) ignore the correlation effect among the attributes in consumer requests. We proposed a multivariate HMM for predicting the high-frequency and multivariate patterns. We applied a modified

Markov assumption on the limited horizon property of correlated sequences and found explicit dependence and appropriately lagged values using the correlation operator. We proposed a modified ARIMA model to predict seasonal-trend request patterns. The prediction errors in a seasonal-trend ARIMA model were further modeled in the multivariate HMM. We also predicted new consumer behavior without history. We found that consumers usually belong to a community and the new consumers' behaviors are similar to their community's behavior. The community generates a multivariate HMM or ARIMA model by aggregating the corresponding models of its members. The model is updated using each new user's performance. We used the community's most recent aggregated model to transform the requests of a new consumer. We evaluated the efficiency of the proposed HMM-ARIMA model using a mixture of Google Cluster resource utilization [109], real-world cloud QoS performance [67] and synthetic data. We found that the average prediction error (NRMSE) of the proposed multivariate HMM-ARIMA was 0.27, which is lower than the univariate models, i.e. ANN, HMM, and ARIMA. The quality of the prediction was better when the correlation density index (CDI) of resource utilization time-series was higher.

In Chap. 3, we also discussed the effectiveness of predicting dynamic consumer behavior in the long-term composition. We started with a simple constraint-based formulation of the IaaS composition. We composed services for the deterministic arrival of requests. We formulated a linear profit maximization objective function. We considered the linear correlation between the operation cost and resource utilization. Although such consideration was not fine-grained according to the real-world cloud providers, it gave a computationally efficient approximation to actual operation costs. We treated the resource limitations as program constraints. As our target was to maximize profits, we transformed the composition to a combinatorial ILP optimization problem. IBM CPLEX optimizer was used to solve the ILP in the experiments. We compared the performance of the proposed approach with greedy and ILP approaches without heuristics. These approaches do not consider consumers' runtime behavior. In the experiments, the proposed ILP based optimization approach maximized both the profit and resource utilization in the long-term. We, therefore, concluded that the proposed IaaS composition framework has the potential to maximize long-term profit and revenue of an IaaS provider.

In Chap. 4, we addressed the research issues in developing the quantitative economic model, and found a solution to the research question—*"How can we transform consumer requests to SLA violations and operation costs?"* One of the fundamental limitations in Chap. 3 was to correlate operation costs linearly with the resource utilization. However, real-world cloud providers use multi-tenant architecture to share their resources which lead to non-linear relationships among SLA violations, operation costs, and resource utilizations. We proposed a new economic model that incorporates dynamic pricing and operation cost modeling of the service requests. As the business models of IaaS providers are similar to business models of utility providers, the demand-driven pricing model was used to construct the economic model for the provider. As Dynamic Bayesian Network (DBN) models succeeded in modeling a temporal dynamic environment, we represented the dynamic pricing behavior as a DBN. The DBN described the correlations among physical resources (computing, storage, and network), QoS values (Availability, Throughput and Response time), demand and the service price. The DBN was incorporated into the long-term revenue and operation cost modeling to calculate the economic valuation of a composition of requests. The operation cost was determined by the server's power consumption. Each running physical server had a predefined threshold of utility that determines a fixed power cost for routine operations. The variable power cost was determined from the workload of the servers. We found that the SLA violation cost depends on the SLA violation penalty rate and the number of SLA violations. We calculated the long-term operation cost using the server power consumption and utility threshold. Hence, it was independent of any particular resource allocation schemes. Real-world cloud providers can use the proposed operation cost modeling without changing their internal resource allocation scheme. In the experiments, we evaluated the performance of the proposed DBN using the dataset of Australian Electricity prices [41] provided by the Australian Bureau of Statistics. We found that the NRMSE of the DBN is 0.3, which is acceptably accurate for real-world predictions.

In Chap. 4, we also addressed the optimization issue in service management, and found a solution to the research question—*"How do we design an effective optimization process for a stochastic arrival of incoming requests?"* We extended the single-valued objective function (Chap. 3) to a multi-valued, non-linear objective function. In this respect, the long-term economic expectations of the provider were represented as a weighted, semantic, multidimensional time-series. Such modeling is more practical than traditional quantitative approaches as the provider can specify its relative preferences among economic operators such as "more" profit or "fewer" SLA violations. Also, we characterized the IaaS service requests by their dynamic resource, QoS requirements and stochastic arrival times. We developed an optimal composition framework that meets the provider's non-linear long-term expectations. As the ILP approach described in Chap. 3 is inapplicable for non-linear objective functions, we first applied a genetic algorithm (GA) for the long-term service composition using the proposed economic model. The genetic optimization approach generates dynamic global solutions considering the runtime behavior of service requests. The proposed approach deals with the non-linear objective functions of the economic model by creating a population of feasible solutions. The GA-based optimization model is "memory-less", incapable of handling prediction errors and optimizing the composition at runtime. If we have different checkpoints to evaluate the performance of a composition, the GA needs to run every checkpoint from scratch. It does not transfer knowledge of one optimization from one checkpoint to another to improve the quality of the composition. Therefore we proposed an innovative Hybrid Adaptive Genetic Algorithm (HAGA) to optimize the acceptance or rejection decision of stochastic user requests. The proposed HAGA is "memory-full" and reserves the global inter-dependency and preference heuristics from the population generated in the previous optimization. The global inter-dependency matrix is the statistical relationship among requests in the generated populations. The global preference heuristic (GPH) is the probabilistic indicator of a request's influence on the fitness of a solution. We used ACO to determine the GPH. We updated the GPH by the fitness of the generated populations containing the particular requests. The heuristics were updated according to the changed environment and were used in the new optimization to generate computationally efficient solutions. We also performed a local search to check that the solution is not stuck at a local optimum. We used these heuristics to repair the infeasible population. The hybrid approach converged to the global composition in an iterative process. In the experiments, the proposed HAGA approach fitted the economic expectation better than the GA, ACO, and greedy approaches, and increased the cumulative fitness by 25% in an 18-month composition period. It also reduced the optimization time at runtime. We, therefore, conclude that the HAGA is more applicable in the real world IaaS composition than the GA and ACO approaches.

Developing a qualitative economic model is another key research challenge for the IaaS composition. In Chap. 1, we mentioned three key research issues in respect of the qualitative economic model, i.e. modeling long-term qualitative preferences, designing an effective sequential optimization process and analyzing the long-term qualitative performances of the provider.

In Chap. 5, we addressed research issues in qualitative economic models, and found a solution to the research question—*"How do we model long-term preferences of a provider as the qualitative economic model?"* The qualitative economic model was represented by a Temporal CP-Net to capture the provider's dynamic business strategies in qualitative service provisions. The acceptance or rejection of an incoming request relied on the models, and accepted requests were committed for the whole period. The dynamic semantics of the preferences was indicated using the Conditional Preference Table (CPT) of the Temporal CP-Net. The temporal mismatch between the service request and the provider's preferences was solved through the semantic temporal segmentation of the request. Moreover, the induced preference graph from the Temporal CP-Net was indexed in a multidimensional k-d tree to effectively compute the global preference ranking of a composition. The total ordering of all the configurations was created using pairwise comparison (ordering queries) of the configurations in the k-d tree. In the experiments, the qualitative ranking of a set of requests was produced 60% faster through the k-d tree indexing than the preference graph.

In Chap. 5, we also found a solution to the optimization research question— *"How do we design an efficient sequential optimization process to follow the qualitative economic model?"* First, we observed different arrival patterns of stochastic incoming patterns. We found that preferring short-term requests over long-term requests usually reduces the effect of previously selected requests in the sequential optimization for most request patterns. We proposed a heuristic-based local optimization approach to accept or reject requests in each segment of a temporal CP-Net. We used collaborative decisions of local optimizations to accept long-term requests in the final composition. In the experiments, we found that these local decisions collectively converged to an acceptable approximate global optimal composition. Next, we improved those heuristics using machine-learning techniques and historical request patterns. Due to the dynamic environment, we used a model-free reinforcement learning called Q-learning. We started by creating a Markov Decision Process (MDP) where intervals of the temporal CP-Net were treated as states, and the service configurations in the k-d tree were treated as actions. We proposed a three-dimensional Q-learning approach to learn the MDP. We applied a unique state policy and policy termination condition to stop multiple execution orders of similar states. We classified the initial Q-values in different distributions using the Kolmogorov-Smirnov test (K-S test). Later, the aggregation of the major historical patterns was used to predict the early Q-values of a new set of requests. In the experiments, we used four types of request patterns, i.e. normal, left-skewed, right-skewed and random distributions. The proposed three-dimensional Q-learning approach generated more accurate results than the heuristic-based sequential optimization approach in different distributions. The proposed method was also efficient in runtime as its convergence time was similar to the heuristic-based sequential optimization approach, given a history of Q-matrices. However, the proposed method converged slowly to build a history of Q-matrices. We conclude that providers should allocate time before the actual composition to finish the offline learning phase. In the composition interval, the provider should continue to learn the Q-values by allocating resources in parallel with the online optimization process.

In Chap. 6, we found a solution to the research question related QoS prediction models—*"How efficiently can we predict long-term QoS performances of the provider?"* We first discussed the importance of predicting the future performance of peer IaaS providers to construct an effective long-term economic model. We then proposed a multivariate QoS prediction model (MQPM) using historical QoS performances and short-term advertisements from the providers to predict future performance. As we considered time-series representations of QoS values, we incorporated multivariate analysis into both ARIMA, and Holt-Winters approaches. The proposed MQPM forecasts for a long-term period (l-step forecast) using a prediction error reduction algorithm. In the experiments, we used a real-world QoS dataset. The proposed MQPM reduced the prediction error by 26% over the ARIMA, Holt-Winters and VAR models. Additionally, MQPM performs better with more time slots in the QoS history. Hence, we conclude that MQPM would be more efficient when there is enough historical dataset, and QoS attributes are correlated. It was found that real-world cloud QoS datasets are mostly correlated. Hence, the proposed MQPM has potential applicability in the real world IaaS composition.

In summary, we have designed an effective IaaS composition framework using quantitative and qualitative economic models. The proposed framework will provide significant momentum to the business of IaaS providers, especially small providers. IaaS service providers will have the technology to compose cloud services with optimal resource utilizations and long-term business strategies. Using the framework, the provider should be able to efficiently predict its clients' dynamic behavior that ensures right-provisions of the resources. The proposed framework should enable an IaaS provider to determine the long-term effect of accepting consumer requests before the service is actually provided. The provider should be able to apply their high-level business strategies in the long-term composition, using the proposed framework. This framework is designed to optimize stochastic consumer requests in a dynamic economic environment. Hence, the provider should be able to compose requests efficiently in the real world. From a small provider's perspective, the proposed framework should enable it to offer high quality and low-cost services in the market. It should provide small investors with leverage to compete with larger service providers.

7.1 Future Work

The book has focused on developing the long-term composition framework from a single IaaS provider. The proposed framework has dealt with the dynamic consumer behavior and the stochastic arrival of requests. It has developed a quantitative and a qualitative economic model to evaluate the long-term profitability of a set of incoming requests. A new metaheuristic optimization approach has been proposed to improve the runtime efficiency of a composition. A machine-learning approach has been applied in the framework to improve the quality of a long-term composition. These tasks have been completed and better performance has been achieved. However, there are other possibilities that have not been within the scope of this book. Some limitations in the developed models are discussed below which could open up pathways for future research based on the context of this book.

In Chap. 3, we only considered high-frequency and seasonal-trend patterns in consumer behavior. Although these patterns are very common in the real world, other patterns such as regime shift may also be found in some consumers' behavior. Our proposed prediction model may not accurately predict those other patterns. A potential avenue of research in this direction is to explore new patterns and to improve the prediction model.

In Chap. 4, we defined checkpoints to regularly update the proposed hybrid adaptive genetic optimization process to compose requests. We did not focus on determining the optimal interval between checkpoints. A potential research direction is to find the optimal interval length between checkpoints. Smaller intervals between checkpoints may be inefficient as possible updates may not be triggered in shorter periods. It may waste computation resources and time. A larger interval between checkpoints may also be inefficient, as all potential changes may be ignored in an optimization in such cases. Further research in this direction could determine the optimal interval between checkpoints in the proposed hybrid adaptive genetic optimization process and thus improve the quality of composition.

In Chap. 5, we developed a long-term qualitative economic model for the IaaS provider. We considered fixed resources for the long-term. In reality, providers continue to add resources through investments and use cloud federations to allocate more resources. We did not focus on these dynamic features in the proposed temporal CP-Net model. The proposed model is insufficiently flexible to sudden changes because the model retains temporal relationships in the induced preference graphs. If the provider wants to change a segment of the model, the whole model has to be rebuilt from scratch. A potential research direction is to add the ability to restructure the temporal CP-Net for the IaaS provider with dynamic resources. It should leverage a wider adoption of the qualitative economic model by the real-world IaaS providers.

As it is difficult to find a real-world IaaS provider's business strategies, we synthetically generated the temporal CP-Nets in the experiments in Chap. 5. Here, the dependencies among the attributes in a CP-Net were randomly generated. Such random assignments may not be semantically accurate and may be an inefficient business strategy. As the purpose of the proposed algorithm is to effectively make decisions according to the given business strategy, we only evaluated the accuracy of a composition using the similarity measure of the given random CP-Nets. As such CP-Nets may be the inefficient business strategies, we did not evaluate the long-term profitability of the IaaS provider using the qualitative economic model. In the future work, we plan to evaluate the effect of an actual real-world qualitative composition to the long-term profitability of an IaaS provider. Hence, one potential research direction is to find an efficient algorithm to generate meaningful and effective temporal CP-Nets that should lead to a profitable long-term composition. Real-world datasets can be collected through interviews with executives of cloud service providers about their business strategies. Subjective qualitative preferences of the consumers could be collected and processed from social media such as Facebook and Twitter. Finally, the experiments could be run in a real cloud environment such Amazon AWS and Microsoft Azure.

In Chap. 6, we developed a multivariate model to predict performances of peer IaaS providers. We may construct an effective long-term economic model using future performances of peer IaaS providers. For example, if it is predicted that peer providers will reduce their prices, the temporal CP-Net needs to be updated to retain their existing customers. However, we did not discuss how such a prediction is used to build better long-term economic models. A potential research direction is to find an efficient model to apply performance predictions in the construction of economic models.

A possible extension to the proposed framework is to compose services for a cloud federation. In the cloud market, it is a natural phenomenon to join in a federation and share each other's resources, while maintaining individual economic models. Conflicting economic models may hinder the formation of such federations. We treat the clustering of economic models with conflict resolution as a future work.

Another possible extension of the proposed economic models is to define and specify a unified, long-term economic model for both cloud consumers and providers. The consumers' economic model will help consumers to select cloud service providers with a view to saving costs and for better QoS satisfaction. On the other hand, the cloud service providers' economic model will assist providers to select service requests with a view to maximizing their long-term economic benefits (e.g. revenue and resource utilization). Such a unified model will characterize, model and capture the inherent consumers' and providers' long-term goals and QoS requirements, using a variety of techniques such as time-based, multi-dimensional, statistical and graph theoretic techniques. In future, our target is to create a foundation for market-driven selection and provisioning of cloud services based on consumers' and providers' long-term economic models.

References

1. Sudhir Agarwal and Steffen Lamparter. User Preference based Automated Selection of Web Service Compositions. In *Proceedings of the ICSOC Workshop on Dynamic Web Processes*, volume 12, pages 1–12, 2005.
2. Mohammad Alrifai, Dimitrios Skoutas, and Thomas Risse. Selecting Skyline Services for QoS-based Web Service Composition. In *Proceedings of the 19th International Conference on World Wide Web (WWW)*, pages 11–20. ACM, 2010.
3. Amazon Inc. EC2 Service Level Agreement, June 2015. Available online at https://aws.amazon.com/ec2/sla.
4. Arun Anandasivam and Christof Weinhardt. Towards An Efficient Decision Policy for Cloud Service Providers. In *Proceedings of the 14th International Conference on Information Systems*, pages 40–48. AIS Electronic Library, 2010.
5. Alexandr Andoni and Piotr Indyk. Near-optimal Hashing Algorithms for Approximate Nearest Neighbor in High Dimensions. *Communications of the ACM*, 51(1):117–122, 2008.
6. Nikos Antonopoulos and Lee Gillam. *Cloud Computing: Principles, Systems and Applications*. Springer Science and Business Media, 2010.
7. Danilo Ardagna, Barbara Panicucci, and Mauro Passacantando. A Game Theoretic Formulation of the Service Provisioning Problem in Cloud Systems. In *Proceedings of the 20th International Conference on World Wide Web (WWW)*, pages 177–186. ACM, 2011.
8. M. Armbrust, A. Fox, and R. Griffith. Above the Clouds: A Berkeley View of Cloud Computing. *Technical Report, University of California, Berkeley*, 2009.
9. Leonard E Baum, Ted Petrie, George Soules, and Norman Weiss. A Maximization Technique Occurring in the Statistical Analysis of Probabilistic Functions of Markov Chains. *The Annals of Mathematical Statistics*, pages 164–171, 1970.
10. Peter P Belobaba. Survey Paper on Airline Yield Management: An Overview of Seat Inventory Control. *Transportation Science*, 21(2):63–73, 1987.
11. Anton Beloglazov, Jemal Abawajy, and Rajkumar Buyya. Energy-Aware Resource Allocation Heuristics for Efficient Management of Data Centers for Cloud Computing. *Future Generation Computer Systems*, 28(5):755–768, 2012.
12. Anton Beloglazov and Rajkumar Buyya. Optimal Online Deterministic Algorithms and Adaptive Heuristics for Energy and Performance Efficient Dynamic Consolidation of Virtual Machines in Cloud Data Centers. *Concurrency and Computation: Practice and Experience*, 24(13):1397–1420, 2012.
13. Jon Louis Bentley. Multidimensional Binary Search Trees used for Associative Searching. *Communications of the ACM*, 18(9):509–517, 1975.

14. Michel Berkelaar, Kjell Eikland, Peter Notebaert, et al. lpsolve: Open Source (Mixed-Integer) Linear Programming System, 2004. Available online at http://lpsolve.sourceforge.net/5.5/.

15. C Guus E Boender, AHG Rinnooy Kan, GT Timmer, and Leen Stougie. A Stochastic Method for Global Optimization. *Mathematical Programming*, 22(1):125–140, 1982.

16. Marko Bohanec, Antoine Messean, Sara Scatasta, Frederique Angevin, Bryan Griffiths, Paul Henning Krogh, Martin Žnidaršič, and Sašo Džeroski. A Qualitative Multi-Attribute Model for Economic and Ecological Assessment of Genetically Modified Crops. *Ecological Modelling*, 215(1):247–261, 2008.

17. Michael Borkowski, Stefan Schulte, and Christoph Hochreiner. Predicting Cloud Resource Utilization. In *Proceedings of the 9th International Conference on Utility and Cloud Computing*, pages 37–42. ACM, 2016.

18. Craig Boutilier, Ronen I Brafman, Carmel Domshlak, Holger H Hoos, and David Poole. CP-Nets: A Tool for Representing and Reasoning with Conditional Ceteris Paribus Preference Statements. *Journal of Artificial Intelligence Research*, 21:135–191, 2004.

19. George EP Box, Gwilym M Jenkins, and Gregory C Reinsel. *Time-series Analysis: Forecasting and Control*. John Wiley & Sons, 2013.

20. George EP Box and David A Pierce. Distribution of Residual Autocorrelations in Autoregressive-Integrated Moving Average Time-series Models. *Journal of the American Statistical Association*, 65(332):1509–1526, 1970.

21. R. Buyya, C.S. Yeo, S. Venugopal, J. Broberg, and I. Brandic. Cloud Computing and Emerging IT Platforms: Vision, Hype, and Reality for Delivering Computing as the 5th Utility. *Future Generation Computer Systems*, 25(6):599–616, 2009.

22. Gerardo Canfora, Massimiliano Di Penta, Raffaele Esposito, and Maria Luisa Villani. An Approach for QoS-Aware Service Composition based on Genetic Algorithms. In *Proceedings of the 7th Annual Conference on Genetic and Evolutionary Computation*, pages 1069–1075. ACM, 2005.

23. Jian Cao, Yihua Wu, and Minglu Li. Energy Efficient Allocation of Virtual Machines in Cloud Computing Environments based on Demand Forecast. In *Proceedings of the International Conference on Grid and Pervasive Computing*, pages 137–151. Springer, 2012.

24. Junwei Cao, Kai Hwang, Keqin Li, and A.Y. Zomaya. Optimal Multiserver Configuration for Profit Maximization in Cloud Computing. *IEEE Transactions on Parallel and Distributed Systems*, 24(6):1087–1096, June 2013.

25. Fabio Casati, Ski Ilnicki, Li-Jie Jin, Vasudev Krishnamoorthy, and Ming-Chien Shan. Adaptive and Dynamic Service Composition in EFlow. In *Proceedings of the International Conference on Advanced Information Systems Engineering*, pages 13–31. Springer, 2000.

26. Fabio Casati, Ski Ilnicki, Li-Jie Jin, Vasudev Krishnamoorthy, and Ming-Chien Shan. EFlow: A Platform for Developing and Managing Composite E-services. In *Proceedings of Academia/Industry Working Conference on Research Challenges*, pages 341–348. IEEE, 2000.

27. Antonio Celesti, Francesco Tusa, Massimo Villari, and Antonio Puliafito. How to Enhance Cloud Architectures to Enable Cross-Federation. In *Proceedings of the 3rd International Conference on Cloud Computing (CLOUD)*, pages 337–345. IEEE, 2010.

28. Sivadon Chaisiri, Bu-Sung Lee, and Dusit Niyato. Optimization of Resource Provisioning Cost in Cloud Computing. *IEEE Transactions on Services Computing*, 5(2):164–177, 2012.

29. Chris Chatfield. The Holt-Winters Forecasting Procedure. *Applied Statistics*, pages 264–279, 1978.

30. Chun-Hung Chen and Loo Hay Lee. *Stochastic Simulation Optimization: An Optimal Computing Budget Allocation*, volume 1. World scientific, 2011.

31. Kun Chen, Jiuyun Xu, and Stephan Reiff-Marganiec. Markov-HTN Planning Approach to Enhance Flexibility of Automatic Web Service Composition. In *Proceedings of the 7th International Conference on Web Services (ICWS)*, pages 9–16. IEEE, 2009.

32. Tang Lung Cheung, Kari Okamoto, Frank Maker III, Xin Liu, and Venkatesh Akella. Markov Decision Process (MDP) Framework for Optimizing Software on Mobile Phones. In *Proceedings of the 7th International Conference on Embedded Software*, pages 11–20. ACM, 2009.
33. P.C. Chu and J.E. Beasley. A Genetic Algorithm for the Multidimensional Knapsack Problem. *Journal of Heuristics*, 4(1):63–86, 1998.
34. Debabrata Dash, Verena Kantere, and Anastasia Ailamaki. An Economic Model for Self-tuned Cloud Caching. In *Proceedings of the 25th International Conference on Data Engineering (ICDE)*, pages 1687–1693. IEEE, 2009.
35. Ashton De Silva, Rob J Hyndman, and Ralph Snyder. The Vector Innovations Structural Time-series Framework: A Simple Approach to Multivariate Forecasting. *Statistical Modelling*, 10(4):353–374, 2010.
36. Haluk Demirkan and Dursun Delen. Leveraging the Capabilities of Service-Oriented Decision Support Systems: Putting Analytics and Big Data in Cloud. *Decision Support Systems*, 55(1):412–421, 2013.
37. Carmel Domshlak and Thorsten Joachims. Efficient and Non-parametric Reasoning over User Preferences. *User Modeling and User-Adapted Interaction*, 17(1–2):41–69, 2007.
38. Marco Dorigo and LM Gambardella. Ant-Q: A Reinforcement Learning Approach to the Traveling Salesman Problem. In *Proceedings of the 12th International Conference on Machine Learning*, pages 252–260. IEEE, 2016.
39. Jae Edmonds and John Reilly. A Long-term Global Energy-Economic Model of Carbon Dioxide Release from Fossil Fuel Use. *Energy Economics*, 5(2):74–88, 1983.
40. Robert J Elliott, Lakhdar Aggoun, and John B Moore. *Hidden Markov Models*. Springer, 1994.
41. Energy Supply Association. Electricity Prices in Australia. Technical Report 02, Australian Bureau of Statistics, 2000.
42. Daji Ergu, Gang Kou, Yi Peng, Yong Shi, and Yu Shi. The Analytic Hierarchy Process: Task Scheduling and Resource Allocation in Cloud Computing Environment. *The Journal of Supercomputing*, 64(3):835–848, 2013.
43. Eyal Even-Dar and Yishay Mansour. Learning Rates for Q-learning. *Journal of Machine Learning Research*, 5(Dec):1–25, 2003.
44. Giovanni Fasano and Alberto Franceschini. A Multidimensional Version of the Kolmogorov–Smirnov Test. *Monthly Notices of the Royal Astronomical Society*, 225(1):155–170, 1987.
45. Joseph Gacinga. The Big Losers in the Cloud Pricing Wars, Mar 2014.
46. Yan Gao, Jun Na, Bin Zhang, Lei Yang, and Qiang Gong. Optimal Web Services Selection using Dynamic Programming. In *Proceedings of the International Symposium on Computers and Communications (ISCC)*, pages 365–370. IEEE, 2006.
47. Sarah Gelper, Roland Fried, and Christophe Croux. Robust Forecasting with Exponential and Holt-Winters Smoothing. *Journal of Forecasting*, 29(3):285–300, 2010.
48. Jan Gläscher, Nathaniel Daw, Peter Dayan, and John P O'Doherty. States versus Rewards: Dissociable Neural Prediction Error Signals underlying Model-based and Model-free Reinforcement Learning. *Neuron*, 66(4):585–595, 2010.
49. Daniel Gmach, Jerry Rolia, Ludmila Cherkasova, and Alfons Kemper. Workload Analysis and Demand Prediction of Enterprise Data Center Applications. In *Proceedings of the 10th International Symposium on Workload Characterization (IISWC)*, pages 171–180. IEEE, 2007.
50. Inigo Goiri, Jordi Guitart, and Jordi Torres. Characterizing Cloud Federation for Enhancing Providers' Profit. In *Proceedings of the 3rd International Conference on Cloud Computing (CLOUD)*, pages 123–130. IEEE, 2010.
51. Íñigo Goiri, Jordi Guitart, and Jordi Torres. Economic Model of a Cloud Provider Operating in a Federated Cloud. *Information Systems Frontiers*, 14(4):827–843, 2012.

52. Google Inc. Compute engine features, 2015. Available online at https://cloud.google.com/compute/.

53. Hadi Goudarzi, Mohammad Ghasemazar, and Massoud Pedram. SLA-based Optimization of Power and Migration Cost in Cloud Computing. In *Proceedings of the 12th International Symposium on Cluster, Cloud and Grid Computing (CCGrid)*, pages 172–179. IEEE, 2012.

54. Jerald Greenberg. Determinants of Perceived Fairness of Performance Evaluations. *Journal of Applied Psychology*, 71(2):340, 1986.

55. A Haji, A Ben Letaifa, and S. Tabbane. Implementation of a Virtualization Solution: SaaS on IaaS. In *Proceedings of the 4th Joint IFIP Wireless and Mobile Networking Conference (WMNC)*, pages 1–5. IEEE, Oct 2011.

56. Taekgyeong Han and Kwang Mong Sim. An Ontology-Enhanced Cloud Service Discovery System. In *Proceedings of the International Conference of Engineers and Computer Scientists*, volume 1, pages 17–19. IEEE, 2010.

57. Qiang He, Jun Han, Yun Yang, John Grundy, and Hai Jin. QoS-driven Service Selection for Multi-tenant SaaS. In *Proceedings of the 5th International Conference on Cloud Computing (Cloud)*, pages 566–573. IEEE, 2012.

58. Mark D Hickman. An Analytic Stochastic Model for the Transit Vehicle Holding Problem. *Transportation Science*, 35(3):215–237, 2001.

59. Charles Hitch. Sub-optimization in Operations Problems. *Journal of the Operations Research Society of America*, 1(3):87–99, 1953.

60. John H Hoag. *Calculus and Techniques of Optimization with Microeconomic Applications*. World Scientific, 2008.

61. E. Hossny, S. Khattab, F. Omara, and H. Hassan. A Case Study for Deploying Applications on Heterogeneous PaaS Platforms. In *Proceedings of the International Conference on Cloud Computing and Big Data (CloudCom-Asia)*, pages 246–253. IEEE, Dec 2013.

62. Walayat Hussain, Farookh Hussain, and Omar Hussain. QoS Prediction Methods to avoid SLA Violation in Post-interaction Time Phase. In *Proceedings of the 11th International Conference on Industrial Electronics and Applications (ICIEA)*, pages 32–37. IEEE, 2016.

63. Ren-Hung Hwang, Chung-Nan Lee, Yi-Ru Chen, and Da-Jing Zhang-Jian. Cost Optimization of Elasticity Cloud Resource Subscription Policy. *IEEE Transactions on Services Computing*, 7(4):561–574, 2014.

64. Dragan Ivanović, Manuel Carro, and Manuel Hermenegildo. An Initial Proposal for Data-Aware Resource Analysis of Orchestrations with Applications to Predictive Monitoring. In *Proceedings of the 7th International Conference on Service-oriented Computing (ICSOC)*, pages 414–424. Springer Berlin Heidelberg, 2010.

65. Dragan Ivanović, Manuel Carro, and Manuel Hermenegildo. Constraint-Based Runtime Prediction of SLA Violations in Service Orchestrations. In *Proceedings of the 9th International Conference on Service-Oriented Computing (ICSOC)*, volume 7084, pages 62–76. Springer-Heidelberg, 2011.

66. Jing Jiang, Jie Lu, Guangquan Zhang, and Guodong Long. Optimal Cloud Resource Auto-scaling for Web Applications. In *Proceedings of the 13th International Symposium on Cluster, Cloud and Grid Computing (CCGrid)*, pages 58–65. IEEE, 2013.

67. Wei Jiang, Dongwon Lee, and Songlin Hu. Large-Scale Longitudinal Analysis of SOAP-Based and RESTful Web Services. In *Proceedings of the 19th International Conference on Web Services (ICWS)*, pages 218–225. IEEE, 2012.

68. Zhang Jin-Hong. A Short-Term Prediction for QoS of Web Service based on RBF Neural Networks Including An Improved K-means algorithm. In *Proceedings of the International Conference on Computer Application and System Modeling (ICCASM)*, volume 5, pages 633–637. IEEE, Oct 2010.

69. George G Judge, R Carter Hill, William Griffiths, Helmut Lutkepohl, and Tsoung-Chao Lee. *Introduction to the Theory and Practice of Econometrics*. John Wiley and Sons 1982., 1988.

70. V. Kantere, D. Dash, G. Francois, S. Kyriakopoulou, and A. Ailamaki. Optimal Service Pricing for a Cloud Cache. *IEEE Transactions on Knowledge and Data Engineering*, 2011.

71. V. Kantere, D. Dash, G. Francois, S. Kyriakopoulou, and A Ailamaki. Optimal Service Pricing for a Cloud Cache. *IEEE Transactions on Knowledge and Data Engineering*, 23(9):1345–1358, Sept 2011.

72. Sheryl E. Kimes. Yield Management: A Tool for Capacity-Considered Service Firms. *Journal of Operations Management*, 8(4):348–363, 1989.

73. Sheryl E Kimes. Perceived Fairness of Yield Management. *The Cornell Hotel and Restaurant Administration Quarterly*, 43(1):21–30, 2002.

74. Sheryl E Kimes and Gary M Thompson. Restaurant Revenue Management: Determining the Best Table Mix. *Decision Sciences*, 35(3):371–392, 2004.

75. John L Kling and David A Bessler. A Comparison of Multivariate Forecasting Procedures for Economic Time-series. *International Journal of Forecasting*, 1(1):5–24, 1985.

76. Matthias Klusch, Andreas Gerber, and Marcus Schmidt. Semantic Web Service Composition Planning with Owls-Xplan. In *Proceedings of the 1st International Fall Symposium on Agents and the Semantic Web*, pages 55–62, 2005.

77. Kleopatra Konstanteli, Tommaso Cucinotta, Konstantinos Psychas, and Theodora Varvarigou. Admission Control for Elastic Cloud Services. In *Proceedings of the 5th International Conference on Cloud Computing (CLOUD)*, pages 41–48. IEEE, 2012.

78. Ioannis Konstantinou, Verena Kantere, Dimitrios Tsoumakos, and Nectarios Koziris. COC-CUS: Self-configured Cost-based Query Services in the Cloud. In *Proceedings of the 34th International Conference on Management of Data (SIGMOD)*, pages 1041–1044. ACM, 2013.

79. Markus Kradolfer and Andreas Geppert. Dynamic Workflow Schema Evolution based on Workflow Type Versioning and Workflow Migration. In *Proceedings of the International Conference on Cooperative Information Systems (IFCIS)*, pages 104–114. IEEE, 1999.

80. Freddy Lécué. Optimizing QoS-Aware Semantic Web Service Composition. In *Proceedings of the International Semantic Web Conference*, pages 375–391. Springer, 2009.

81. J. Leonard. Dynamics of Cloud-Based Software as a Service in Small Communities of Complex Organizations. In *Proceedings of the 47th Hawaii International Conference on System Sciences (HICSS)*, pages 3778–3787. IEEE, Jan 2014.

82. Nikolaos Leontiou, Dimitrios Dechouniotis, and Spyros Denazis. Adaptive Admission Control of Distributed Cloud Services. In *Proceedings of the International Conference on Network and Service Management (CNSM)*, pages 318–321. IEEE, 2010.

83. Frank L Lewis, Draguna Vrabie, and Kyriakos G Vamvoudakis. Using Natural Decision Methods to Design Optimal Adaptive Controllers. *IEEE Control Systems*, 32(6):76–105, 2012.

84. Lu Li, Mei Rong, and Guangquan Zhang. A Web Service QoS Prediction Approach based on Multidimensional QoS. In *Proceedings of the 6th International Conference on Computer Science Education (ICCSE)*, pages 1319–1322. IEEE, Aug 2011.

85. Meng Li, Zhebang Hua, Junfeng Zhao, Yanzhen Zou, and Bing Xie. ARIMA Model-Based Web Services Trustworthiness Evaluation and Prediction. In *Proceedings of the 12th International Conference on Service-Oriented Computing (ICSOC)*, pages 648–655. Springer Berlin Heidelberg, 2012.

86. Xiaolin Li, M. Parizeau, and Rejean Plamondon. Training Hidden Markov Models with Multiple Observations - A Combinatorial Method. *IEEE Transactions on Pattern Analysis and Machine Intelligence*, 22(4):371–377, 2000.

87. Heejin Lim, Richard Widdows, and Jungkun Park. M-loyalty: Winning Strategies for Mobile Carriers. *Journal of Consumer Marketing*, 23(4):208–218, 2006.

88. Wei-Yu Lin, Guan-Yu Lin, and Hung-Yu Wei. Dynamic Auction Mechanism for Cloud Resource Allocation. In *Proceedings of the 10th International Conference on Cluster, Cloud and Grid Computing (CCGrid)*, pages 591–592. IEEE, 2010.

89. Wei Lo, Jianwei Yin, Shuiguang Deng, Ying Li, and Zhaohui Wu. Collaborative Web Service QoS Prediction with Location-based Regularization. In *Proceedings of the 19th International Conference on Web Services (ICWS)*, pages 464–471. IEEE, 2012.

90. Zaki Malik, Ihsan Akbar, and Athman Bouguettaya. Web Services Reputation Assessment using a Hidden Markov Model. In *Proceedings of the 7th International Joint Conference on Service-Oriented Computing (ICSOC)*, pages 576–591. Springer-Verlag, 2009.
91. Zaki Malik and Athman Bouguettaya. Reputation Bootstrapping for Trust Establishment among Web Services. *IEEE Internet Computing*, 13(1):40–47, 2009.
92. Microsoft Inc. Virtual Machine and Cloud Service Sizes for Azure, Apr 2015. Available online at http://msdn.microsoft.com/en-us/library/azure/dn197896.aspx.
93. Kevin Patrick Murphy. *Dynamic Bayesian Networks: Representation, Inference and Learning*. PhD thesis, University of California, Berkeley, 2002.
94. Bipin B Nandi, Ansuman Banerjee, Sasthi C Ghosh, and Nilanjan Banerjee. Dynamic SLA based Elastic Cloud Service Management: A SaaS Perspective. In *Proceedings of International Symposium on Integrated Network Management (IM)*, pages 60–67. IEEE, 2013.
95. George L Nemhauser and Laurence A Wolsey. *Integer and Combinatorial Optimization*, volume 18. Wiley New York, 1988.
96. D. Niyato, S. Chaisiri, and Bu-Sung Lee. Economic Analysis of Resource Market in Cloud Computing Environment. In *Proceedings of the 1st Asia-Pacific Services Computing Conference (APSCC)*, pages 156–162. IEEE, Dec 2009.
97. Seog-Chan Oh, Dongwon Lee, and Soundar RT Kumara. A Comparative Illustration of AI Planning-based Web Services Composition. *ACM SIGecom Exchanges*, 5(5):1–10, 2006.
98. S. Pacheco-Sanchez, G. Casale, B. Scotney, S. McClean, G. Parr, and S. Dawson. Markovian Workload Characterization for QoS Prediction in the Cloud. In *Proceedings of the 4th International Conference on Cloud Computing (CLOUD)*, pages 147–154. IEEE, July 2011.
99. Ranjan Pal and Pan Hui. *Economic Models for Cloud Service Markets*, pages 382–396. Springer Berlin Heidelberg, 2012.
100. Suraj Pandey, Linlin Wu, Siddeswara Mayura Guru, and Rajkumar Buyya. A Particle Swarm Optimization-based Heuristic for Scheduling Workflow Applications in Cloud Computing Environments. In *Proceedings of the 24th International Conference on Advanced Information Networking and Applications (AINA)*, pages 400–407. IEEE, 2010.
101. Michael P Papazoglou and Willem-Jan van den Heuvel. Blueprinting the Cloud. *IEEE Internet Computing*, 15(6):74, 2011.
102. Ronak Patel and Sanjay Patel. Survey on Resource Allocation Strategies in Cloud Computing. *International Journal of Engineering Research and Technology*, 2, 2013.
103. John C Platt. Fast Training of Support Vector Machines using Sequential Minimal Optimization. *Advances in Kernel Methods*, pages 185–208, 1999.
104. Hai Qian. PivotalR: A Package for Machine Learning on Big Data. *The R Journal*, 6, 2014.
105. Fang Qiqing, Peng Xiaoming, Liu Qinghua, and Hu Yahui. A Global QoS Optimizing Web Services Selection Algorithm based on Moaco for Dynamic Web Service Composition. In *Proceedings of the International Forum on Information Technology and Applications (IFITA)*, volume 1, pages 37–42. IEEE, 2009.
106. Lawrence Rabiner. A Tutorial on Hidden Markov Models and Selected Applications in Speech Recognition. *Proceedings of the IEEE*, 77(2):257–286, 1989.
107. Jinghai Rao and Xiaomeng Su. A Survey of Automated Web Service Composition Methods. In *Proceedings of the 1st International Conference on Semantic Web Services and Web Process Composition (SWSWPC)*, pages 43–54, Berlin, Heidelberg, 2005. Springer-Verlag.
108. Charles Reiss, Alexey Tumanov, Gregory R Ganger, Randy H Katz, and Michael A Kozuch. Heterogeneity and Dynamicity of Clouds at Scale: Google Trace Analysis. In *Proceedings of the 3rd Symposium on Cloud Computing*, page 7. ACM, 2012.
109. Charles Reiss, John Wilkes, and Joseph L. Hellerstein. Google Cluster-usage Traces: Format + Schema. Technical report, Google Inc., Mountain View, CA, USA, 2011. Available online http://code.google.com/p/googleclusterdata/wiki/TraceVersion2.
110. Stanley Reiter and Donald B Rice. Discrete Optimizing Solution Procedures for Linear and Nonlinear Integer Programming Problems. *Management Science*, 12(11):829–850, 1966.

111. Ganesh Ram Santhanam, Samik Basu, and Vasant Honavar. Web Service Substitution based on Preferences over Non-functional Attributes. In *Proceedings of the 6th International Conference on Services Computing (SCC)*, pages 210–217. IEEE, 2009.

112. Andrew J. Schaefer, Matthew D. Bailey, Steven M. Shechter, and Mark S. Roberts. *Modeling Medical Treatment Using Markov Decision Processes*, pages 593–612. Springer US, 2004.

113. Dieter Schuller, Artem Polyvyanyy, Luciano García-Bañuelos, and Stefan Schulte. Optimization of Complex QoS-Aware Service Compositions. In *Proceedings of International Conference on Service-Oriented Computing (ICSOC)*, pages 452–466. Springer, 2011.

114. Margrit Sessions, Keith Breed, and Carl Hamilton. Pricing the Cloud 2016–2019. Technical report, London, 2016.

115. Guy Shani, David Heckerman, and Ronen I Brafman. An MDP-based Recommender System. *Journal of Machine Learning Research*, 6(Sep):1265–1295, 2005.

116. Bhanu Sharma, Ruppa K Thulasiram, Parimala Thulasiraman, Saurabh K Garg, and Rajkumar Buyya. Pricing Cloud Compute Commodities: A Novel Financial Economic Model. In *Proceedings of the 12th International Symposium on Cluster, Cloud and Grid Computing (CCGRID)*, pages 451–457. IEEE, 2012.

117. Evren Sirin. *Combining Description Logic Reasoning with AI Planning for Composition of Web Services*. PhD thesis, University of Maryland at College Park, 2006.

118. Evren Sirin, Bijan Parsia, Dan Wu, James Hendler, and Dana Nau. HTN Planning for Web Service Composition using SHOP2. *Web Semantics: Science, Services and Agents on the World Wide Web*, 1(4):377–396, 2004.

119. Barry C Smith, John F Leimkuhler, and Ross M Darrow. Yield Management at American Airlines. *Interfaces*, 22(1):8–31, 1992.

120. Murray Stokely, Amaan Mehrabian, Christoph Albrecht, Francois Labelle, and Arif Merchant. Projecting Disk Usage Based on Historical Trends in a Cloud Environment. In *Proceedings of the 3rd Workshop on Scientific Cloud Computing Date*, pages 63–70. ACM, 2012.

121. T. Thanakornworakij, R. Nassar, C.B. Leangsuksun, and M. Paun. An Economic Model for Maximizing Profit of a Cloud Service Provider. In *Proceedings of the 7th International Conference on Availability, Reliability and Security (ARES)*, pages 274–279. IEEE, Aug 2012.

122. Tram Truong-Huu and Chen-Khong Tham. A Game-Theoretic Model for Dynamic Pricing and Competition among Cloud Providers. In *Proceedings of the 6th International Conference on Utility and Cloud Computing (UCC)*, pages 235–238. IEEE, Dec 2013.

123. Wei-Tek Tsai, Xin Sun, and Janaka Balasooriya. Service-Oriented Cloud Computing Architecture. In *Proceedings of the 7th International Conference on Information Technology: New Generations (ITNG)*, pages 684–689. IEEE, 2010.

124. Tom Vercauteren, Pradeep Aggarwal, Xiaodong Wang, and Ta-Hsin Li. Hierarchical Forecasting of Web Server Workload using Sequential Monte Carlo Training. *IEEE Transactions on Signal Processing*, 55(4):1286–1297, 2007.

125. Ngo Anh Vien and Marc Toussaint. Hierarchical Monte-Carlo Planning. In *Proceedings of the 29th International Conference on Artificial Intelligence (AAAI)*, pages 3613–3619. AAAI Press, 2015.

126. Hongbing Wang, Shizhi Shao, Xuan Zhou, Cheng Wan, and Athman Bouguettaya. Preference Recommendation for Personalized Search. *Knowledge-Based Systems*, 100:124 – 136, 2016.

127. Hongbing Wang, Jie Zhang, Wenlong Sun, Hongye Song, Guibing Guo, and Xiang Zhou. WCP-Nets: A Weighted Extension to CP-Nets for Web Service Selection. In *Proceedings of the 10th International Conference on Service-Oriented Computing (ICSOC)*. Springer, 2012.

128. Hongbing Wang, Xuan Zhou, Xiang Zhou, Weihong Liu, Wenya Li, and Athman Bouguettaya. Adaptive Service Composition based on Reinforcement Learning. In *Proceedings of the 8th International Conference of Service-Oriented Computing (ICSOC)*, pages 92–107. Springer, 2010.

129. Christopher JCH Watkins and Peter Dayan. Q-Learning. *Machine Learning*, 8(3-4):279–292, 1992.

130. Kevin Werbach. Syndication: The Emerging Model for Business in the Internet Era. *Harvard Business Review*, 78(3):84–93, 1999.
131. David E Wilkins and Roberto V Desimone. Applying an AI planner to Military Operations Planning. Technical report, DTIC Document, 1993.
132. Wayne L Winston and Jeffrey B Goldberg. *Operations Research: Applications and Algorithms*, volume 3. Duxbury press Boston, 2004.
133. Rich Wolski, James S Plank, John Brevik, and Todd Bryan. Analyzing Market-based Resource Allocation Strategies for the Computational Grid. *International Journal of High Performance Computing Applications*, 15(3):258–281, 2001.
134. Linlin Wu, S.K. Garg, and R. Buyya. SLA-based Resource Allocation for Software as a Service Provider (SaaS) in Cloud Computing Environments. In *Proceedings of the 11th IEEE/ACM International Symposium on Cluster, Cloud and Grid Computing*, pages 195–204, 2011.
135. Linlin Wu, Saurabh Kumar Garg, and Rajkumar Buyya. SLA-based Admission Control for a Software-as-a-Service Provider in Cloud Computing Environments. *Journal of Computer and System Sciences*, 78(5):1280–1299, 2012.
136. Hong Xu and Baochun Li. Dynamic Cloud Pricing for Revenue Maximization. *IEEE Transactions on Cloud Computing*, 1(2):158–171, July 2013.
137. Wenbo Xu, Jian Cao, Haiyan Zhao, and Lei Wang. A Multi-agent Learning Model for Service Composition. In *Proceedings of International Asia-Pacific Conference on Services Computing Conference (APSCC)*, pages 70–75. IEEE, 2012.
138. Yagiz Onat Yazir, Chris Matthews, and Roozbeh Farahbod et al. Dynamic Resource Allocation in Computing Clouds using Distributed Multiple Criteria Decision Analysis. In *Proceedings of the 3rd International Conference on Cloud Computing (CLOUD)*, pages 91–98. IEEE, 2010.
139. Zhen Ye, Athman Bouguettaya, and Xiaofang Zhou. QoS-Aware Cloud Service Composition Based on Economic Models. In *Proceedings of the 10th International Conference on Service-Oriented Computing (ICSOC)*, pages 111–126. Springer Berlin Heidelberg, 2012.
140. Zhen Ye, Athman Bouguettaya, and Xiaofang Zhou. QoS-Aware Cloud Service Composition Using Time Series. In *Proceedings of the 11th International Conference on Service-Oriented Computing (ICSOC)*, volume 8274, pages 9–22. Springer Berlin Heidelberg, 2013.
141. Zhen Ye, Xiaofang Zhou, and Athman Bouguettaya. Genetic Algorithm Based QoS-Aware Service Compositions in Cloud Computing. In *Proceedings of the 16th International Conference on Database Systems for Advanced Applications (DASFAA)*, pages 321–334. Springer Berlin Heidelberg, 2011.
142. Cheng Zeng, Xiao Guo, Weijie Ou, and Dong Han. *Cloud Computing Service Composition and Search Based on Semantic*, pages 290–300. Springer Berlin Heidelberg, 2009.
143. Liangzhao Zeng, B. Benatallah, A H H Ngu, M. Dumas, J. Kalagnanam, and H. Chang. QoS-Aware Middleware for Web Services Composition. *IEEE Transactions on Software Engineering*, 30(5):311–327, May 2004.
144. Meng Zhang, Xudong Liu, Richong Zhang, and Hailong Sun. A Web Service Recommendation Approach Based on QoS Prediction Using Fuzzy Clustering. In *Proceedings of the 9th International Conference on Services Computing (SCC)*, pages 138–145. IEEE, June 2012.
145. Qi Zhang, Lu Cheng, and Raouf Boutaba. Cloud Computing: State-of-the-art and Research Challenges. *Journal of internet Services and Applications*, 1(1):7–18, 2010.
146. Qi Zhang, Quanyan Zhu, and Raouf Boutaba. Dynamic Resource Allocation for Spot Markets in Cloud Computing Environments. In *Proceedings of the 4th International Conference on Utility and Cloud Computing (UCC)*, pages 178–185. IEEE, 2011.
147. W. Zhang, C. K. Chang, T. Feng, and H. Y. Jiang. QoS-Based Dynamic Web Service Composition with Ant Colony Optimization. In *Proceedings of the 34th Annual Computer Software and Applications Conference*, pages 493–502. IEEE, July 2010.
148. Yilei Zhang, Zibin Zheng, and M.R. Lyu. WSPred: A Time-Aware Personalized QoS Prediction Framework for Web Services. In *Proceedings of the 22nd International Symposium on Software Reliability Engineering (ISSRE)*, pages 210–219. IEEE, Nov 2011.

149. Yingjian Zhang. *Prediction of Financial Time-series with Hidden Markov Models*. PhD thesis, Simon Fraser University, 2004.
150. Xinchao Zhao, Boqian Song, Panyu Huang, Zichao Wen, Jialei Weng, and Yi Fan. An Improved Discrete Immune Optimization Algorithm based on PSO for QoS-driven Web Service Composition. *Applied Soft Computing*, 12(8):2208–2216, 2012.
151. Zibin Zheng, Hao Ma, M.R. Lyu, and I. King. Collaborative Web Service QoS Prediction via Neighborhood Integrated Matrix Factorization. *IEEE Transactions on Services Computing*, 6(3):289–299, July 2013.
152. Zibin Zheng, Xinmiao Wu, Yilei Zhang, M.R. Lyu, and Jianmin Wang. QoS Ranking Prediction for Cloud Services. *IEEE Transactions on Parallel and Distributed Systems*, 24(6):1213–1222, June 2013.